PRAISE FOR *DATA EXCELL*

"Every page of *Data Excellence* succeeds in a remarkable feat: translating years of experience, mistakes, successes and insights into a real practical training course in data excellence. The original metaphor of the 'Data Personal Trainer' who trains corporate 'Data Athletes' is not just a stylistic device, but the key to transforming complex concepts into a concrete and accessible path. I highly recommend this book to anyone responsible for organizational change, from Chief Data Officers, to digital transformation leaders, to all those who want to move beyond talking about being 'data-driven' and start truly embodying it, day after day."
Franco Francia, Vice President of DAMA Italy and CEO of Inema and FIT Strategy

"Roberto Maranca's humanitarian and philosophical approach to data is assessible, actionable and inspiring for all of us that wants to make a real difference with data."
Caroline Carruthers, bestselling author and CEO of Carruthers and Jackson

"Organizations that lead the market are those that master both the art and science of turning their assets into value: money, materials, talent and data. This has become increasingly clear with AI's insatiable hunger for data. The organizations of the future recognize that data is a team sport, and *Data Excellence* neatly outlines how to train those teams into top performance."
Stijn Christiansen, Co-founder and Chief Data Citizen, Collibra

"Set at the interface of leadership, culture change and technical data expertise, this book holds a unique position in the market to enable us to understand the conditions that are critical to drive value from data into our businesses. Roberto Maranca tackles the most challenging of topics, such as driving value and embedding operating models without losing the complexity of them and the muti-faceted principles that a leader must attend to for success. He shows us how and why embedding data at the heart of our organization is critical but immensely complex and outlines beautifully the vast responsibility that data leaders hold today. Sectioned into pillars and brought to life with models and workable examples ensures accessibility for mid-range and senior leaders from across all professions. Thought-provoking for us all."
Johanna Hutchinson, Group Chief Data Officer, BAE Systems

Data Excellence

*How data leadership can drive stronger
organizational performance*

Roberto M Maranca

KoganPage

Publisher's note
Every possible effort has been made to ensure that the information contained in this book is accurate at the time of going to press, and the publishers and authors cannot accept responsibility for any errors or omissions, however caused. No responsibility for loss or damage occasioned to any person acting, or refraining from action, as a result of the material in this publication can be accepted by the editor, the publisher or the author.

First published in Great Britain and the United States in 2026

Kogan Page
Kogan Page Ltd, 2nd Floor, 45 Gee Street, London EC1V 3RS, United Kingdom
Kogan Page Inc, 8 W 38th Street, Suite 902, New York, NY 10018, USA
www.koganpage.com

EU Representative (GPSR)
Authorised Rep Compliance Ltd, Ground Floor, 71 Baggot Street Lower, Dublin D02 P593, Ireland
www.arccompliance.com

Kogan Page books are printed on paper from sustainable forests.

© Roberto M Maranca 2026

The moral rights of the author have been asserted in accordance with the Copyright, Designs and Patents Act 1988.

ISBNs
Hardback   978 1 3986 1480 2
Paperback   978 1 3986 1479 6
Ebook   978 1 3986 1481 9

British Library Cataloguing-in-Publication Data
A CIP record for this book is available from the British Library.

Library of Congress Control Number
2025036090

Typeset by Integra Software Services, Pondicherry
Print production managed by Jellyfish
Printed and bound by CPI Group (UK) Ltd, Croydon CR0 4YY

To all of you data heroes and heroines: notwithstanding your imposter syndrome, you know that's what you really are

CONTENTS

LIST OF FIGURES AND TABLES

PREFACE

Thank you for joining me on this journey through the world of *data excellence*. Before we commence, I thought it would be useful to make a short excursion into my past, and explain how my passion for data excellence came to be, as it will doubtless shed some light on many of the concepts I am going to convey.

Although I gained a solid academic grounding in Greek, Latin and philosophy, from a very young age I also developed a keen interest in the digital world, like many attracted by the rise of video gaming in the 1980s. Later, my passion for planes led to a Masters in Aeronautical Engineering (itself a necessary substitute for a career in the Air Force). My thesis, demonstrating that you could use a combination of the finite element method and an operational research base algorithm to minimize the weight of an airframe, was all about creating a computer program. Little did I know that was my first encounter with what today might be called artificial intelligence, and in 1992, though I was lucky enough to have my own computer, it had a whole 2 megabytes of RAM (forgive me for tutting when somebody spins up a terabyte of cloud space to play with data just because they can!).

My compulsory service in the Italian Army that inevitably followed university surprisingly made that digital thread stronger, as I was taught 'the art of fixing PCs and the things attached to them'. Arguably, this landed me my very first job on the helpdesk at Nissan. I came to understand that I was now an 'IT guy', which wasn't too bad because, as a bespectacled young man with a love for videogames and computers, I was never far away from the term 'nerd'. But these were the 1990s and computers in the workplaces were becoming as essential as desks. I was lucky enough to meet great leaders and colleagues who taught me everything under the technological sun, from hardware and software to networking, to wide area networks and mobile communication, then email and then... the internet! So, the 'nerd/IT guy' was elevated to a much more integral part of the business.

Then came GE Capital. When I first joined this huge company, I only knew about its aircraft engines, and could not imagine it was even doing long-term rentals (i.e. company cars). 17 years later I could have probably written a book on the whole meatball! But GE Capital was the forge in which my IT technical curiosity was melted into business value and subsequently recast as a passion for data. I was fortunate to have had a superbly passionate and empathic leader – Kevin Griffin was my CIO for nine consecutive years. It was he who trusted my versatility enough to let me lead a kaleidoscopic variety of topics, of which the most important for my future career was undoubtedly Basel II. Basel II is a regulatory framework that requires financial institutions to calculate a certain amount of capital to keep on their books. Such amounts previously formed a fixed percentage of their asset risk, but with Basel II it became a calculation based on many more data attributes. I was effectively 'loaned' to the regulatory risk team as their IT guy, under the lead of another legend, Michael Sicsic. Michael had this very GE-like idea of responding to a global regulation in a global and standard manner across all the banks of the enterprise. For readers who know a little about banks and regulation, even in these times of clouds and webs it sounds pretty ambitious, so imagine the scale of the challenge almost 20 years ago! 'How can you have something standard and centralized when every bank has its own specific processes, every national regulator has its own data model and operates in a different language...? It simply can't be done!' whined the chorus of naysayers.

And yet we did it!

To succeed I had to become more than an IT guy, I had to learn the lingo of risk and finance, and even become proficient in *Bundesdatenschutzgesetz*, the German grandmother of the General Data Protection Regulation (GDPR). I realized the importance of agreeing on a definition before accepting what the subject matter expert tells you to map that field into. Often this unfortunate individual turned out to be the person who happened to draw the short straw. I grasped why even if on day one all the files you received were right, putting in place format or 'quality' control for the subsequent interfaces could make the difference between making the regulatory deadline or missing it. Thus, it is no surprise that a few years later, when I saw the first job description of a chief data officer, for once in my working life, I clearly saw what I wanted to be! Although not all the details were clear, at least the road to Damascus was bright and open and I could get back in the saddle (from the proverbial fall) and ride on.

Since then, in the last ten years, I have dedicated myself to becoming a good data officer with the genuine goal of ensuring that the business really gets the most out of that data. It has been a rollercoaster of successes and failures, but an enriching experience none the less, as I had the time to reflect, plan, test and adapt. Some if not all of the ideas in this book were concocted on rainy days when you ask yourself why people are unable to see the blindingly obvious, shiny, virtuous way in front of them but instead opt for that dark, Excel-ridden side alley. As a final data point of my journey, in the last few years, due to a combination of gardening leave, a global pandemic and a midlife crisis – and especially because I bought a popular insurance product that trades your health data for vouchers and discounts – I have become active to the point I am restless and fidgety without my daily exercise fix. In another arena of this self-improvement drive, I have experimented on myself the dos and don'ts of Change with a big 'C', which is an essential part of what follows in these pages.

01

Is it all about data?

WARMING UP

- What is data and why is it so important in today's world?
- What are the misconceptions and the expectations of data in the wider world?
- Who are the data personal trainers and the data athletes?
- What is a 'pandedomenistic' world?
- What are the three reasons why we need data excellence?

Why organizations need data

Achieving business success is usually determined by making the right decision at the right time so an action yields a beneficial outcome. What makes a decision right, or in fact the best possible course of action, is situational awareness and the understanding of what links the action to the intended outcome. Saying that data is the lifeblood of business should come as no surprise, since awareness, understanding, postulation and, ultimately, knowledge are all an output of information processing, which in an ever-digitizing world is experienced in the form of digital data. Therefore, to successfully perform a new strategic initiative, to dominate a new market, to integrate a new business, or to change an operational process, a series of decisions must be made. The reality is that those decisions *consume* data – and the better the data the better the decision and the lower the risk of failure. Even more importantly, data allows us to measure the effect of the decision once it is made and to learn what made that decision right or wrong, and that means more data.

Common misconceptions about data

Data is everywhere, and data is everyone's business, not just data officers' or heads of data, but also business professionals at all levels, hence this book is for everyone who is convinced that one can only thrive if one's decisions and actions are based on good data. However, from product managers and product development to marketing managers, all can succumb to commonly held misconception about data, and be hindered in effective decision making or, worse, fail in their missions. Thus before delving into what the world of data entails, let us tackle these common clichés, and demonstrate why it is imperative to avoid them.

Data is not IT

This has been my bugbear since the beginning of my initiation into this field. I have been in information technology (IT) for most of my professional life; however, this is the biggest misunderstanding that business professionals fall into when trying to achieve their ambitions using data. To cave in and concede that data is just a technical problem with a technical solution and miraculously 'this application should make it all better' is simply too tempting. It is also the most common epitaph on the tombstone of many first-time data officers, as they are so busy building 'stuff', convinced that the new, shiny toy is cool and attractive. They are sure that their customers will come. But in the end they do not, because technology alone does not deliver value and what is left is a cost that has not generated any measurable benefit for the organization. Make no mistakes, good technology is absolutely essential to data, as data does not live in the ether but in the bit and bytes of the machines; however, we shouldn't confuse the container with the content.

Data is not AI

At the risk of upsetting all the data scientists I know, I would argue that the pendulum could perilously swing from the mistaken belief that data is IT to the other extreme position that 'artificial intelligence (AI) is all we need'. Such is the quasi-magical lure of AI that it can become a means to all ends for the data officer. But this is a pitfall that is camouflaging the harsh reality: AI and its derivative areas (gen AI anyone?) are the elite field at which you can only excel when you have mastered all the disciplines of data you have trained in long and hard. Instead, the common perception is at present that AI is magic, free and simple, none of them being true of course and, as a result of this tunnel vision, organizations can literally hallucinate on AI, being presented with recommendations that are based on poor data and valid only for a very narrow type of use cases, effectively remaining in a constant 'proof of concept' phase that never scales to the full size of the enterprise.

Data is not the new oil

The British mathematician, data scientist and leading data pioneer Clive Humby famously described data as the new oil. Humby said that, like oil, data in its raw form is of little use. It requires processing and refinement to produce value. Looking back (and at the same time peering into the future), I would argue that data is more like the technology of nuclear fusion we could one day master. We have been aware of data's existence for decades. First, we were *passively* gaining power out of data, then we learnt to harness its simpler digital form (like nuclear fission) and now, with the *combination* of cloud, AI, generative AI and quantum computing, we have just unleashed its fusion-like awesomeness. And exactly like at the dawn of the nuclear era, we are now scrambling to establish new paradigms and building a fit-for-purpose data economy, and scratching our regulatory heads on how to govern the proverbial genie out of the bottle. Most importantly, we are also exploring widely how to design a risk/reward framework that would serve us as a compass, as we know that both data and nuclear power can be used for both good and evil.

Data as a team sport

'Data is a team sport, isn't it, Roberto?' my experienced data friend concluded in a LinkedIn exchange. And it finally really hit me:

Data is *not* IT!
Data is *not* AI!
Data is *not* the new oil!
Data is a *SPORT*!

If you are not convinced, ask a data leader and they will tell you the amount of physical and mental strength that it takes! However, less facetiously, there are many similarities between data and the sporting world: it is definitely not an innate skill, and it requires nurturing, zealous training and mental resilience. The whole enterprise has to act as a team in order to succeed, and, no matter how many solo champions you might have in the team, without leadership, coaching and dedication to create a harmonious environment you will never reach peak performance.

Introducing the data excellence approach

Here we are at the starting blocks. If data is a sport that you want to excel at, this book advocates that data excellence is the discipline you have to practise. Two main protagonists are going to be our focus: the *data athletes (DAs)* – the business leaders who strive to use data to achieve the ultimate performance for their teams; and the *data personal trainers (DPTs)* – the data practitioners who are applying their experience in data to ignite the data athletes' ambitions. The role of the data personal trainer is to prepare and coach their organization to professional excellence and capabilities through a long-term sustainable performance plan. In this conceptual data excellence gymnasium, I will explore the boundaries, expectations, challenges and practices that both personae will need to master in order to succeed in their professional lives, which by virtue of data are undergoing an epochal transformation.

The emerging need for data

If data is a sport, it is crucial to understand its places, rules, fixtures and, of course, its asks on the data athletes' fitness. The successful data personal trainer will need to develop a solid understanding of the condition of the playing field, who the best performers are, what they are doing to be the best and what the crowd is cheering for, as it will help them to gauge the likelihood of success for their data athletes and then adjust their training to enable higher performance. In my experience, I have found seven aspects related to external circumstances that are crucial to understand whether you will succeed in helping your organization harness data and use it effectively to achieve the desired results.

1) *Data is everything: A pandedomenistic world*

Data as a representation of reality has been with us for many centuries. In Ancient Greece, the philosopher Socrates famously said 'Know thyself.' He meant of course that the foundation of one's (spiritual) growth is the awareness of one's potentials and limits. Putting this in a modern context, Socrates asserts the importance of good metadata, knowing the combination of qualities and concepts that defines him. Similarly, Plato's *Theory of the Forms* argues that the perfect forms are the concepts we all share as pure knowledge and that the physical reality is just its imperfect copy. This can be likened to the work of the first documented Information Governance Architect. Finally, we can also view 'reasoning' of modern graph technology as nothing more than a large-scale implementation of Aristotle's syllogism.

These are age-old ideas, but the difference today is the almost infinite power of digital technology. In today's world, digital data overlays and extends our reality. When speaking at the IRM UK data conference in May 2018, I labelled this phenomenon as *pandedomenistic* (from Greek words meaning 'everything is data'). I managed to raise a few eyebrows; nevertheless what I wanted to stress was the fact that there is a new dimension of reality and it is made of data. While everyone is in search of the new monetization opportunities that data offers, pandedomenism is the conceptual leap that both our data athletes and data personal trainer will need to make. It is about thinking about data less as bytes coming out of a screen and more as a new element that will unlock amazing opportunities for the organizations that can properly develop a holistic approach. For example: taking the concept of digital twin up from the single asset to the enterprise level is where a complete pandedomenistic model of the organization could offer incredible opportunities for simplification, cost optimization and operational resilience.

2) Digital warp speed

I once saw a viral meme online which said something along the lines of, 'Who was behind your company's digital revolution? The CEO? No! The CIO? No! Covid!' I see that a bit differently. The truth is the time was ripe to take a step towards a more digitized way of working and that readiness saved us from much more dire consequences. The pandemic simply took us beyond a point of no return and certain changes are now going to be structural, though far from stable and settled. Although we might feel that we have been bounced back to where we were before 2020, it is not the case. A hybrid work pattern, for instance, far from being a benefit, has become an expected feature of an employment contract. Data has a huge role to play in creating a solid support for the kind of collaboration that a video call does not yet allow, and in creating more transparency, for example providing an off sync but real time accurate status of a cross-functional complex project, enabling 20th-century leaders to step nimbly into the 21st century.

Another example is the dramatic acceleration of digital payment. Point of sales battery operated devices for contactless payments are now ubiquitous – cash and data are now properly interoperable.

3) Digital neo-humanism

No matter how much AI you unleash on business processes, there is no way that, at the time I am writing this in 2025, an algorithm can predict with 100 per cent certainty that given a certain input X a customer would buy Y. This is not because statistics, on which data science is based, is an imprecise science. It is due to the fact that making a decision (like buying something) includes a good deal of non-deterministic emotions. *What* is bought is not really significant. Whether it is a product, service, charitable idea, investment or even a company, at the end of the business-to-business (B2B) transaction there is always an *H*, a human who is making a decision based on seemingly chaotic or irrational psychological processes. This is the reason why, once all the friction of the tool is removed and a seamless digital experience is truly achieved, we will have entered a neo-humanistic digital age where business success will be based in greater proportion on understanding humans and the decisions and choices that they make. Naturally, all of this remains valid as long as Alexa chooses a song because Alexa's algorithm recommends one that *I* might like based on *my* listening patterns. The day Alexa picks a song *it* likes we will have crossed the threshold into a very different world, and although recent examples of artificial intelligence are increasingly better at mimicking tastes, we are still far from this quintessentially human feature. Nevertheless, our world is becoming more and more pandedomenistic. The more digital our lives become, the more sophisticated and almost almighty technologies are deployed, the more longstanding human issues are pushed into the foreground for us to tackle. Let me quote from the tragedy *Antigone* written by the Ancient Greek dramatist Sophocles in 441 BC to illustrate this:

> Many wonders, many terrors, but none more wonderful than the human race.
> Or more dangerous. These creatures move across the white-capped ocean seas
> blasted by winter storms, carving their way under the surging waves engulfing
> them. With their horses they wear down the unwearied and immortal Earth,
> harassing her, as year by year their ploughs move back and forth [...] There is

no event their skill cannot confront – other than death – that alone they cannot shun, although for many baffling sicknesses they have discovered their own remedies. The qualities of their inventive skills bring innovation beyond their dreams and lead them on, sometimes to evil and sometimes to good.[1]

In this chorus, Sophocles exposes the wondrous beast who is simultaneously capable of both almost-miraculous acts and heinous crimes against its own species, of senseless exploitation of the environment on which lives depend and of Machiavellian misdeeds. This beast is of course the human being. I am struck by the affinity of Sophocles' words with the modern world's struggle for peace, human rights, sustainability, trust, honesty and selflessness. We can conclude that nothing has changed, the central problems of humanity have not been solved by any of the technological advancements of the last 25 centuries, and technology alone is obviously not an answer. The social and behavioural sciences attempting to answer the 'big questions' must merge with the hard sciences and create a sort of new renaissance where data will play the pivotal role in solving, amongst the others, the paradox of achieving growth for everyone at a sustainable cost. Thus, my choice of the personal trainer metaphor emphasizes the need for a new balanced set of skills to succeed: the change agent operating in such a digital neo-humanistic environment must have exceptional emotional intelligence and sociological insight together with mastery of technical sciences, as the powerful formula to lead their clients to a successful and sustainable achievement of their ambitions.

4) Neo-Luddism

Precisely because of the pandedomenistic world and the spectacular amount of change that comes with it, it becomes more and more evident that our brain has limitations, even if it is considered the most complex machine in the universe. The gelatinous mass roughly 1,500 ml in volume on average has evolved over thousands of years to respond to very precise survival needs. In a space of time infinitesimal in comparison to the time it took for the brain to develop, we are now experimentally pushing the envelope of the brain's performance, bombarding it with obscure and almighty, almost magical, technological wonders, radically changing the environment in which the brain operates. As a result, the fight-or-flight mechanism is triggered and exacerbated by the innate angst of inadequacy. Instead of dreaming about flying cars like in the 1960s, people show a broad mistrust towards everything that is harvesting their data to possibly absorb their knowledge and one day to get rid of them as workers. Without doubt, the more the pandedomenistic world shows its workings, the more a creeping neo-Luddite sentiment grows. So, our data athlete's performance might be undermined by regarding data with prejudice – as a force that dehumanizes, destroys jobs and subjugates the digital have-nots. In this instance the DPT may have to tackle the concerns of key stakeholders, demystifying as much as possible the aura of sorcery that sometime surrounds data initiatives, especially AI, to increase the buy-in and engagement.

5) Data sovereignty

What is data sovereignty? Data sovereignty is the concept that digital data is subject to the laws of the country in which it is collected and stored. You might think of this as state-sponsored Luddism but in fact the notion of data sovereignty is nothing new. The Peace of Westphalia of 1648 is seen by many as the birth of the modern state: a state that for the first time had its sovereignty. Sovereignty is the right of the state to govern key aspects of its entity, associated with its own laws, customs and especially religion, within geographic borders.

However, the pandedomenistic world we live in has no borders. Data has been moving in and out of countries effectively oblivious to the local laws – and in some cases intentionally so. More recently, states have realized that they are bleeding data and the economic opportunities that go with it through their borders, while also exposing their societies and businesses to potential harm. As a result, they are reacting by restricting flows of data across their borders. And the more the world becomes unstable, the more this data protectionist trend increases. For example, the Cybersecurity Law in China (2017) creates a new category of 'important data', which is really a catch-all class related to the Critical Infrastructure Information Operator (CIIO) whose data cannot leave China. The General Data Protection Regulation (GDPR) in the EU (2018) limits the export of data in states with 'inadequate' privacy laws. The number of policies (and indeed the imagination of said regulators) will only increase, and there are now plenty of websites to track online how many of these policies are in the making.[2] If you expect these regulatory policies to be focused on personal data, you will be disappointed as only about one-third of them are scoped around personal data. There is a lot more sovereignty out there on other data that is way more important to a state, such as high IP data, critical infrastructure and economic data. So where previously firms, especially multinationals, would have enjoyed the global free flow of data, which in turn allowed process globalization, service outsourcing and ubiquitous cloud services, for the data athletes geographic restrictions on data have the potential to become a potentially insurmountable hurdle if not properly factored into the design of the company data flows.

6) Responsible data

You cannot write a book about data today without talking about artificial intelligence (AI). And since 2023 it has also been impossible not to add 'generative' when illustrating the acceleration AI has undergone in the last few years. AI has been around for decades, its first working examples dating all the way back to the 1950s. However, the conditions are now ripe for its giant leap, which means that data leaders are at a fork in the road. Turn in one direction and you go down the path of data utopia: believing that AI is the ultimate force for good and the pandedomenistic world is one of prosperity and opportunities for everyone. Think about the advancement in pharmacological drug design using AI which has reduced testing on animals and humans while maintaining efficacy. Turn in the other direction and you are on a path where AI is going to be what the neo-Luddites are fearful of: the destroyer of free will and social equality. Advanced AI can make weapons more deadly, influence elections, destroy someone's reputation with deepfakes or even, in a banal fashion, render entire job types redundant.

Hopefully the future will not be so polarized, but we cannot deny that this is a critical moment. Personally, I find it astonishing that, given the potential harm our profession could cause, codes of conduct and professional responsibility are still broadly left to self-regulation. Behaving responsibly when working with data and championing ethical conduct is therefore essential for the data personal trainer. And, typically, that takes the form of introducing the correct amount of doubt in the development phase. We will find in Pillar II that being data-driven is all about moving from questions to statements, but in data ethics, dogmatic certainty could be disastrous. Explaining the risk of treating data irresponsibly to executives could be tricky as per the above-mentioned misconceptions. However, here is a simple idea that, in different guises, I use to make the issue real. A survey with two simple made-up questions for a group of business leaders:

1 'Your product is software and hardware devices supporting facility managers and you are about to close a very lucrative deal with a prospective client, a hotel chain in, let us call it, a very conservative

region of the world. However, the client is demanding that you make a simple change to the product so that it will detect and report when a certain room key is spending the night in a different room. Would you make the change?'

2   'Our sales development team had a hackathon, and they are postulating that cross-referencing the public social media feed of their sales account representative and their visit, i.e. going to visit them only when they are 'happy', can increase the orders by 25 per cent. Would you authorize that?'

The answers usually come back as an almost perfect 50/50 split. The conclusion that I offer to the audience is that either response would have been legitimate for a business. The point is to have the difficult conversation to agree on a course of action and to have a documented rationale to stand by it.

7) Sustainable data

The last point of my whistle-stop tour around the context in which data as a team sport is practised, is much closer to home and embedded in our line of duty itself. Put simply, we data leaders help create data on data. A lot of what we do is about creating better data but a lot more is about producing more data. Just think about data quality. Yesterday you would have had a dashboard with its payload of data. Now you have measurements of quality dimensions for each one of your *critical data elements* somewhere in your systems and that has consequences. The main one is that, as I write this, the industry is pretty much in agreement that data centres, the places where most of our data is kept alive, have overtaken general aviation in terms of CO_2 emissions.[3] Even more sadly, only about a third of that data is actually 'live', i.e. really used. Our pandedomenistic world has the potential to accelerate the problems of its real-world companion. So, if there were not enough expectations on the data leader already, a sustainable approach to data must also be an integral part of our modus operandi. I will explore in Chapter 14 what the concrete actions are to be more parsimonious with resources, for example enhancing our data retention capabilities to minimize the data hoarded in data centres. Neglecting this would be deeply hypocritical, because all the well-intentioned posts about the importance of data for humanity and the AI for good pledges would ring hollow in the face of not truly confronting climate change.

Why being good at data is hard

Given the complex circumstances affecting data we have just explored and the constraints they place on data leaders, is it so surprising that data programmes are struggling to be successful? I am not aware of any company that would be able to certify that they are *excellent* at data. We will discuss what data excellence means and its three pillars in Chapter 2, but it would be difficult to find a data officer or a data leader who, away from the limelight of a conference, podcast or published article, will not confess that their journey has been hard going, with plenty of failures, compromises and pivots. Although all data personal trainers know that the highest data quality is a must and that everyone should be conversant in data modelling and artificial intelligence, there are inherent challenges to establishing what we commonly call, and soon will properly define, a data-driven organization. Having gone through my fair share of these challenges, I have found the following three to be the most towering obstacles data professionals face:

- Data is tribal.
- Data is an afterthought.
- Data value is hard to quantify.

Let us examine each of these and consider both how they impact the way we approach data leadership and how data leaders can overcome them.

Data is tribal

At some point in our careers, most of us have found ourselves in front of a typical assessment, made internally or led by a third party, in which an alleged 'siloed approach' is blamed for the inability of an organization to spread their wings in unison and become a digital and data unicorn. As a data leader, I have found that the word 'silo' misdirects us towards trying to fix a system or a procedure, because we associate the silo with a systemic problem, a physical impenetrable set of barriers that must be removed. It might be complex, long or cumbersome (you wouldn't settle for a suboptimal solution), but I have very seldom found a system or a process that was impossible to modify in order to achieve a certain outcome. Worst case scenario, systems and processes can be replaced with more fitting solutions.

Instead, what I have frequently experienced is people resisting or leaning into a change just temporarily, only to slowly fall back into their old habits.

How many times have our companies tried to implement a 'No agenda, no meeting' policy? We all agree that it will improve collaboration and productivity, and yet it only works for a short while, then more or less everyone returns to the habit of inviting colleagues to a one-hour gathering with a few vague words from which to glean the expectations. Why is that? As human beings we yearn to belong. This is a powerful instinct that has served us well as a species, as we feel safer and look after each other in an affinal group. Similarly in an organizational environment, to be part of the finance or marketing team (whose respective bosses-chieftains might not share the same opinion) or being the team enclaved in a new company after an acquisition surrounded by the buyer's teams, reinforces a bond of 'us versus them'. A *tribe* forms and proudly states its customs, habits, taboos and dialects in antithesis to the *other*. Now, imagine all these clans occupying adjacent territories – the Sales Mountains, the Finance Plains, the Hills of IT – and imagine data like a river that flows across them. In theory it should connect them and allow for trade and prosperity, moving knowledge around the territories. But in practice a tribal approach to data means that every tribe tries to impede the flow, or worse pollute the water, heedless of the implications downstream. Sooner or later this data-water will end up in the hands of third parties (e.g. customers, investors, regulators, etc.) who, uninterested in the identity of the polluter, would be only able to assess that the water is contaminated (i.e. the data is not good enough) and take their trade somewhere else. Thus, the first hurdle of the data personal trainer is to navigate the very sensitive issues of different cultures, expectations and habits of different teams. This is why Pillar I dedicates plenty of space to addressing the issue of augmenting the company culture with a common culture of data.

Data is an afterthought

The world is constantly changing, and the pace of change is accelerating. Digitalization, innovation and technological progress fundamentally transform whole industries and radically change consumer demands. Consequently, businesses must change too in order to pre-empt and win in this unpredictable business environment.

Within organizations, such pressure to match this continuous transformation translates internally into strategic initiatives, programmes and projects. Over the years, businesses have learnt that taming and riding change is a struggle for survival, so managers have been playing increasingly the role of change agents and not just supervisors. Correspondingly, project management and change management certification have become a must, whether you are a new or experienced manager. They now form core blocks of training programmes in managerial and leadership skills. In the last 40 years, with the advent of information technology, with increasingly more processes undergirded by hardware and software, the notion of change expanded to encompass the digital part of the change, as digital is an essential part of achieving the desired outcome. It did not happen immediately. Having started as an 'IT guy', I can attest that for a while the system change was happening in isolation, and, at times, even in contrast to the business change. Nowadays everyone is fully aware that to manage change you must change the processes, change the system and change the people (i.e. training and engagement). It is now the turn of the data to be forgotten!

THE CONSEQUENCES OF DATA FORGETFULNESS

Data forgetfulness starts at the very beginning: the business case might highlight a problem that needs solving and recommend an investment. However, the way the solution is outlined fails to identify its dependency on data. Such failure carries over to the project charter and also possibly to the definition of 'done', i.e. the checklist of the project to-dos, where data-related tasks such as quality management do not appear because the focus is solely on a process or a system. The project team focuses on writing business requirements based on the above. As a result, nobody adds any specific data requirement (e.g. adding a new element, classifying an existing one) and so the design prescribes process and system architecture changes that do not include a design for data change. A test phase is launched in earnest at the end of a laborious build, and the results are not as expected – indeed the beneficiary of the change (e.g. the business entity) discovers just before the planned go live date that the data is not good enough, hence the solution cannot be signed off.

Scramble mode kicks in. However, the project is well beyond the point of no return: most of the budget, or even more than the planned budget, has been spent and so as a last resort the project manager strikes a deal to proceed to a sign-off with a vague commitment to resolve the data issues in 'business as usual'. Unfortunately, our complex business machines are optimized and lean, which means that there is no slack capacity to swallow significant amount of data remediation backlog. The change just implemented has lowered the standards (quality, integrity, etc.) of the company data.

In fact, the more complex the business becomes (think mergers and acquisitions, market growth, geographical growth, overextended infrastructures, multiple regulations, etc.), the more difficult designing and implementing an optimal data change becomes. Suboptimal data changes, in turn, create more complexity in a virtually unstoppable process that sees more and more changes affected by regression, i.e. delivering unforeseen and mostly adverse results even in areas not seemingly connected to the original change.

DATA DEBT

Procrastinating over the data issues we have discussed equates to an 'I owe you' of data because sooner or later that issue will need to be remediated and such remediation will cost someone's time or, interchangeably, money. For instance, a new business unit is created in an organization, but because this is done in a hurry the architecture is not very integrated with the rest of the system. The organization cannot update all the downstream systems with the new entry in the business unit list in time for the launch. Instead, they issue a 'workaround' to the operations team, saying that in case they do not find the new business unit name in their systems to leave it blank. This is just another way of saying 'I owe you (some data fixing)' because some business unit executive will want to see all the opportunities, orders, invoices of their unit nicely listed and aggregated, so the data team will need to go back and fix that. How many times does that happen? Too many to count, but if we add all of these 'I owe yous' together, we compute what I call the *data debt*. Data debt is the cost to make 'all data fit for all purposes' – the theoretical amount that would be necessary to pay out to satisfy all the requirements of all data consumers (internal or external), so that their expected value from data is attained.

The growth of data debt is the main cause of the complexity of data, to the point that data debt is effectively the ballast that slows down or even sinks digital transformations. How? Usually, such transformations are first started in a 'hub'. The hub tests a new digital product that nowadays almost always uses some kind of artificial intelligence. The scientists in the hub gather data about the process they are trying to transform. They analyse, curate, normalize and cleanse the data and prove the hypothesis using this extremely purified version of data. A proof of concept (PoC) is born. The PoC is expanded and it is now implemented in an 'easy' area. This is again done with great care under 'sanitized' conditions, and the pilot succeeds. The management is finally convinced. Their appetite is wetted by the possibilities and the 'scale-up' is decided. Scaling up means to be subjected to the full brunt of the real business operations, meaning a very imperfect data environment, with high levels of data debt. Not having been prepared for such different, variable conditions, it all turns out to be too much. The little digital miracle drastically degrades its performance until being rendered completely useless. And so, the revolution fizzles out in a small experiment that was costly, but, of course, ended in a bevy of lessons learnt that are going to be duly archived and ignored next time round. In Pillar II, the aspiring DPT will learn about their quintessential duties, how to avoid the forgetfulness of data by embedding new rituals and changing the way the business changes.

Data value is hard to quantify

Data might be the lifeblood of digital, and digital might be the future, but as we have discussed, there is an inception point to the data journey. To set an organization in motion, it is necessary to apply energy. Energy in business comes in the form of investment, funds and labour, for which a return is expected. In engineering you would measure an increase in pressure, speed or temperature, but here you will be measuring an increase in revenue, reduction in churn, reduced losses, increased customer satisfaction, etc., so, in one word, data! Data measures whether we are effective at transforming our business and improving the fundamental key performance indicators (KPIs) of a given process.

In order to achieve such performance improvement, an idea has to be sold speaking the language of the business: a *business case*. Following on from the two previous points, not only might we have clans selling each other ideas that are based on completely inconsistent concepts, formulated in a different language, but also their assessment of the costs might have completely missed the underlining data debt. For example, a marketing team writes a business case about powering their marketing strategy with a very complex measure that uses many customer fields, but, when deployed in production months after, the formula is found to yield a usable value less than 50 per cent of the time, as key data is missing.

However, and here comes the final blow, together with underestimating the inherent issues with data the business cases will invariably miss the linkage between the quality of the data they depend on and the business outcome they intend to achieve, creating diverging results. The proposer of the business case will not be able to prove or correlate any tangible business outcome deriving from the creation or improvement of a certain data delivery, the cost of which, depending on the complexity of the effort, might be substantial. When asked about the tangible benefit that the outcome would return on the investment, on the one end the answer could be a disappointing time saving by team members no longer required to perform the tedious task of extracting data, manipulating it in Excel and then sticking it on a PowerPoint. This would be a hard sell to the CFOs, who are justifiably laser-focused on the bottom line and would find it difficult to see this as a quantifiable benefit. On the opposite side of the spectrum, though, the even worse happens: an overinflated benefit statement comes in claiming that a dashboard alone would generate double-digit growth, which would of course be too good to be true. Ultimately, having moved somehow beyond the impasse of the return on investment, for the data personal trainer the true paradox then comes from asking how 'good' the data will need to be. Here the non-data-fluent business leader (data athlete) will have a very binary answer: 'Either it is perfect, or I can't use it.' This is because they miss the causal connection between the data's 'goodness' and the gradient of the value created. 'Perfect' is a laudable ambition but a very expensive one, and we will learn how the DPT will break this apparently irreconcilable deadlock.

In summary, a tribal approach to data would unavoidably create an internal data Babel that would increase the likelihood of not delivering a good change, with benefits we would be unable to quantify. And this is what we are all set to tackle in the remainder of this book. The following three parts will each build up one pillar of data excellence, each one dedicated to resolving the three challenges described above.

COOLING DOWN

- In the digital world, data is the lifeblood of business that powers good decisions.
- Data is not IT, not AI, but a team sport, with data athletes and data personal trainers.
- Data athletes are the business leaders who strive to use data to achieve the ultimate performance for their teams.
- Data personal trainers are data practitioners applying their experience in data to unlock the data athletes' best.

- The more the world becomes pandedomenistic, the more the human being makes the difference and must be at the centre of our change efforts.

- There are three challenges that our data athletes face:

  o Data is tribal.

  o Data is an afterthought.

  o Value from data is hard to quantify.

Notes

1 Sophocles. *Antigone*, First Stasimon, episodes 332–78.
2 United Nations. Data protection and privacy legislation worldwide, UNCTAD, 2024. unctad.org/page/data-protection-and-privacy-legislation-worldwide (archived at https://perma.cc/2H3K-763J)
3 D R E Ewim. Impact of data centers on climate change: A review of energy efficiency, *The Journal of Engineering and Exact Sciences*, 2023, 9 (6), 15.

02

The data excellence approach

WARMING UP

- What is the definition of data excellence?
- What is the difference between data excellence and data governance?
- What are the three pillars of data excellence?
- What is the role of the data personal trainer?
- How do data journeys start in organizations?

What is data excellence?

Data as a sport to excel in

I vividly remember the days in which data conferences were all about data governance and data quality. The data governance sessions covered policies and controls whilst the data quality talks all focused on finding a technological solution, amongst the many on offer, which could solve all the company's issues. The most used adverb was of course 'automatically', the fashion in which everything would have been solved, feeding the unrealistic expectations of an effortless journey to become good at data. Nowadays, these conferences have a very different tone and focus. *Culture*, *value* and *ethics* are no longer talked about by only a small group of visionaries in the corner. Instead, roundtables, panels and fireside chats on the 'soft' aspect of implementing data programs are filling the agendas. Nevertheless, due to the presence of almighty tech forces in the data arena, there remains an overpowering fragrance of 'there must be an app for it', i.e. there must be a fast and painless technical solution, a killer app that will cure all the company's data ailments. This is a perception that stubbornly persists in the minds of our data athletes.

Who can really blame them for wanting an easy solution? Like novice competitors, organizations look for a path of least resistance when approaching the problem. This is down to indolence. It is a natural safety measure that aims at avoiding gold-plating of business endeavours, i.e. adopting a solution that is unnecessarily complex or too refined for the problem that it tries to solve. But the reality is that companies often end up paying considerable sums for solutions that promise wonders but do not deliver.

REAL-WORLD EXAMPLE
Master data management

Kevin is the business intelligence lead for a medium size financial service firm. Kevin's boss has given him *carte blanche* to fix the data in a particular area of the firm that has come under the scrutiny of the regulator. The data reported externally has been inconsistent during the last few quarters, especially their customer data. Like many other financial services institutions, Kevin's company has made a good many acquisitions, and integration activities have not always delivered a consistent set of customer data. There are still multiple points in the company where customer records are created and achieving a common master has been a struggle. Although Kevin has a good technical background and his team is pretty proficient in moving data around the company, this is not a reporting or analytic issue.

At the latest data conference, Kevin has seen demonstrated a product that once installed, the provider says, could deliver a single view of the customer. The price is not cheap, but he has got *carte blanche* and so the contract is drafted, the purchase order is cut, and the licence activated. However, Kevin's legacy infrastructure environment does not sit well with the new technology the master data management (MDM) tool is based on. Unexpectedly, one of the previously acquired company's team reveals they have their own homemade MDM solution that works well, and they are unwilling to phase it out. The pilot that Kevin embarks on to prove the viability of the tool takes a long time as the essential resources required for its success are also the ones involved in the day-to-day regulatory reporting, But the nail in the coffin for the initiative comes from an error in interpreting the product pricing model, which, overnight, doubles the cost of the solution when applied to the company's entire customer base.

Such an approach is not dissimilar to buying a state-of-the-art treadmill believing you will be able to compete with professional athletes in a marathon after only a couple of very intensive sessions. Unfortunately, experience tells us that only two outcomes are likely in this scenario: one is injuring oneself and the other is being humiliated as one's performance is incredibly distant from the professional marathon, assuming that the race is not abandoned pathetically early. In a business context you might experience both, under the guise of financial losses (injuries) and reputational damages (embarrassment). Think about the hosts of customer centre chatbots that have been launched without properly curating and organizing the data and the processes behind, with the net result of customer satisfaction being floored.

The definition of data excellence

Seeing data as a sport that organizations need to excel in is a powerful analogy. Today firms are expected to perform at a level that is unprecedented if they aspire not just to survive but to thrive in the new era of digital neohumanism. It might sound clichéd to mention this, but just consider privacy regulations like GDPR and the expectation of complying fully with the so-called 'right to be forgotten', which prescribes that all personal data that is no longer required for company use should be disposed of. That alone is still a very tall order for any company on the planet. Only someone who has ever stared at the recesses of the technology infrastructure could understand the speed and ramification of data across the company systems. Yet it is rightfully expected that, in case of personal data, especially if sensitive, an organization should be accountable for its whereabouts. To know where all the data is and to manage it consequently is an exceptional ability, and it is this expectation of 'excellence' that inspired me to formulate the definition of *data excellence*, the concept at the heart of this book:

> Data excellence is an enterprise-wide stance that seamlessly combines a specific set of data practices to deliver a comprehensive foundation for *how* an organization deals with its data. It has got at its core a data centric modus operandi that connects sound data abilities to measurable value, increasing the likelihood for an organization to succeed at its strategic ambitions.

Data excellence makes an organization excellent at what it intends to do. As a result of mastering certain practices, the data-excellent organization is recognizable by its strong data culture, robust and resilient change process that takes care of data and the ability to quantify the value it derives from data. Like an Olympian's performance, data excellence is not *achieved*, it is *pursued* along a path of permanent augmentation that continuously coun-teracts the challenges we explored in Chapter 1: the tribal nature of data, the lack of a method to take care of data in the key moments of change, and the absence of a clear mechanism to predict value creation. Let us now take a moment to clarify how data excellence differs from data governance, as too often what we do is collectively defined as data governance to a point that sometimes even our teams are simply called data governance teams.

The initial common misunderstanding is between governance and data governance. Governance is a system that increases the likelihood of reaching and maintaining a certain target performance. It is not specific to data. For instance, a sovereign country *governs* its land, so its laws are complied with to achieve a desirable outcome for its citizens. Data governance is instead a *process* that allows approved data consumers to obtain data that satisfies their consumption requirements, in accordance with the company's approved standards of traceability, meaning, integrity and quality.[1] Therefore, the data governance process is an integral part of the desired operating model compa-nies need to establish to make usage of data a reliable and dependant part of their business operations. However, it would be too reductive to classify our data practitioners' envelope of activities as 'data governance', or, even worse, to relegate it to an action of pure 'governance'. Nevertheless, a jour-ney to data excellence must be *governed*, i.e. understood, championed and appreciated in terms of its cost. Naturally it will include as a constituent part the deployment of adequate data governance, but equally it will comprehend other essential elements I will describe later, such as organiza-tional focus on data, how data use cases are collected and executed, and how data is monitored and valued.

The data excellence gym

'We are what we repeatedly do. Excellence, then, is not an act but a habit.' This quote credited to Aristotle can help us understand how excellence is achieved. A habit is established by repetition of an action, and repetition is not accidental, it must be intentional. So to achieve excellence a strong mindset is required, not only to push through the physical (and mental) discomfort that practising a new action will initially create – as the old saying goes, 'No pain, no gain' – but also to feed the hunger for going beyond, as repeating the same action in the same way will over time require less and less effort, so it is easy to get complacent and plateau at a level that is below what one's personal best could be. Deciding to run 5km every day will take weeks to achieve, but in a few months it could be the easiest part of someone's day. Is that achieving excellence? Not really, as excellence implies being comparatively much higher than the norm. Here expert help is required from a coach or a trainer able to put those repetitive workout sessions into the right upward trend of increasing strain, to achieve and maintain peak performance. You might not be able to beat a world record, but you would have achieved the best you can.

Transposing the above into a business environment, producing the best product or delivering the best experience to customers is, in most cases, the main strategic aim of companies, so their intent is to excel in their mission and be better than their competition. Data is a crucial factor to achieve such a performance in a digital world. Excellent data fuels excellent business. However, as discussed above, data is not yet a *habit* and that's why data excellence requires the expertise of the data personal trainer.

I am introducing here the concept of the data excellence gym. It is a conceptual place where, supported by data personal trainers, data athletes practise the habit of excelling at data and learn how to establish the rituals that will improve business performance. It is my harmless mind trick to shift the common approach to data from a 'fast food' mentality to a mindset of improvement through guided exercise. Aside from the three challenges mentioned above, I've observed that, for many, asking for data is like placing an order from a menu that they do not completely understand, perhaps based on pictures, and to politely queue until the order has been delivered. They do not care about the process and they believe that a simple instruction should be enough to obtain what they want, just to find out that is not always the case and they are disappointed. Instead, the data excellence gym metaphor emphasizes the point that to be able to consume the right data and create value requires a solid partnership, in which both parties, the data athlete and data personal trainer, commit for the best results, in the complete understanding that data is not just the DPT's job and it requires the DA's effort too. It is not transactional but transformative.

The three pillars of data excellence

Like the stereotypical Greek structure, we can picture the data excellence gym resting on a stony base of data foundations with an airy triangular, marble-clad gable of value at the top. The weight of the gable is born by three solid columns – the three pillars of data excellence (Figure 2.1):

- *Pillar I – The mindset:* To start and sustain a revolution in the company culture to facilitate data excellence. In this pillar I describe how to use the

FIGURE 2.1 The three pillars of data excellence

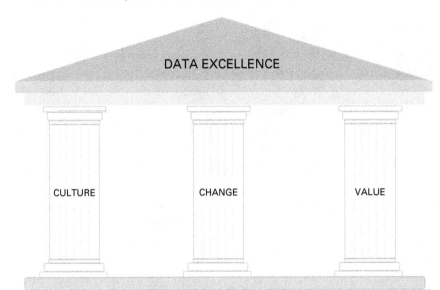

strategic intent to foster a corporate mindset that yearns to excel at data. It goes from establishing the right tone at the top, it is reinforced with the help of new roles like the data domain owners, and it is propagated to all levels by meticulous communication and engagement plans that align behaviours to the excellence goals.

- *Pillar II – The method:* To embed in the existing processes and procedures the necessary methodological alterations that realize data excellence. This pillar takes care of changing the way change is done, as every change is both an opportunity to improve the data environment and a risk to increase data debt. Here the Data Excellence Operating Model is fully described as the basis to operationalize such a shift, inclusive of the crucial monitoring and controlling phase.

- *Pillar III – The value:* To appraise the improvement in performance, correlating the value creation that comes from consumption of better data to the improvement in the outcome achieved by better decision-making processes. The idea of likening data to a product is the centrepiece of this pillar, together with the illustration of valuation methodologies that increase the likelihood to deliver on the business case hypothesis.

The data personal trainer

The role

The centre stage of the data excellence gym is occupied by the data personal trainer (DPT). This alias refers to all those data practitioners who have over the years become the essential change agents of the data revolution. The heads of data, heads of enterprise data, chief data officers, chief data and analytics officers and now, more imaginatively, chief intelligence officers who have been leading the charge to revolutionize data in their companies – either by desire or by default but always with passion. In the figure of the data personal trainer I am amalgamating years of experiences, personal and shared by others, who by virtue of the transversal nature of data have realized that you need to act from within the core business processes and side by side with all key stakeholders. They have understood that quality is in the eye of the consumer of data and hence they have dedicated more time to decipher unspoken intentions for the results not to disappoint. They have learnt that those intentions often reveal misjudgement and overoptimistic assumptions and hence they have finessed the way to hold the conversation about who has to put in the real effort (i.e. the athlete, not the trainer), while reassuring in words and in deed that they will be there to provide support and encouragement all the way along.

Different data journeys

Although there are no material impacts on the tenets of data excellence, it would be useful to trace back the genesis of data programmes, as it is useful to know where one has come from. History has value and organizational history explains the culture and its workings, and helps to uncover lurking variables that might affect the effectiveness of our schedules as DPT. Every company will have accumulated emotional scars and made big mistakes whose aches and echoes are still felt and might manifest with reluctance or reticence incomprehensible to an external observer. Equally, there might have been proud moments and historical achievements that would be dangerous to call into question. Any personal trainer would want to be aware of such pain points and muscular strengths before defining the best regime for their trainees.

I have observed broadly two fashions in which companies have come to embark on a such endeavours. The first and most common data journey is the one initiated by 'heroes', leaders of a function or unit. Enlightened by an intuition, these leaders start their data journeys in pure 'Skunk Works' style, as conceived by American aeronautical engineer Kelly Johnson. They gather the resources and a handful of like-minded colleagues and push the envelope in untried ways. Their survivability and scalability, even when some success is achieved, is always uncertain. This is because they themselves have now emerged as a tribe and therefore their impact on data is restricted to their own territories.

The other form of data journey has an external origin, where there is a non-negotiable demand for better data. This could take the form of a crisis or more commonly a regulatory change. Basel II, GDPR[2] and BCBS 239[3] are all clear examples of external origins that put in motion the events creating the majority of the data leader roles we see today. The potential pitfall of an externally imposed data journey is that this becomes too focused on a tick-box exercise. Instead of following the adage 'to be, rather than to seem', the bare minimum to be compliant is attempted, often on a separate plane from the reality of the business and is then repeated many times in slightly different ways for subsequent regulations. A quick scan of the flows of information would reveal that there is a 'core' that supports the main business processes, and that core is surrounded by a constellation of end points that, taking data from the core, is feeding siloed regulatory reporting solutions. Here each one extracts a slightly different set of data from the systems of record in the core, and each one adapts that extract to the specific need of the regulation. Aside from the evident proliferation of flows, which increases infrastructure and maintenance cost, the potentially fatal flaw of this set-up is the impossibility of answering consistently to the same question coming from two different regulators about the data in different reports. Here the reconciliation of different data manufacturing lines (later we will call them data supply chains) is very difficult, unless of course, the company has done an excellent job of making all the data that flows in all the different end points consistent, but that, in my experience, almost never happens.

The issue could be just accumulated complexity whereas it is easier to start from scratch when a new regulatory requirement comes in rather than harmonizing it with the existing legacy. However, the real challenge is that modern regulations, like the latter two mentioned above, are increasingly principle-based. What that means is that the regulators are like the parents with messy teenager children who have been trying for years to educate their kids on the need to remove all the toys from the floor, only to find said toys shoved under the bed. After asking their untidy offspring not to use the bed as a bin, at the next inspection they find that the jumble has simply moved to the cupboards! So, the frustrated parent-regulator issues a simple order 'Be tidy!', so no list of tick boxes is available. Likewise, at the centre of the regulations there are tidy terms like 'adequate', 'accurate', 'transparent', 'effective' – principles that are difficult to demonstrate compliance with, without complying by outcome, i.e. regulatory compliance is a by-product of the act of doing business well, so a habit!

Whatever its genesis might have been, at a certain point in that journey, the management – our data athlete – feels a higher performance could be achieved if the whole enterprise commits to it. And so, they come across the notion of the data officer, and, after a long gestation, a decision is made to hire 'one of those'. Peer pressure is high and advisors are insisting that all successful companies have 'one of those' because, of course, data is the new oil!

Hiring the data officer

The first hurdle to overcome when hiring a new data officer is creating the job description. What does the data officer really do? It is astonishing that the same question that we posed 10 years ago, and which we have spent many hours debating as a group of data enthusiasts, is still fundamentally unresolved. After a decade, our craft is in fact still a craft and not a science. Even if it were a science, the challenges we have explored in the data arena would require precise tailoring to a company's unique conditions. In fact, that tailoring is immediately evident in the first attempt at a data officer job description, written at best by a 'boutique head hunting' partner with very little knowledge of data, and, at worst, crowd-sourced by the executive committee, by collecting everyone's wish list in an incoherently long laundry list of 'things to fix'. I have read many of those and I have seen this role been asked to take on an incredibly broad spectrum of responsibilities, from implementing data lakehouses to increasing search engine optimization (SEO) and, crucially, being able to handle the media in case of a data-related incident.

In my experience, it would only take a few small adjustments to increase the success in matching the need with a suitable candidate. Leaving as independent variables the recruitment process and the 'chemistry' between the hiring manager, the role's stakeholders and the new recruit, I have seen job descriptions that clearly show that the internal talent acquisition team and the external partner have produced a viable description. Externally they had performed serious market research, resulting in them using the right terminology – rather than just throwing in the current buzz words – and created a consistent set of responsibilities that one could see well suited in the same role. Finally, the compensation package was within the expected range of the role and the type of candidates they were approaching. On the internal side, it was evident that a good deal of thinking had gone into the problems that the role should tackle and the positioning and the high-level composition of the data organization (more on this in Pillar I) had been sketched in such a way that allows the candidate to see a trajectory but still with room for their personal contribution to the direction. So, in summary, unsurprisingly good market research on naming and compensation, an honest 'behind the scenes' view of the current situation, a coherent set of expectations matching the problem the company wants to solve with the role are the best premises for finding the best candidate.

The job description has been published, then the true dilemma comes: *buy* vs *upcycle*. What I mean by this is you can either open to the external market and bring in a well-known data expert, or pick one of the existing internal heroes and promote them to become the lead for the enterprise. Both approaches are viable, but they have pros and cons. In the case of buy, you should be able to onboard a proven data expert, free of internal baggage and emotional attachment to the past and able, with the proverbial fresh pair of eyes, to look candidly at root causes and bring to bear the power of data. However, they will need to learn about the company and its agility or lack of, and win the trust of the different tribes, who may find it hard to embrace the 'outsider' telling them to change and do something new they do not completely understand.

On the other hand, upcycling an internal resource would put in the post someone who, in theory, 'knows our ways' and could have an easier journey to gain buy-in and trust, as hopefully they would have an established network and possibly some reputational credit to cash in from good deeds done in the past. However, their approach to data might be more based on common sense than subject matter expertise, so the speed at which progress is made could still be slow and susceptible to mishaps, like the one that happened to Kevin in the above example.

Whichever option is chosen, the elected one will find themselves facing a quasi-messianic expectation of speedy results and material value creation in an environment where data debt has grown steadily, and the process issues, known but sadly neglected, have depleted the once-agile lean mass of the organization. That is where data excellence flips the axis of the problem: data excellence stipulates that the data athlete should not ask what the data personal trainer can do for the data. Instead, the data athlete should learn to express clearly what their objectives are and follow the data personal trainer's regime to achieve them.

And it starts from the first commonly ask deliverable to the newly arrived data officer/data personal trainer: 'Give us the *data strategy*!' There cannot be a pre-formatted, readily concocted data strategy. No matter how deep your expertise in data might have been, you need a clear and articulated business strategy first.

COOLING DOWN

- Excelling at data is like excelling at a sport – buying the latest and greatest gym gadget, alone, does not make you an Olympian.

- Data excellence is a holistic posture; data governance is a process essential to it.

- To become excellent, a habit that is continuously improved must be established.

- The data excellence gym has three pillars: mindset, method and value.

- Whether your data journey starts from within or is imposed from outside (regulations) there comes a moment when a DPT is needed to excel.

- Hiring the first DPT (you might call them chief data officer) is tricky, but you can help yourself by putting together a good description of the role.

- There is no 'data strategy', there is only a 'business strategy' enabled by data.

Notes

1 P J Thomas. An in-depth interview with experienced chief data officer Roberto Maranca, 2018. peterjamesthomas.com/2018/05/10/an-in-depth-interview-with-experienced-chief-data-officer-roberto-maranca/ (archived at https://perma.cc/L8BT-65GZ)

2 European Union. Regulation (EU) 2016/679 of the European Parliament and of the Council of 27 April 2016 on the protection of natural persons with regard to the processing of personal data and on the free movement of such data, and repealing Directive 95/46/EC (General Data Protection Regulation), 2016. eur-lex.europa.eu/eli/reg/2016/679/oj (archived at https://perma.cc/3659-MEM4)

3 Bank for International Settlements. Principles for effective risk data aggregation and risk reporting, 2013. www.bis.org/publ/bcbs239.pdf (archived at https://perma.cc/N63F-HD46)

Strategies and tactics for cultural change

03

The data culture

WARMING UP

- Is the concept of culture applicable to companies too?
- Do leaders drive culture or is it formed historically by random events?
- What is the best position for the data team to win the cultural challenge?
- How does the DPT deal with the top management?

What is culture?

We have already touched on the tribal nature of data owing to company culture, but for clarity's sake let's define what culture is. For that I like the definition that Sir Edward Burnett Tylor gave in 1871:

> Culture or Civilization, taken in its wide ethnographic sense, is that complex whole which includes knowledge, belief, art, morals, law, custom, and any other capabilities and habits acquired by man as a member of society.[1]

So can companies have a culture? Dissecting this definition, it seems that we could describe the company as a societal subset with capabilities, e.g. company policies, knowledge, customs and habits which are acquired by its employees as part of their affiliation to this group. Everyone must be familiar with the types of phrases thrown at the new recruits: 'This is not the way we do things here', 'We prefer to say it this way', 'You are not supposed to say that', 'We work this way', 'We call it that'. Such learning is supposed to assimilate the new starters into the existing 'society' to avoid friction or faux pas, while the assimilated quickly adapts to feel part of the new group. Famous examples of company culture are Netflix's 'freedom and responsibility' or Google's '70–20–10 rule', designed to create a true sense of 'who we are' for employees to affiliate themselves with.

So, no need for the services of an anthropologist – the answer seems to be a resounding yes, companies have cultures. Data requires new habits, norms and capabilities to be embedded in the company. Therefore, the first pillar of data excellence is dedicated to creating the right culture that is receptive of data – and by design I used the word mindset to highlight the vectored and focused intention that has to be the basis of the cultural change. If the tribes are to be unified, a strong resolution must be in place to sustain the motivation that would propel the organization along the data journey.

The importance of culture for the success of data

From a quick search in my archive, I was able to trace the first appearance of the word 'culture' as something essential for the success of data in a presentation to my management team at General Electric (GE) in early 2015. In over 30 slides I described the journey undertaken up to that point, outlining the essential components of a robust and effective response in the form of an ideal 'temple'. This presented column-like workstreams of change supporting a 'governance and enterprise risk' roof and solidly sitting on a foundation of 'augmented organizational culture'. In one key page about the experience garnered in the first year, the tagline at the bottom was revealing: 'Changing the culture of the company is vital, but it is the trickiest bit!'

This was the company in which I had spent 14 years, thus far the majority of my working life, and so I knew pretty well 'the way we worked'. GE was highly networked, mostly by design, and many leaders had multiple functional reporting lines and cross-team responsibility; it was seen as a perk having to respond to only one boss. My previous roles were all in IT but even then I observed that the technology alone would not serve everything and any project could have been successful only if all the 'ecosystem of stakeholders' were favourably aligned. The point I am stressing is that 'acceptance' and 'adoption' are two crucial steps to success. Neither of them is deterministic or automatic, there is no quid pro quo or mechanism to implement them: people have to accept and adopt, and people would actively buy into something they feel is not alien to them, something they can understand and trust as good for them, and therefore they adopt as a new norm and new rituals. Looking at the problem of making GE Capital, my business unit, good at data, and good at it in a way that a US and European regulators could be satisfied, on the back of my Basel II experience I instinctively grasped that there would have been no application or software alone capable to achieve that, though cloud computing, data lake technology, blockchain, etc., had shown that nothing was technically impossible, and it was clear that to truly achieve data excellence a change of lifestyle was required. Change had to be achieved in the most complex component of any enterprise: its people. I didn't know then, but soon I would have had empirical data to demonstrate it.

In 2016 the Gartner chief data officer (CDO) survey was launched and, being in a data officer position, I was invited to participate together with more than 100 other data officers or heads of data, which at the time was a very representative sample. A comprehensive assessment of the 'hottest' role in the business was conducted, the questions aimed at performing an ideal X-ray of its genesis, position and status. One of the questions became in the next few years a sort of barometer of a CDO's success: the participant was asked to rank the top three roadblocks to the success of data initiatives, and it was demonstrated that more than half of the answers identified 'cultural challenges in accepting change' as the number one internal roadblock. This answer stayed as number one until the 2023 edition, which showed 'skills and staff shortages' at the top, with culture still in solid third place.[2]

Change acceleration process

At this point I would like to connect my quasi-instinctive reaction to this problem with the most important training that General Electric was imparting to its leaders, known as the change acceleration process (CAP). At the beginning of the 1990s, true to GE's engineering approach, the question posed to the management was why were so many perfectly conceived technical changes failing to deliver the business benefit that they were engineered to achieve? The answer was low acceptance of the change. The culture resisted change, failed to embrace the behavioural change that would have made the change most effective, and in a new era of constant change that was disastrous. CAP, which provided a very pragmatic toolkit to make change effective and sustained, became mandatory for everyone in GE. To this day I practise religiously many of its tenets, one of them being 'Always check for understanding and check for agreement.' So it was natural that, when faced with the task of injecting something as new and alien as data, my focus was quickly taken away from the 'simple' and convenient targets in the foreground, those of implementing the hardware and software mechanics. Instead, at the centre, the big target on which the success of the whole enterprise depended, was cultural change.

Later my determination was further strengthened when I started comparing my experiences with the others in the same position. Almost by chance I entered the data conference circuit where I could compare notes with other data leaders like me, who had been on the journey for much longer. Here were financial institutions trying to comply with their regulators' high data demands, still struggling to make the data thing stick. Data officers were being regularly hired, tried and fired. It was calculated at the time that the average the lifespan of a CDO in the post was 17 months! In this atmosphere of high expectations, the honeymoon period was soon over, and the magic dissipated in the face of steep bills that accounted for very little value.

Toning the top

Why culture needs to come from the top

Masujro Hashimoto, Thomas Edison, Henry Ford, Sampson Lloyd and John Taylor, Adolphe and Joseph-Eugene Schneider; in my career's chronology these are the founders of my past employers. Companies are born out of an individual's idea, and become a legacy of that original idea, which their leadership strives to live up to, fulfilling their mission while continuously interpreting that original idea. In the way I defined culture above, culture is the mechanism of furtherance of that idea, it is indeed the will of a corporation, and thus top down. This is evident in companies still directed by their original founders, and it is somewhat more subtle in big corporations where successive generations of leaders would have steered the original culture, especially when facing a crisis, for example the shift on safety culture that followed BP's Deepwater Horizon disaster or the Equifax trust campaign to restore customer confidence after their data breach. So, if we want the company culture to embrace data it is important to say a few words on the positioning of the data team in relation to the top, and on the governance or 'influencing model'. We need to tone that top into shape so the top can then set the tone in line with the level of data ambition.

Positioning of the data team as a key factor of success

Data is the latest addition to the organizational set, and it is still in flux through the ranks of enterprises, a dynamic that creates a spectrum of hierarchical reporting lines. In the past those lines were mostly the remnant of the initial genesis of a data journey. The 'boss' of the data team was the hero that trailblazed the start of something new in the way reporting was done and, seeing the project through its initial success, naturally wanted to control the journey.

More recently, a more designed approach to the data-driven company has emerged, one where you might have expected a certain level of standardization around the positioning of the data team. Instead, looking at one of the most recent data surveys, the demographic of CDOs shows almost half of them still reporting to the chief operating officers and chief information officers, albeit in declining numbers.[3] On the other hand, chief digital officer rose in rank, while an increasing share, currently more than a quarter, is dispersed within the 'others' category (i.e. reporting to other executive roles). The coveted reporting line to the CEO is only between 10 and 20 per cent and disappointingly steady. This stubbornly low level of reporting to the CEO perhaps speaks to a perceived undervaluing of the CDO role within many organizations. However, in full disclosure I am definitely in the 'should not report to the CEO' camp, so I am not too disappointed, for reasons I will outline in the following section.

Designing an effective reporting line for the CDO

It is difficult in our very nonstandard craft to make absolute statements and it would contradict what I said above about the digital neo-humanistic approach if I now affirmed that the CDO reporting lines are the sole predictor of their prospects. There is a rich set of independent human variables that are going to be more important for the outcome, albeit highly unpredictable, than just how far the data lead sits from the top. However, it would be nice to operate an analysis of variance to establish whether the success of CDOs (whichever way one defines it) is more likely when reporting to the CEO. Nevertheless, without labouring the point too much, I believe that insisting that the CDO sits in the executive committee of certain companies can backfire. This is because, no matter the increased power that comes with the position, the lens of the one person responsible for data sitting at the top can create a permanent distortion to the culture, whereby data is that team's problem, not mine. During his tenure as CIO at GE, I remember Gary Reiner telling us how, during the highest of executive committees, if the projector suffered a technical glitch, no matter the seriousness and strategic weight of the matter he was presenting, all eyes immediately fixed on him to draw a screwdriver and repair the issue. Rolling forward a few years, I believe that one chair in the boardroom occupied by data could perpetuate that tribal sense, by which there is now a data police/helper/housekeeping that flushes all bad data away.

So, if real life shows that there is no standard answer to the question of where a CDO's reporting line goes, as suggested by the increased share of 'others', this signals that, as a data personal trainer presented with the chance to create or redesign the data organization, instead of imposing my preconceived textbook view, I should be open-minded and assess the unit or function which, at that moment in time, has the best chance of success.

The first step of that assessment should include a first memorandum of understanding with the top management on what it really takes to be excellent at data. This is far from a generally shared concept so it must address preconceptions. In the majority of cases that I have observed, either with prospective employers or second-hand information, being good at data is hindered by the three misconceptions covered in Chapter 1: 'Data is IT', 'Data is AI' and 'Data is the new oil'. During an interview for a CDO role I was once asked (and it was a good question) what I would have wished the interviewer to personally do in order to enable my success. I surprised them by answering that, beyond the mobilization of money and resources, the real enabler of my success would be whether the interviewer could use their authority to make two colleagues from different parts of the business overcome their entrenched thinking to agree on a common position. This emphasized the importance of 'breaking data silos' and what this really means, in my view. That surprised them, because increasing *definitional integrity* – the ability to call the same thing with the same name across the whole organization – is not the first thing that people associate with data excellence. Since then I have made that example a standard part of the expectations I set out to new data athletes.

Organizational models and their influence on the data team

A powerful reporting line will turn out to be futile if it is not accompanied by a structure that stitches the data team into the fabric of the organization and allows it to influence the culture. Here, once again, a keen situational awareness of the existing organizational model has to be achieved in order to then craft the data team accordingly. Three types of generally accepted model types of organization are recognized: centralized, decentralized and federated, as per Figure 3.1.

FIGURE 3.1 Organizational models

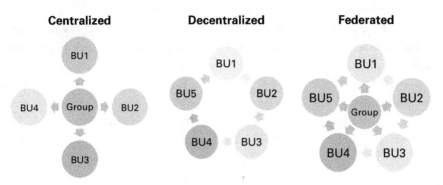

A centralized model is characterized by a central 'group' function which manages the business unit (BU) in a strong top-down 'command and control' type of governance – the 'group' is at the helm. Policies and procedures are the by-laws issued centrally, and control frameworks are in place to check whether the BUs are in compliance with the desired strategy.

Most 'traditional' financial services organizations have this model in place; risk, finance, HR, operations functions would be centralized, accountable for the overall strategy and standards of execution and deal with business units, usually associated with their product lines, e.g. consumer banking, insurance, commercial banking, leasing. It is a model that in 'regulated' industries is associated, in theory, with greater control and consistency. Its detractors point out that, from an innovation point of view, this model lacks agility as the BUs have little autonomy.

A decentralized model has no central fulcrum and relies instead on a common goal and loose collaboration amongst the business units. Here the BUs have the power to chart their own destiny and as long as results are achieved no real standardization is imposed.

You might think this model would be suitable just for young companies that are going through a series of diverse portfolio acquisitions. In fact, this has been implemented with success by some decently large manufacturing and media companies. It is usually the response to a fast-moving market that has seemingly no minimum common denominator, i.e. very customer bespoke, speed of response is crucial and standardization is seen as unnecessary red tape. However, in a downturn this model might be exposing a weakness; when productivity and cost reduction are a factor of survival, it struggles to reduce costs due to the variation (read duplication without similarities) in processes, systems and of course data, of approaches in a loosely coupled organization, or it is less able to perform consistently. Equally, in such a model it would be very challenging to serve global customers, when they would be expecting, and most of them do, a consistent customer experience across different geographies, i.e. dealing with different units.

A federated (or franchised) organization is the hybrid of the two and philosophically it aspires to create a sort of *yin–yang* balance. Here the pull for standardization from the centre stays in dynamic equilibrium with the centrifugal forces of customization from the edge of the business units, which is where innovation usually happens.

Successful examples of such an organization model can be found typically in the giant fast-food companies. The group issues a set of corporate defined rules that are sacrosanct and should not be breached, but the BUs have an agreed degree of freedom to satisfy their customers. Example: the marketing, the branding, the architecture and furnishing of the points of sale would be tightly controlled, but certain product recipes would be at discretion of the unit, assumedly more in tune with the local customer needs. It is a tricky dynamic balance of push-and-pull that successful companies resolve with a pristine information flow process that constantly brings instances of innovations from the periphery (BUs) into the centre (group) where innovation becomes a standard that is then pushed back to the edge.

It is not my intention to dwell on the pros and cons of the different models, suffice to say that a DPT must observe and craft its action routes while cognisant of the company dynamics, possibly mimicking them: it would be pointless, for example, to adopt a centralized model for the data organization in an overall decentralized company. It is fair to say that sizeable companies are finding themselves leaning more and more towards a federated model, which does not deliver the agility of a decentralized one but allows a certain amount of control. This is due, partially, to the fact that the monolithic company built around a command and control centre, if it ever had achieved any real success, in a digitally enabled, fast paced world struggles to sustain the pace of change, but it is also due to a markedly different intention of human relationships within organizational hierarchy, where empowerment of front lines and diversity of thinking are scientifically demonstrated to foster more sustainable growth.

Whichever the model of the organization, the data organization should be moulded to support it, with special attention to not becoming isolated or overinflated. Indeed, in any organization if the data team is more than 10 per cent of the total workforce, something has gone wrong, as you can't have more trainers than trainees, unless the trainers are the ones supposed to compete, meaning that the duties that were expected to be carried out by data athletes are now the responsibility of the data team. And yet, to reach that 3–5 per cent of total workforce, which I maintain is optimal for the stability of the journey, this might still be a long and hard journey if only obtained through organic growth (i.e. net new hires), even assuming a fat blank check from the CFO allowing for a doubling of resources year-on-year. To describe this with simple maths: for a company of 1,000 people, I would judge as an optimal size 40 full-time equivalents (FTEs) in the data team. Then let's assume a starting point of just the CDO/DPT together with three heads of department, so it would still take four years to reach the optimum size, which is a very long timeframe to become impactful across the whole organization. Instead, the biggest advantage here is one of speed of growth: enrolling or annexing existing 'data enclaves' under the franchise banner creates a much bigger team of data personal trainers, at a speed that would be impossible to sustain with centrally led, organic growth.

Working out the top

Eventually, the top job of data has been filled and, notwithstanding the shortcomings of the job description, the data team has been positioned and is poised to operate within the given organizational model. It is now time to start the work of the data personal trainer.

Toning the top tone

'Tone at the top' is the behaviours that are shown by the top leadership as a marker of the company intent: they represent models for the rest of the company to imitate, and tone at the top is especially critical in relationship with ethical stances that the organization is taking when facing systemic crisis or reputational backlashes. However, if proactively displayed, tone at the top effectively is a primary objective of the data excellence first pillar (the culture), as it verbalizes the corporate culture in manifestos, policies and corporate communication. Also it allows me to employ the play on words of 'toning the top tone' as the first challenge of the data personal trainer, as culture has to be toned up in its data muscle at the very top. Here, access is essential, and it is not a given that the DPT would be at earshot distance from the board or the executive committee (ExCom), or (better) be seen as a confidant by one of the ExCom members, or (even better) be part of the ExCom; however, whatever the starting position, the first task is to identify a suitable avenue to the top. In general, that can be achieved in three ways:

- *Contractual power.* This is the shortest to achieve when the DPT has had leverage in attaining a position that has got the access to the top that is required, though it is the quickest to be lost, and requires exceptional political skills.
- *Reputational credit.* The DPT has been known for a while in the company, and in their new role they are staking their reputation on this novel thing called 'data' as they are trusted in trying a fresh approach.
- *Navigational skills.* The DPT slowly builds up their network of allies and believers, applying good data work and, not without a hint of a Machiavellian approach, influences up the ranks until they are able to connect with the top.

'Public' commitment

It doesn't necessarily mean posting a long announcement on social media or issuing a press release, but, internally, the wider communication about the new intent about data and the fulfilment of a position that has got clear accountabilities around the journey of data is a definite must. Plenty of data officers have made the costly mistake of underestimating this need for 'vocalization' of an agreement that becomes commitment before the workforce. The thought is that it is 'implicitly obvious' that the organization is committed, as in the end I have filled the position and I have been given some budget, and maybe insisting on over-captioning the new team might be felt like just pleasing one's ego, the CDO as *prima donna*. In fact, this is a first test of resolve that the leadership has to pass, as any first step towards improvement is the admission of an existing problem. The second step is to tell someone, as once it is written down and communicated, pride in 'walking the talk' would prevent a hasty withdrawal from the intent to improve on data when the going gets tough. The format and timing of the commitment might vary depend on the company, the genesis of the journey and, of course, the culture. But in any case, the recommendation for the DPT is to remove any possible obstacles and facilitate it, working directly with the communication team, finding existing *loci* where the message can be posted, and drafting the comms. The time spent might seem disproportionate to the immediate outcome – an email, a presentation, a pdf manifesto – but it is a worthwhile investment.

All enterprises, of a certain size, try to encode their culture in tangible artefacts, which would encapsulate the spirit of their vision and values. Usually that takes the form of yearly renewal of a pact between the employer and employee going through a document and attesting to that document. It would usually state the commitment to ethical conduct in business versus the key parties of suppliers, customers, employees and regulators, and, more recently, it would focus on sustainability and diversity ambitions. A first victory for the DPT would be for their data athletes to agree to instil in the code of conduct a tangible call-out to data excellence, and, if we recall the seven external trends mentioned at the beginning of the book, pledging something about responsible AI or personal data rights would probably be welcome with open arms, and so the very first ritual is established!

The 'big picture'

Once access to the top is secured and positive affirmation has been given, any personal trainer will start setting 'the big picture' for their athlete. The big picture is a conceptual exercise to depict a vision of a potential future state where the trainee sees themself in a highly desirable status. As such it is used to create an attractive vision to motivate the trainee to embark on a challenging journey. Here is when the DPT must spare no energy to penetrate the business jargon to extract its mission and its strategy. The big picture must be a 'to be' status where there is a clear enabling role for the data to play. A fitness assessment should then follow to understand the gap between the ambition and the current level of data ability, but I will describe that in Chapter 5.

For example, a consumer bank wants to provide above-and-beyond duty of care for customers in distress, for instance in the case of critical illness diagnosis or bereavement. In particular they want to focus on those customers who hold multiple products (e.g. current account, insurance and/or car leasing) who find it stressful having to notify their predicament to all the different customer lines of the same bank and more often than is desirable receive inconsistent treatment. The goal is for the customer to only have to communicate once with any of the customer care lines, and then that message would not only be conveyed to all other product lines the customer has a relationship with but also the appropriate action(s) would be put in place, e.g. a loan repayment delayed for a family loss or mail communication switched to braille for a vision impairment.

The big picture that the DPT should propose in this case would take the form of one or multiple stories (these are called data consumer stories, which I explain in more detail later in the book). For example, 'I am a customer of Bank X, and I have recently been diagnosed with cancer. I am very concerned about my finances, but I know that I just have to call any of the bank's helplines and, thanks to my identification and a letter from my GP, the helpline will take care of it across all my products.' The DPT would explain to the bank how this ambition can only be achieved by creating and maintaining a true customer 360-degree view that connects customer, products and 'what if' scenarios.

It is a marathon, not a sprint

Outlining the 'big picture' should have already dispelled such misconceptions, but in the spirit of vocalizing for positive commitment, the DPT should intercept and address any belief that data is like a 'single project' or a 'just another program' with an end date. Of course, milestones and short-term objectives should be agreed (how do you measure improvements otherwise?) but it would need to be as clear as possible and relayed by the management as frequently as possible that, in data, there is a before and an after, meaning that sustainable results are only achieved with a true change of lifestyle: as the business changes and evolves to match trends, competition and customer needs changes, so data excellence ambitions have to be raised.

Making preparations for a journey requires us to stock up principally on resilience, so that change is tangible and durable. One way of realizing what form the 'big picture' is going to take is the use of simple metaphors. One I have used successfully is that of a marathon. In one of my data roles, I designed and had realized a simple cartoon that compared the desire of excelling at data with running a marathon. A runner is seen running on the screen, accompanied by a voiceover asking, 'Would you run a marathon if you had never trained for it before? Certainly not...'. The point was simple but full of opportunities for analogies. Nobody would run a marathon without duly training for it, but training alone would not be enough; an appropriate diet, resting regime and, equally important, mindfulness would all be required. The analogy is that excelling at data requires disciplined training, but the 'company mindfulness' is the winning factor, something that was probably not emphasized enough at the time we made that cartoon. Instead, it was aimed more at disproving the idea that an IT tool, here symbolized by a high-priced gym machine, would make you a data champion.

Beyond the metaphor, then, connecting with the top also from a non-technical level is essential to reinforce that resilience. One effective option, also fuelled by the excitement over AI, is to propose bidirectional mentoring, where, using the 'excuse' of teaching about AI, the DPT can be formally paired up with executives and instil in them a non-buzzword-related understanding of data and its potential for creating that 'company mindfulness' for rainy days.

Not everyone is a data cheerleader

Finally, it is perfectly fine not be as passionate about data as the DPT, and, as mentioned at the beginning, this book is also trying to address the ones that, unlike me, don't particularly fancy practising conceptual modelling, or are not impressed by an intricate data lineage diagram. We should always assume that the vast majority of data athletes want to do the best at work, that they genuinely care for their colleagues and that they want to satisfy their customer needs. So, aside from the public commitment to the big picture mentioned above, in which an unequivocal commitment to the journey of data excellence is expected, when it is down to the single individuals at the top it would be unfair for the data personal trainer to expect that the whole of the board or the executive committee devote themselves to become data enthusiasts or specialists, not excluding that some might. A good measure of success would be for each one of them to be able to articulate how data would contribute to their missions.

Engaging the data international Olympic committee

While the organization is being set up, the roles that have been established are being recruited for and the strategy is being percolated, it is critical to keep the data athlete motivated, as at the very beginning it is easy to lose focus. Maintaining the rhythm necessary to achieve data excellence requires more than just the data personal trainer, who might have a short role-life span.

In all companies there are one or more functions which control the performance of the business. These 'control functions' are like the bodies that regulate competition, as they define how performance is measured and set the rules. If the aim is to embed data in the culture, after human resources and finance, then these are the next set of people the DPT would want on their side. Whether they take the form of a risk team, an audit team or simply an internal control team, these functions have in common a spasmodic need for good data, as without it they cannot be in control. Data is the evidence that proves performance and it is normal practice for the control function either to have access to process data, e.g. data that is produced in the course of executing a process, or to issue a data request to analyse a unit's performance. In either case, the ultimate win–win scenario is convincing the leaders of these control functions that good data practices are a necessary condition for effective controls, and that after-sales, a special magic happens. If an auditor or controller is going around asking about 'sources of authority', 'data governance' and 'data quality', or if there are data requests to appraise a business unit's 'data maturity', our data athletes will find themselves caught in a pincer movement that firmly drives them towards more virtuous behaviour towards data.

Enterprise risk frameworks, once the sole prerogative of financial institutions, are now widely adopted in many industries, and I will dedicate ample space in Pillar II to how data risk is essential to deliver data excellence, but for now I will just mention a few essential concepts. Risk management is implemented to mitigate the occurrence of an issue that causes a type of loss (e.g. reputational, financial, operational), so keeping a record of the losses is an important part of the framework to determine the effectiveness of the mitigation, as it can only be proved over time ('With our current access control we assume that the risk of seriously being hacked is once a year'). The content of that *losses database*, as it is commonly called, is a treasure trove the DPT should seek access to, as it is the key to bind the alliance with the control functions. The information is highly confidential and so its custodians would be reluctant to share, but the shrewd DPT would argue that they need only aggregate information about losses having data as root cause, and hopefully access would be granted for the company's sake. A reputational blunder due to inadvertent leakage of information, an outage on the company website because of a change that created regression (i.e. an unforeseen problem), a business decision made with inaccurate data that created a commercial problem are all cases in which our data athletes breached the rules and were penalized due to their underperforming data excellence, so embedding it should be an easy enough conversation. It proves that embedding the precept of data excellence in the risk assessment of the company should have a direct impact on the reduction of the losses, and that is how the control functions could be recruited as DPT helpers, just as if an auditor during their field audit work were to start to ask someone to show their metaphorical data quality muscle, that someone will definitely work harder to improve them.

After all, nobody wishes to be called out by or to disappoint the control functions. Consequently, the recommendations of the DPT are listened to more attentively and deemed more noteworthy.

Amongst all the control functions, there is one that is probably the most vital to infiltrate: that of the project management office (PMO). Sometimes called the change office or strategic initiatives, this is the function that has the overall responsibility for funding and overseeing the strategic agenda of change. There might be more than one, managing different types of portfolios, but these are the places where I go first to understand the intent, the mindset of what is being attempted strategically. And here I have to infer the relationship between these priorities and the data, or the capabilities of data. These are the 'competitions' that the DPT has to prepare the DA for. Among the typical symptoms of the DA not being ready for such contests is the lack of anything in the business case or in the planned expense related to making the data fit for its intended consumption, which, as we now know, will cause the project to run over schedule and/or over budget. The simplest example of such a failure is a project that is supposed to deliver a decision support system such as a dashboard or a cockpit, where the presentation layer and the data supply chain (i.e. the pipeline that connects the different systems to propagate the data from the source to the target) are technically complete and functional, but sadly it is found out only during the final testing that the data is not good enough to provide minimum viability of the solution. The investment to repay the data debt was never planned because the right questions about the acceptance levels of data were never asked, so the project either fails or goes through a long phase of 'improvements' where all hands are to the pump to fix the data – a poor performance indeed.

Data Workout 1, at the end of this part, will go more into the detail of how to create a portfolio of data excellence initiatives to minimize the risk that programmes forget about the investment in data. I will practically show how that essential interlocking with the change or portfolio teams could be achieved, perhaps starting with a simple addition of the information denoting dependency on data, and then gradually moving towards listing the types of data involved or, even better, including in the initial assessment (whether for a business case or risk assessment) useful checks for potential risks to data or expectations of quality levels or general standards. The speed at which the interlocking would expand is to be wisely throttled, exactly like an exercise routine that increases in its effort, because the portfolio owners are usually already fighting an adoption battle, and if their processes are over-loaded with more information requests this could quickly see the data athletes giving up altogether, labelling the request 'overwhelming'. Instead, even with a gradual approach it should be possible to measure very early that initiatives where data is planned in advance would perform better in predict-ability and reliability of outcome, thus gaining the data athlete's buy-in to push for more information upfront in search of even better performance.

COOLING DOWN

- Company culture is crucial to the data excellence of an organization.

- There are three types of organizational models: centralized, decentralized, federated (or franchised). Each can be successful when properly managed, and organizations can change model over time.

- There is no real standard reporting line for the data organization, as the capability accountable for the overall execution of a data revolution depends on the history and culture of the company.

- The top of the organization, being the most important contributor to the company culture, has to be guided in 'toning up' in its data muscles through effective influence and energetic encouragement by the DPT.

- The control functions (risk, compliance, audit, etc.) play a pivotal role if the DPT manages to strike an alliance of intents.

Notes

1 E B Tylor (1871) *Primitive Culture: Research into the development of mythology, philosophy, religion, art, and custom*, J P Putnam's Sons, New York

2 Gartner. Gartner survey reveals less than half of data and analytics teams effectively provide value to the organization, 2023. www.gartner.com/en/newsroom/press-releases/03-21-2023-gartner-survey-reveals-less-than-half-of-data-and-analytics-teams-effectively-provide-value-to-the-organization (archived at https://perma.cc/QV5P-GL6D)

3 Wavestone. Data and AI leadership executive survey 2024. www.wavestone.com/en/insight/data-ai-executive-leadership-survey-2024/ (archived at https://perma.cc/79MF-JF82)

04

Introducing data roles

WARMING UP

- Who are the data personal trainer helpers?
- What do they do?
- Why is data domain ownership the toughest discipline?
- Introducing the data excellence triumvirate.

The winning team

Very often underestimated, the change of company culture hinges on a transformation of human resources. If there is something new to do, someone should have that in their job description, or completely new roles should be drafted. That is not as obvious as it seems, as there are firms allegedly very forward in their data journey, but in which the new recruits attracted by a glamorous-sounding posting for a data role find themselves mislabelled as 'database administrator', 'IT specialist' or 'system engineer'. These are by all means absolutely respectable and important roles for the functioning of the company. However, the mislabelling of a new recruit role, frequently dismissed with a 'The company directory is wrong' shrugging of shoulders, signals to someone who has just made an important bet on a new workplace that there might be a mismatch between the offer and the appreciation of their skills, and with the war for good talent we are all in, the seed of a doubt will grow into very sour fruit. So, fixing the human resources (HR) job code taxonomy is not just a data task, it is also part of the data revolution, because describing who does what in the organization is all part of the acknowledgement that data is not just a project but rather a change of lifestyle.

Getting HR onto a training regime

Possibly even before finance, HR is the place where you, as the DPT, should go next and start to enthuse data excellence practices, as they are the key avenue of new blood entering the organization. Ironically, however, often the relative immaturity and fragmentation of their data can make HR an almost insurmountable obstacle if tackled at the very beginning. Analysing the genesis of a data programme in the organization performed above, HR is seldom the place where it starts, because the attention is focused on an area that is expected to be in closer relationship to value generation, like sales or after-sales, but in my view it is not sustainable to expect that sales are data-driven and digitally ready, while everything that is supporting their work life isn't. Of course, with the introduction of various privacy regulations in the last decade, HR departments were forced to improve the handling of their data, as even in a business that doesn't processes any sensitive customer data HR, by nature of its mission, is always in scope of such compliance requirements, and with data privacy and protection, fragmentation of systems and heavily manual processes are costly weaknesses that have to be mitigated. Nevertheless, being compliant with GDPR (Europe) or the California Consumer Privacy Act (CCPA) or China's Personal Information Protection Law (PIPL) doesn't necessarily mean being excellent at managing personnel data, and given it is HR who need to buy into the new list of roles to initiate the cultural change, it is essential that the DPT commits time to create an effective relationship with their human resources team.

REAL-WORLD EXAMPLE

Everyone likes data, and their fondness for data inevitably leaks into the creativity reflected in the job titles that are created in the absence of existing guidelines. At the beginning of my engagement on a data excellence journey, I have made it a habit to run a simple exercise to start focusing minds. No matter how fragmented or broken employee data might be, there would always be a 'company index' or an 'employee directory' with a list of all the employees and a minimum set of identification data, like name, surname, office address, phone number, department, job title. It should be relatively easy to run a quick search on how many job titles have the word 'data' in it. The results could be insightful and scary at the same time, as in a decent size company the list could include literally hundreds if not thousands of different job titles, from the more mainstream ones such as 'data analyst' and 'data scientist' to the more outlandish 'data controller' or 'data ninja'. Furthermore, the spread across the different departments reveals important clues on nascent or established data tribes that it would be important to connect in the federated or franchised model explored in Chapter 3. Also, the point made above around fixing the taxonomy to better attract talent becomes ever more tangible as a rationalization of roles is required to prevent unfair treatment of employees having equivalent roles but with different job titles and different pay grades.

Data excellence roles

Data is a team sport, as already mentioned, so I would like to describe in more detail the make-up of the winning team that, with the HR buy-in, should be put in place. In Table 4.1 I present an outline of the key players that it would be important to identify that either match existing roles or are creating anew.

TABLE 4.1 The data excellence roles

Chief data officer (aka the data personal trainer)	Accountable executive whose role is to define the data excellence approach for the company. They are the interpreters of the company's ambitions and translators of those into rituals that reinforce the culture and methodology of data to achieve value and impact.
Business data officer (aka DPT deputy)	Accountable for embedding data excellence within a country/division/function, they represent the CDO locally. They should be matched to the constituent parts of enterprise. Their role involves mainly advocacy of the CDO's messages and being ambassadors of data excellence.
Data domain owner (DDO)	Set what 'good looks like' for the data associated with their domain of expertise (e.g. sales, service, pricing). Their efforts contribute to the creation of data standards that are used to track the conformity of the data fitting within the said domain.
Data domain architect (DDA)	Responsible for the articulation of the data standards set by the DDO in the data architecture of the organization. They act as a design authority, assessing design for change in software applications, and data flows, recommending improvements to reduce risk of data issues and increasing conformity to the data standards. For example, prior to the deployment of a new analytic platform, they would validate the sources to be connected and suggest a data quality assessment (and potentially a remediation plan) prior to deployment in order to maximize the accuracy of the outcome. Their duties should be kept segregated from other roles labelled as architect, e.g. solution architect.

(continued)

TABLE 4.1 (Continued)

Data consumer (aka data athlete)	Use a given set of data to derive value. As such they are responsible for the clear articulation of the data requirements, i.e. what data is needed and how acceptable it is. They champion the action or initiative that is setting or amending the data supply chain from which they are consuming (data change).
Business application owner (they can be data athletes too)	Accountable for the business outcome of a software application supporting one or many business processes they oversee. As regards data excellence, for the scope of data the application contains, they are accountable for the compliance of the data standards defined by all DDOs, e.g. if the application contains customer addresses, the customer address standards defined by the DDO for the customer data domain.
Data stewards	Generic role describing those responsible for monitoring, assessing and improving data standards on behalf of application owners. Usually, they are organized in teams operating on issue remediation types of process, for example they will be accountable to manage the customer data when requested by a customer or when a monitoring process has detected an anomaly (e.g. change of address, misspelling of name/identity, contact information).
IT application owner	Leads the technical activity to maintain operational availability and reliability of a software application, inclusive of the software changes, fixes and upgrades and enabling infrastructure. For data they are responsible of the technical measures to assure security and integrity of application contained data.

From the list in Table 4.1, we spent quite a long time in the previous chapter talking about the data personal trainer and, by extension, about the business data officers, who are their local representative and advocates. So, here I am going to focus in more detail on the two most important roles that will help the DPT in achieving the cultural change: the data domain owner and the data domain architect. These roles are as pivotal as they are misunderstood, given that the concept of 'ownership' and 'architecture' are broad and crowded with other roles performing already something similar, so tweaking the names to resonate with the different data athletes' sensitivities will also be important. No matter the names, though, a good data personal trainer will press persistently on their HR teams to have the names agreed and embedded in their job code/type list and, if never done before, the DPT will experience the seemingly disproportionate length of time that it takes to change a key referential, as it involves more than adding an entry to a list of value. In fact, it is changing an axis of measurement which has material ramification across all the processes and analytics that are using it. In this case, the change would have a wide effect, from the talent acquisition process to the learning and development processes and all the way down to the access management systems. This challenge could constitute one of the first practices that could test the most important role that data excellence is relying on: the data domain owner.

The data domain owner

REAL-WORLD EXAMPLE

In all my career, one of the moments in which I felt I came closest to being fired was around 2010. At the time I was leading the business intelligence team, which delivered reports and analytics for the GE Capital EMEA business, so the majority of those were of enterprise type. One day a major project landed on my desk. It was the blueprint for a super-duper dashboard that had been deemed to deliver to the CEO a perfect view of the KPIs of our business unit on a monthly basis (by the way, I think that was the first time I had heard the term 'KPI'). This would have been a set of roughly 100 KPIs measuring the entire European business in all its product lines across a variety of performance aspects essential for the conduct of the business. My team's role was, 'simply', to accept the request, designing the user interface (UI) and user experience (UX) and, of course, to deliver and operate it, having obtained the sign-off from business testers. The project got stuck at business test as some KPIs could not be signed off, and after a few iterations things got ugly as we were holding back the entire launch. What was happening? Two business testers, both of whom were quite senior, sitting in different countries, had a slight difference of opinion about the formulation of the KPIs. As it happened, one's definition if applied made the other tester's definition appear in the 'red' zone of the KPIs, and vice versa. I was just the IT PM, and after many back-and-forths, was unable to break the tie. Delivery of the monthly KPI dashboard was now seriously delayed so, in a last-ditch attempt to resolve the impasse, I tried to find somebody above the two testers who could arbitrate. But nobody would tackle the two leaders or had enough time to spend on the problem to come up with a negotiated strategy, so I failed. Later in my first days as data officer, I learnt that what I had experienced was a 'lack of data domain ownership'.

The role of the data domain owner

Of all the data disciplines that exists, the one of 'ownership' is the most difficult and the most essential to master. It is the most apt set of muscles to train
against the data tribalism mentioned at the beginning of this book, and
although this alone is not sufficient in order to establish a culture of data, it
is essential. First it is necessary to clarify the term, as data ownership is
frequently referred to as the mere 'possession' of the data in situ, a sort of
guardianship and stewardship which a specific team are encouraged to exert
over the data that sits in their territory, i.e. their data systems of record. 'Data
owner' is a synonym for 'application owner' or 'IT owner'. In the most
mature cases there is a distinction made between a 'technical owner' and a
'business owner'. This type data ownership is specifically aimed at protecting
the physical data from undesired events like deterioration, loss and/or leakage and, as a role, focuses on protection and security aspects. Unfortunately,
an expectation of data quality is also often bestowed on these 'data owners',
as they own the application and the application users or anyone else that
might use the data contained in their application would complain if the data
were not of 'good quality'. The problem is that such expectations of performance are not tied to a standardized measure of performance, and that's
where things go wrong.

To explain, the application owner tends to drive data quality, or data
standards in general, based on their point of observation, i.e. their application. If we stay with a simple example of customer data, let's say I am the
application owner of an opportunity management system. This is the system
that salespeople use to capture the potential leads that can then be converted
into customer orders. Whether bought or built, such software would require
sound customer classification as an important attribute to analyse and
improve performance. However, this might not be the only opportunity
management system in the company. Maybe this one is only used for a
certain portfolio of products, and for sure there are going to be other systems
that manage important 'customer classification' attributes. The zealous
application owner would certainly try to control the quality of the attribute,
but how are they able to guarantee that customer classification is the same
across all the organization if their jurisdiction is confined to the single system
they own? Establishing a lingua franca of everything related to data is the
gap filled by data domain ownership.

In any company, everyone wants to be a data athlete nowadays and they
need data to perform in their competitions. Whether understanding what is
the best marketing or pricing strategy that would increase sales, distilling

customer feedback from the killer app innovation (maybe with a sprinkling of AI on top!) that would sweep the market, or accurately assessing the value of a targeted acquisition, these are only a few of the team challenges that are enabled by data. However, in the absence of a data personal trainer, the act of consuming data for those performance would be a 'many-to-many web of requests and provisions'. I will describe later the relationship between data intelligence and level of reusability, but for now let's say that in an immature data environment virtually all data athletes try to consume data independently as a single, seldom-repeated act, because the time it takes to find and to be sure that the existing data is 'good enough for them' is not factored in their planned activities. As a result, they identify where the data they believe they need is. They then request it and that's where the data tribalism strikes. The data athlete asks for the data they think they need in the form they need it, but in most cases that data does not exist in that form. So, the data owner responds to the requests with 'This is what I have'. The data athlete then responds with a request for the data in a form they need, only to receive the stock answer, 'Sorry, I have no budget [or no time] to adapt the data to your need.' This back-and-forth goes on for a while until the data athlete, pressed for time, finally tries to resolve the problem by 'post-processing' the data in question in an attempt to adapt it to the new need.

If you scale such behaviour at the company level, then a myriad of similar exchanges is happening every day, everywhere. Evidently this data tribalism is a complex dynamic within organizations that is costing them dearly in time and resources. What is the solution? One answer is to introduce a third party to this 'many-to-many' relationship: the data domain owner (DDO). Who are they? They are business partners who, by position, experience or acquired knowledge, have a vested interest in and the authority to be the last word on what a given business term means. They are the masters of business language in a specific domain, the owners of 'meanings'.

I will define how to design the most suitable data domain model in more detail in Chapter 8. For now, it is suffice to say that domains of data are defined sets of homogenous data to foster standardization and prioritization. This standardization is achieved through the formalization, publication and governance of the domains, whilst prioritization is achieved through data consumer stories, as part of the Data Excellence Operating Model presented in Chapter 9.

Scouting for the data domain owner

The data domain owners are difficult to find, not just because the concept of ownership is misunderstood, but also because 'ownership' evokes additional responsibility. To assign additional responsibilities to tackle an issue that is not visibly connected to one's priorities, or worse looks like 'boiling the ocean', is very challenging. So, having found myself in many robust conversations in which a prospective data domain owner was very reluctant to be one, I have identified two actions that can be very effective in convincing them to step up. Firstly, I explain clearly why their experience and status makes them suited to take on this responsibility. Secondly, I clarify that data domain owner is not a role and my intent is not to change the career trajectory of a future chief risk officer into that of a chief data officer; rather, I am simply asking them to add a few data tasks to their existing role. Over time, those two actions have become a useful identikit and task list that can be seen in Table 4.2.

TABLE 4.2 The data domain owner

What a DDO looks like	What a DDO does
✓ They occupy a senior role in the organization.	✓ They refine/redraw the boundaries and the structure (i.e. subdomains) of their domain.
✓ They are a recognized authority in the fields related to their role, they are a subject matter expert.	✓ They provide (or oversee the provision of) unambiguous definitions for all the terms and concepts that belong to their domain.
✓ Though they have a good understanding of the importance of data, they may not necessarily be an expert.	✓ They arbitrate incongruence between data consumers and data providers in order to guarantee the resilience and stability of data definitions.
✓ They are proven agents of change, having led or leading substantial programme of transformation.	✓ They define and oversee the implementation of data standards (e.g. quality, access, retention, classification, security) for business terms that will be assigned to their domain, in alignment with global policies and rules.
✓ They are bridge builders with the instinctive capacity to build a consensus.	✓ They chair councils, communities or fora dedicated to the governance of the domain.
✓ If there is a process ownership framework or similar infrastructure (e.g. journey, streams, capability) they are a process owner.	✓ They are actively involved in programmes of change involving their domain.

Note that they are not expected to be in charge of standards compliance (i.e. fixing the data gaps deriving from assessing the standards versus the data), as that would create a conflict of accountability around the role. In any sizeable company the data domain owner would almost certainly not be hierarchically in charge of all the places in which the data they own conceptually would be stored physically and processed. Therefore, being accountable for compliance, wherever the data is held in the organization, would create an impossible demand for accountability, i.e. either the DDO would need substantial resources to operate the right stewardship of data or they will be left with an unrealistic 'influencing' expectation on the many application (or data) owners. The already reluctant data domain owner would quickly learn that with every additional rule added to the data they own (however advantageous) another set of data issues would be added to their backlog of problems to solve. Under these circumstances, such an expansion of accountability would have a counterproductive effect on the DDO role. Instead, they should be regarded as the rule makers of the data disciplines, who rely on trained data athletes to perform at their best within the rules.

Of all the tasks that the DPT undertakes, the engagement of the DDO is probably the toughest, as the people identified by Table 4.2 are, usually, already oversubscribed by the company to be deployed in its critical initiatives or operations, so adding a task to the their task list is almost an impossible challenge, especially once they understand the type of effort it could involve. We might approach a moment in which the gathering of data intelligence on the firm would be eased by generative AI tools, but the human intelligence associated with discerning and choosing what 'it is' for the company would be an aspect difficult to escape from. Further, experience of the usage of the identikit in Table 4.2 has taught me that new DDOs fall into two distinct types: those keen to play a part in supporting the business but fearful of taking on too much accountability, and a second type who struggle to understand the rationale of such a role and don't see why they should meddle in this 'IT thing'. In both cases, how you train your DDO is a task that needs to be planned and requires the DPT to turn up their emotional intelligence levels to the maximum.

Training the DDO

In Chapter 8, together with change management and its ritualization, I will propose a structured set of 'training sessions' for DDOs in order to tone them up to peak performance. Here I would like to provide the keen DPT with some tips on how to motivate the data domain owner to enter the arena and start working out.

REAL-WORLD EXAMPLE

One interesting case I encountered in the past taught me that the reluctance around becoming a DDO might have deeper cultural roots. In my scouting for owners, I arranged a conversation with someone who everyone was pointing to as the most revered expert in customer assets. This person had been in the company for a long time and had devoted their working life to the mission of establishing, curating and advocating good data about the products they owned. This is a crucial data domain to have under your control if your company wants to give its customers the best possible post-sale experience and so maximize retention.

During my explanation of the DDO role, they realized that their name had been publicized across the company as the go-to person for customer assets and they became visibly perturbed. Moreover, when I told them their opinion would override that of a 'senior leader' in the company, they looked truly horrified. How could they possibly be more knowledgeable than senior management? I could not have asked for clearer evidence of data tribalism. If the highest paid person's opinion (HIPPO) of the chief is expected to hold all the answers, the path to a data-driven company is permanently blocked.

I took this challenge as a test of data excellence methodology and spent a considerable amount of time –over a year – in making them an effective data domain owner. And in the end they became one! The strategy to achieve successful DDO performance hinged on the twin axis that should be the adopted by the DPT: safe environment and motivation. It was important to show in practice that the data excellence ecosystem that I was setting up would create a safe environment for the domain knowledge they were entrusting us with, so that knowledge would be ratified as company standard and not as just their opinion, with a robust process to arbitrate differences and evolutions. Second, breaking the 'many-to-many' data consumer–data provider closed loops, mentioned above, and exposing them to a wider set of use cases to which they could provide their expertise and measure tangible positive effect, created a strong motivation to be involved and active.

The data domain architect

The second role I would like to focus on, the data domain architect (DDA), has a distinct function. Where the data personal trainer is about coaching and mentoring and the data domain owner is concerned with writing the rules of the game, the DDA acts as the referee. Over the years I have found that in the matter of data, as in any other field, a 'judicial' role is highly recommended. What I mean by this is that it can be very useful to introduce someone who is going to 'call a spade a spade', or speak truthfully and plainly, during a critical moment of change and who will assume a leadership role in the 'data design authority' (discussed in more detail when we focus on Pillar II). Usually, the architects own the design and there are many variations of the role called 'data architect'. I am not going to indulge in a long disquisition on the types and merits of each of these variants, as that is not the focus of this book. However, I will make a point later about how achieving data excellence requires that its precepts are studiously embedded 'by design' rather than being, again, an afterthought. So, whether added as a task to the existing task list of a generic data architect, or created *ex novo* as a brand-new role, a data domain architect is needed. Preferably located in an independent group but vertically aligned to one (or more) domain, the data domain architect is the missing leg of the stool that brings about a new awareness of how to excel at data. While the data domain owner is the articulator of the standards, the data domain architect is their interpreter and demiurge (designer of the physical world). Through their design artefacts, they adjudicate what good design accomplishes through the best data standards. Their role can be described by the following responsibilities.

Mitigate the risk to data in a given project

The DDA should have visibility of an early read on the effect on data owing to material changes (project, program or epic) generated by the business strategic intent, and they should be able to influence the overall design in order to mitigate such risks. For example, a project that is supposed to analyse sensitive customer data and deliver it to a restricted number of priority data consumers should have extra-stringent monitoring and controls along the different steps of the data flow

Design a flow of data to maximize compliance with the data standards

The DDA is responsible for implementing in the flows the data standards ratified by the data domain owners whose data is being processed and consumed. For example, if the DDO for customer data indicated a source of authority for a particular customer data set, it would be the duty of the DDA to design and provide assurance in the build review phase that the data flow originates from the correct source.

Assurance about as-is

The DDA is involved in the assessment of existing data flows, either on an ad hoc basis or following incidents or issues, to determine whether they are complying with the standards, compiling a list of gaps for the application and IT owners to close. For example: if an existing customer-facing application has experienced a data incident whereby customer data was exposed, the DDA would analyse the full source-to-target flow with transformations, processes and control, to determine potential data flow control failures and recommend remediating actions.

Liaise with the other architects to evolve the target data architecture harmoniously

Other data architectural roles include application, infrastructure and security architects. The DDA's role, once it has been harmonized with these, would need to focus on the topology and risks to data flows from usage rather than the underlining technology or security measures.

The DPT, DDO and DDA are thus involved in what I call the *data triumvirate*, as can be seen in Figure 4.1, where a triparty collaboration forms a virtuous circle that moves the company's data culture and maturity further along the path of data excellence.

FIGURE 4.1 The data triumvirate

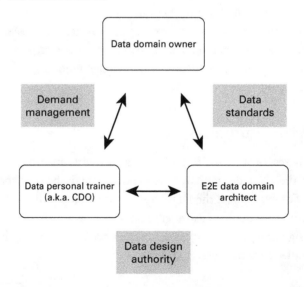

What the DPT collects from the DA as an ambition is brought to the DDO as an ask of standardization of requirements, which is then prescribed by the DDA in their design and ultimately goes back to the DPT who then coaches their DA to improve.

REAL-WORLD EXAMPLE

Miriam is an eager data athlete working for the after-sales team of an automotive company. She wants to make sure that all her dealers can communicate promptly issues with their products when in warranty because she has got some anecdotal evidence from their customer service line that the company is not honouring the warranty periods and customers are upset. Miriam wants to establish a new 'warranty claim report' to check whether warranties are paid on time. She also wants to classify warranties in different buckets (body, engine, transmission, electronics) but knows this classification doesn't exist in the company yet. Miriam engages her DPT, Fujiko. Fujiko adds Miriam's case to her portfolio and, analysing the requirement, realizes that there is potentially a new classifier for warranty data that did not exist before. Consulting the data catalogue of the company, she determines that Xavier is the data domain owner for the service data domain that includes warranty data. Xavier is asked to opine on this new classifier and recommends that it should be named 'fault in warranty type', be classified as 'public' type of data and be connected to the existing warranty definition data as part of the service management application. The use case is taken by Fujiko to the next step where Alan, the DDA for service managements, reviews existing flow from the service management application to the service business intelligence (BI) analytics system, where he recommends the report should be built, and modifies the existing data model to include 'fault in warranty type', its possible values and the design of quality rules to check the validity of the fields to be created along the flow. Fujiko executes the project with the help of her IT teams and Miriam can now accurately observe where faults are happening earlier than expected and feed back improvements to the respective design teams.

The need for funding

Having delved first into the roles and HR matters, I would like to focus briefly on the other foundational element of our cultural change, funding. In Data Workout 1 at the end of this part we will practise the embedding of data in the portfolio of initiatives through proper funding. Also, in Chapter 13 I will describe the funding model associated with the productization of data, as data excellence, seen as an extended list of new 'exercises' to be practiced in the company, necessitates 'energy' and that energy, ultimately, must be funded by investment.

However, in this short section I would like to focus specifically on a simple model for workforce planning to socialize and agree with the finance partners. Perhaps the DPT role is reporting to the CFO and thus far might have had an easier path to fund headcount, or, in other encouraging instances, there has been a resolute reorganization of all existing data resources into one sizeable team (as articulated in the previous chapter). Even so, being identified as an army of new people with a not entirely clear scope and value could create issues at the end of the honeymoon phase. So, it is important to demonstrate a strategic approach to manage resources. The idea is to separate the type of resourcing supporting the data athlete's need into three different types: surge, established and commoditized:

- *Surge:* An external influx of resources is needed, as internally the specific skill is unavailable or not at an adequate level, and/or the thought leadership is sought to implement a new process or operating model.

- *Established:* Roles are staffed in the organization, as designed and required skills are available.

- *Commoditized:* Processes are mature, and some sub-processes are identified as non-core or with transferrable knowledge. Overall cost can be reduced through business process outsourcing.

So, independently of whether the funding model of the company prescribes to staff resources associated to projects, hence timebound, instead of permanent or engage consultants on a time and material basis or fixed price, I highly recommend that the DPT thinks about the data excellence team above as a coherent workforce, planning to socialize and regularly carry out reviews with their stakeholders.

COOLING DOWN

- HR and finance are two key foundational elements of the cultural change.
- A quick analysis of job titles containing 'data' can be insightful.
- Data domain ownership is a business owned data task that augments data intelligence.
- Data domain owners are experts who have authority on data standards.

- Data domain architects design data flows to comply with DDOs' data standards.

- The data triumvirate comprises DPT, DDO and DDA to create a virtuous circle of increasing data intelligence.

- Funding is another foundational element of cultural change, and there are three types that can support the data athlete's need: surge, established and commoditized.

05

Data charter, data disciplines and data fitness assessment

WARMING UP

- Light the data excellence torch with the data charter.
- Introduce the data disciplines to create some order in the data athlete's mind.
- Get ready to change with the data fitness assessment.

What is the data charter?

In Chapter 3 I explored the tips and tactics to tone the top of the company and to make those in power 'vocalize' their commitment in public as an anchor to their resolve in pursuing the journey of data excellence. Here I would like to describe another act of clarity needed to facilitate cultural change. It is about providing an easy guide to what data is and how people should think about it. It can be constituted as the first bridge between the vocalization of the leadership and the instantiation of an internal governance of the venture the DPT is trying to bring people on. The temptation is often to issue a bunch of policies to add to the company's policy portal. The problem with this approach is that not all companies have a Pavlovian reflex to comply with a new policy, and even in the organizations that have that reflex staff may be suffering from fatigue after years of ever-changing policy and overlapping controls. Instead, a good DPT will equip themselves with a simple manifesto of what they want the organization to achieve, something that can articulate the principles of good data in no more than one or two pages. Ideally, these principles should be reflected in the company code of conduct, where one exists. This data charter, as I call it, forms the basis of the documentary scaffolding for data excellence, outlining with succinct sentences, principles or rules, new concepts or expectations that the company desires to accomplish.

Over the years I have seen a few versions of a data charter. Below is a specimen that I found most effective based on five principles and expressed as a pledge that the generic < The Company> should take in order to excel at data.

<THE COMPANY> DATA CHARTER

Principle I – Data is governed: <The Company> establishes strong governing bodies, championed by senior leadership to govern the journey of data excellence. These governing bodies (e.g. existing or set up new councils, forums, steering committees) drive alignment between the growth strategy and the standards of data required within <The Company>'s risk appetite.

Principle II – Data is standardized: <The Company> defines and adopts standards for all its data, in order to reduce ambiguity, increase quality and provide assurance about safe access and sharing, with the ultimate goal of providing data fit for decision making.

Principle III – Data is resilient: <The Company> implements adequate measures to prevent its data from being adversely affected by external or internal process, system or organizational changes.

Principle IV – Data is compliant: <The Company> complies in a timely and satisfactory way with applicable related laws and regulations, and sets for its data, which is subject and evidence of such compliance, higher standards as required.

Principle V – Data is ethical: <The Company> fosters responsible behaviour in its sourcing, processing and usage of data, and implement safeguards to avoid harm to human beings or infringement of their rights.

The issuance of the data charter should follow existing rituals of officiality and should be preceded by an accurate impact analysis on the existing policy corpus of the organization. Especially if an incumbent data policy is being replaced, it is imperative that the launch of the charter is sanctioned with official approval from the management and is followed by a clear process of withdrawal of any previous policy, and issuance of an amended version of existing impacted policies. For instance, the information security policy might have referred to previous data policy, so the charter's wording should be instead adopted in the new version. The data excellence torch has been lit!

Introducing data disciplines

The data charter is just the starting point from which the documentary backbone for data athletes branches out. I have conceptualized it as a simple framework (Figure 5.1), divided into three initial tiers of increasing data excellence detailed content. The framework tiers match the evolving internal journey and provide guidance on how to perform best. Thus, in the second tier the data disciplines are defined as the description of distinct fields of data activities for the data athletes to get involved with. Each discipline is explicitly mapped to the data charter's principles to reinforce their positive contribution to the charter's ambition. As disciplines can be broad topics, to further simplify each one is then broken down in sub-disciplines, so for example the vast topic of data management has, as one of the sub-disciplines, the more narrowly defined data quality management, detailing what is expected to manage data

FIGURE 5.1 The data excellence document framework

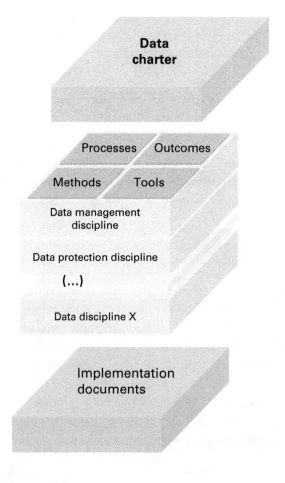

TABLE 5.1 Sub-disciplines of data management

Sub-discipline	Definition	Objectives	Practices	Outcomes
Data governance	The orchestration of an effective and controlled data consumption for all data consumers	• To allow the definition, communication and implementation of the principles, policies, tools and metrics for data management • To assure appropriate data usage	• Set and enforce data policies and standards • Enable data ownership • Own issue resolution • Oversee compliance with all applicable regulations	• Governance model • Data policies and standards • Business glossary • Data ownership catalogue • Data standards • Data issue log • Data risk register
Data operations	The creation and implementation of an operational environment for the end-to-end activities involving data	• To ensure operational excellence for all aspects of data management • To satisfy internal and external stakeholders' availability and reliability expectations	• Define the data operating model(s) • Set and manage data supply chains • Appoint qualified operational leaders • Monitor operations	• Data operating model(s) • Data flow maps • Data access controls • Data sharing contracts • Process management tool • Operational control framework
Data architecture	The practice of designing a system structure to deliver a desired set of data outcomes	• To enable the effective management of data throughout the organization • To transform business needs into operational data structures	• Design, build and maintain conceptual, logical and physical data models • Create and maintain a data asset catalogue • Execute data discovery • Establish an enterprise data architecture practice	• Entity diagrams • Conceptual data model • Logical data model • Physical data model • Data asset catalogue • Data modelling tool • Data architectural standards

(continued)

TABLE 5.1 (Continued)

Sub-discipline	Definition	Objectives	Practices	Outcomes
Data quality management	The combined set of planning, implementation and control of the quality of business-critical data, in order for it to match consumption requirements	• To increase the value of organizational data and utilization opportunities • To reduce the risks and costs of poor data quality • To improve organizational efficiency and productivity • To protect and enhance an organization's reputation	• Identify critical data elements • Execute data profiling • Design and implement data quality rules • Perform data quality issue management • Execute root cause analysis and prioritization of permanent preventative actions • Carry out quality assurance and monitoring	• Business rules and data quality standards • Data quality rule dictionary • Data quality engine • Root cause analysis document • Quality assurance confirmation document • Data quality issue repository
Reference and master data management (RD/MD) management	The capability of managing and sharing core data and golden data taxonomies from one standardized, trustable source of authority	• To reduce business insight ambiguity • To enable the effective management of data quality • To reduce data risks	• List golden taxonomies and master sets • Define RD/MD architecture standards • Assure mastering of data in target system • Coordinate stewardship and maintenance processes	• RD/MD data sets • List of sources of authority by data set • RD/MD lifecycle procedures
Metadata management	The capability to collect at scale and with accuracy the metadata (i.e. the information associated to digital data) of the organization	• To increase the strategic use of data providing context • To increase operational efficiency through data reusability • To reduce regression with more accurate impact analysis	• Define metadata management strategy • Understand metadata requirements • Define metadata architecture • Model metadata • Oversee metadata life cycle	• Information model • Business data lineage • Technical data lineage • Horizontal and vertical data lineage • Metadata repository

Data use case management	The process of defining and implementing the procedures, tools and techniques to manage the delivery of change initiatives involving data	• To assure that data is properly embedded and taken care during programmes or project management by adapting the change methodology work and educate change teams about their impact on data	• Set up data excellence roles • Identify data domains impacted by the change • Develop a data solution design • Develop an impact assessment • Develop an implementation and monitoring plan	• Data use case portfolio • Data requirement • Data design principles • Change implementation and monitoring plans
Data ethics and culture	The competence to address ethical implications owing to the sourcing, processing and consuming of data	• To define the handling of information ethics matters • To create structured support for staff dealing with ethical issues • To foster a culture of care and transparent behaviour in the processing of data	• Oversee data use cases for ethical implications • Identify risk factor and sensitive practices • Communicate with and educate staff • Monitor and maintain a defendable position	• Data ethics board • Project ethical checkpoint • Data code of conduct • Ethics training programme • Awareness of ethical data issues • Engagement and incentives programmes

TABLE 5.2 Sub-disciplines of record management

Sub-discipline	Definition	Objectives	Practices	Outcomes
Record origination and discovery	The inventory and classification of business records, existing and newly created	• To assure that all records generated by business activities are identified and properly listed • To ensure that legal and regulatory requirement pertain to records are complied with	• Assign record identifier and associated metadata • Name and list records consistently based on their business area • Define record definition and capturing methodologies (e.g. APIs)	• Record inventory • Record tagging • Record repository tool
Record storage	The practices and logistics of physical and digital record storage	• To reduce exposure to record leakage or damage • To comply with internal and external policies	• Design and implement appropriate storage facilities • Enforce adequate handling record measures • Monitor storage capacity and performance levels • Implement and maintain a disaster recovery plan for the storage	• Storage capacity plan • Record locator maps • Record storage infrastructure
Record access and retrieval	The procedure to grant access to records following security and control standards	• To ensure effective and efficient retrieval and use of data and information in unstructured formats • To secure confidentiality of information	• Implement record access control procedures • Generate and monitor record access logs • Ensure records systems are designed to support the provision and restriction of access as per access rules	• Access and permission rules • Access logs • Record systems list

Record retention processes	Establish specific instruction on record retention and accessibility	• To comply with business rules and legislation • To support business operations • To ensure availability of information	• Define record owners • Define and implement record retention schedules • Avoid software and operating systems obsolescence which affects record retrieval	• Record owners list • Record retention schedules • Record management system
Record disposal	The processes associated with enacting secure record destruction	• To action record retention schedules • To reduce company liability owing to over- or under-retained records • To optimize physical and electronical space and maintenance costs	• Implement a govern workflow for destruction of records • Implement adequate technology measures complying with regulatory expectations (e.g. pseudonymization vs masking) • Review disposition actions prior to implementation to ensure records' requirements have not changed • Keep an audit trail of every disposal	• Record disposal workflow • Record disposal technology • Disposal audit trails

quality. Each sub-discipline in turn has a definition of the sub-discipline itself, the business objective that it pursues, the practices that are performed in line with it and the expected outcomes as artefacts and tools.

Based on my experience, I suggest starting with four data disciplines to be lined up under the data charter: data management, data science, data protection and record management, as the necessary foundational elements. Each discipline has a consistent scope of activities, in which the data athlete could become familiar with 'what good looks like' at a higher level. For example, to break down the complexity, each discipline could be articulated in sub-disciplines (e.g. data quality management is a sub-discipline of data management, holding the lower-level detailed view of what comprises good quality management). With the intention of exemplifying the structure of these documents, below I have provided a DPT starter pack containing a first draft of each priority discipline and associated sub-disciplines.

Later in this chapter I will show the connection of the disciplines and the assessment of our data athletes, whilst later, concerning Pillar II, I will present a more in-depth description of some sub-disciplines that are essential to transform the way we change. Finally, unlike the charter, the disciplines are to be evolved over time and further tailored to the organization, therefore the introduction of the concept here is just to offer a reasonably holistic initial list of what data athletes are expected to accomplish when they pledge to become excellent at data.

Data management discipline

This is defined as 'the' discipline of data, similarly to the mentioned misnomer existing between data and data governance. Hence, for clarity, I am here defining it as the discipline specific to the activities and processes required to govern data, making it resilient and compliant. The related data charter principles are: I, II, III, V (see box on page 63). The sub-disciplines of data management are listed in Table 5.1.

Record management discipline

This discipline is defined in the industry as the one responsible for the efficient and systematic control of the creation, receipt, maintenance, use and disposition of records, including the processes for capturing and maintaining evidence of and information about business activities and transactions in the form of records,[1] where a record is information maintained as evidence in pursuance of legal obligations or a business transaction, e.g. a supplier contract or a customer call recording, and often it is shorthanded erroneously

TABLE 5.3 Sub-disciplines of data science

Sub-discipline	Definition	Objective	Practice	Outcome
Data collection	The process to identify and retrieve the data required in a data science experiment and to assess its value, quality and reliability	• To enable testing of hypotheses in data science initiatives • To follow correct information security procedures	• Detail data requirement and gain approval • Identify sources of authority and profile data • Provision of necessary access to source and data storage	• Data profiling • Use case source list • Explorative data set ready for analysis • Data acquisition tools
Data analysis and hypothesis	The ability to develop hypotheses and to build statistical (or other types) inference models based on the data collected	• To confirm the viability of a business assumption that would create value through data insights	• Integration of analytic results with operational systems • Initial data analysis and hypothesis • Data insights and findings • Enhancement plan • Integrate/align data for analysis	• Data domain map • Statistical analysis tools • Algorithmic model and asset register
Model build	The capability of apply statistical analysis and machine learning to develop a model that would make predictions or support decisions	• To confirm the viability of the hypothesis and deliver a reliable scientific model	• Perform model learning and calibration • Assess the evolution of the model • Confirm model results with existing data	• Algorithmic model and asset register • Model training tools • Data science libraries • Model calibration and accreditation results
Scale up	The process of embedding the proven experiment in the operating model of the company	• To provide full business benefit from the investment • To reduce operational risks	• Execute full-scale test • Integrate with existing architecture • Establish model pipelines • Implement and monitor production controls	• Operating control framework • Scale test results • Model engineering tools • Data pipeline management tools

TABLE 5.4 Sub-disciplines of data protection

Sub-disciplines	Definition	Objectives	Practices	Outcomes
Governance	The process of exerting control and authority to deliver adequate protection of data that is sensitive from a strategic or compliance standpoint	• To orchestrate the implementation of the policies, tools and metrics for data protection • To ensure the data protection policy and procedures are adhered to and embedded within the organization and by its third party provider • To assure adequate risk management and compliance	• Define data protection framework • Define, communicate and enforce the data protection strategy • Set and implement data protection policies and standards • Ensure the organization remain compliant with all data related regulations	• Data protection policies and standards • Third parties' contract compliance • Information management guidelines • Verification of compliance controls
Data privacy	The process of defining, implementing and managing controls to protect personal data and ensure compliance with regulations and obligations	• To allow a common understanding of data privacy across the organization • To demonstrate compliance with personal data regulations • To industrialize such compliance with adequate tools • To manage data breaches potentially resulting in risks to persons' rights or freedom	• Provide an internal record of the information of all personal data processing activities • Define and implement data protection impact assessment • Provide data protection design principles • Define processes to notify data breaches • Provide data protection oversight • Manage third party responsibilities in processing personal data	• Privacy by design • Data protection impact assessment • Data breach notification • Key internal controls • Privacy audits • Registry of processing • Data subject access request tool

Data security	The process of protecting sensitive and important information vital to business operations.	<ul><li>To establish adequate data security controls</li><li>To determine how to protect data and how to comply with customer and business partner security requirements</li><li>To detect and respond to data security incidents</li><li>To define data security threat profile and risk appetite</li></ul>	<ul><li>Define and enforce data classification</li><li>Implement controls and procedures</li><li>Define security access control processes</li><li>Assess and respond to threats</li><li>Implement encryption standards and security protocols</li></ul>	<ul><li>Data classification policy</li><li>Encryption standards</li><li>Access control procedures</li><li>Endpoint security standards</li><li>Identity management procedures</li></ul>
Data persistence	The process of making data resilient to potential risks of corruption and destruction owing to major unforeseen events	<ul><li>To identify critical data for critical processes</li><li>To assess critical scenarios, threat and control failure mode</li><li>To define and implement a defence for the current and potential data security threats</li><li>To define a data breach communication at corporate level</li></ul>	<ul><li>Define and implement business continuity plans</li><li>Define and implement incident reporting procedures</li><li>Implement data breach response</li><li>Test regularly all of the above</li></ul>	<ul><li>Business continuity plans</li><li>Critical process map</li><li>Critical supplier and customer list</li><li>Incident reporting procedures</li><li>IT disaster recovery procedures</li><li>Emergency response procedure</li></ul>

as 'data retention'. If you are surprised to find record management here, which in the past was probably the Cinderella of all activities related to data, note that in a world where digital is forever, the ability of a corporation to retain only the records that are necessary for its processes and to dispose of the ones that are no longer needed is becoming increasingly the focus of regulation and the fulcrum on which trust from third parties hinges. The related data charter principles are: II, IV, V. The sub-disciplines of record management are outlined in Table 5.2.

Data science discipline

It is difficult to formalize a discipline that has been evolving with almost exponential acceleration in the last few years, and so I have tried to focus on the core processes and capabilities to make it, as much as possible, technologically agnostic. In its simplest definition, data science is using scientific methodologies, such as probability and statistics, coupled with information technology, to extract insight and knowledge from data. This makes the definition valid from the simple arithmetical inference you can play with Microsoft Excel Scenarios to the generative AI explosion we are witnessing these days. As such, the data science discipline depends heavily on the other disciplines, e.g. metadata management, data ethics, data security. The related data charter principles are: II, III, IV. The sub-disciplines of data science can be viewed in Table 5.3.

Data protection

The data protection discipline is a broad topic that encompasses the activities, processes and tools in place to safeguard company-sensitive information from leakages, corruption or improper access and usage, increasingly demanded by regulatory compliance. Often confused with data privacy and data security, I prefer, in line with standards as DAMA, ISO and regulations such as GDPR, to see these as sub-disciplines of the overarching concept of data protection. The related data charter principles are: I, II, III, IV. The sub-disciplines of data protection are outlined in Table 5.4.

Having disciplines and sub-disciplines initialized simplifies the prioritization and issuance of specific policies and standards. Whilst the disciplines are a high-level picture of what would be required to fulfil the ambitions of the charter, the implementation documents are bridging that picture to a use

FIGURE 5.2 Data charter structure

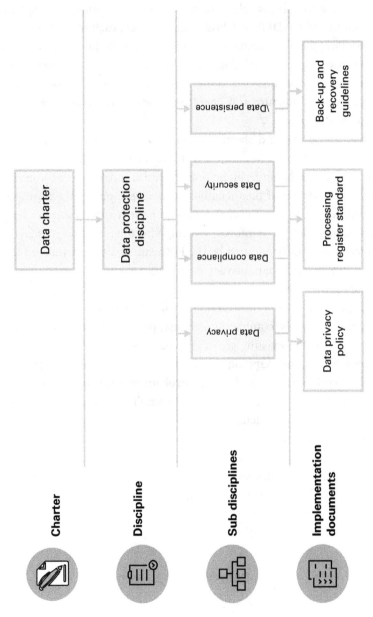

case. For instance, having issued the data protection discipline, and its sub-disciplines about privacy, a data privacy policy would be one of the implementation documents that would respond internally, in line with the discipline and sub-discipline, to the use case of fulfilling compliance with regulations like GDPR or CPRA. Furthermore, such regulations are usually prescribing the maintenance of a register of all the business procedures that are processing personal data. Therefore, a process register standard to capture, describe and maintain a list of processing, together with the prescribed architecture and operating model, would be issued as a further 'how to' document.

Figure 5.2 can and should be expanded to show the corpus of ratified company documents in aid of a graphical chartering of the change. As data is tribal, so are the underlining policies and standards, so an accurate inventory and mapping of the incumbent structure supports the transition to the new structure. In fact, the charter/discipline structure in some cases could be connecting, and so reinforce, existing documents. The present HR data privacy policy only adopted by the HR team could be promoted to become the company-wide data privacy policy once solidly aligned to the discipline of data protection.

Depending on the information availability and the size and age of the organization, duly completing this mapping of the data excellence documents versus the existing set might take weeks or even months. However, once finalized, the mapping should be a living structure maintained by the DPT in collaboration with the control functions responsible for company policies, which in many cases is the compliance team. In the past I have experienced initial reluctance in using names that usually are not associated to a policy architecture, i.e. charters and disciplines; however, once shown the practical usage that the DPT makes of them in the assessment of the data fitness of the data athletes, as described in the next section, the initial reluctance typically gives way to acceptance and even adoption in other subject areas (e.g. cybersecurity).

Data fitness assessment

What is fitness for the data athlete?

The ratification of the data charter and the data disciplines defines a new internal yardstick, and the natural next step is to assess our data athletes against these. We can use these guidelines to create a first view of what the inherent envelope of their performance is. It is back to day one in the fitness club, when the wishful gym-goer expresses their desire to run a marathon and, knowing what a marathon entails, the personal trainer assesses their current fitness to determine what regime to introduce to achieve that goal. The absolute value of weight, muscle mass, height or resting heart rate is useless data by itself – those elements must be interpreted together and in relation to the athlete's intent. If the question 'Can I become a sport champion?' is pointless without context, so is the question 'Can I become data-driven?' Driven to do what, for who and when? A good personal trainer would never dismiss outright even the most fanciful dream of sporting ambition, because a dream is a powerful motivator. However, based on their observation, their honesty will need to prevail and so a verdict of 'maximum entitlement' based on the individual potential ought to be returned. In data terms this means to define the envelope of the possibilities for the organization, given its culture and DNA. Although everything is possible, should a blue-collar manufacturing company entertain the medium-term ambition to become a digital-native media business? Correspondingly, the personal trainer sits their trainee down and engages their client in a conversation about their life story, psyche and goals, even before assessing their fitness. As a crucial part of the picture, the data personal trainer must also become intimate with the surrounding story, the organization as a whole and the environment in which the data athlete will perform, as this is the basic cornerstone on which building the winning data excellence formula is based. Thus, whenever I am asked about 'my' data strategy, I reply, 'Tell me your business strategy and I will tailor a data strategy to support it.' Once the contour of the picture is created, it is about filling in the frame.

So how do you lead your athlete into accepting that they need a data fitness assessment? From their standpoint, they have hired an expert, and experts give answers to questions, they don't reply with more questions. However, as pointed out above, very simple questions ('Am I fit to run a marathon?') might not have a simple answer. Thus, a comprehensive assessment that brings together multiple data points and models them in a way that could simulate whether a human body could withstand the stress of a 26.2 mile run should be justifiable. The first time I was exposed to this type of assessment in a business context was when I started dealing with regulatory compliance in the role of CIO for GE Leverage Finance between 2005 and 2008. When the board asked for the answer to the simple question 'Are we complying with regulation X?', even if a yes or no answer were given it would always be followed by disclaimers and descriptive documents, evidencing the compliance in relationship to different parts of the regulation, which would have made such an answer unpalatable to an audience used to 'simple' answers. What I learnt then is that if you start from the expected regulatory outcome and you break it down into the capabilities, processes and skills that will generate that outcome, and then you score the company (even at department or unit level) on how well those components are in place, the yes/no answer can be transformed into a numeric answer.

For example, preparing for the BCBS 239 regulation mentioned in Chapter 2, as one of the possible catalysts of the data journey, we broke the regulation down into the six key expected outcomes:

1 Adequate governance and infrastructure.

2 Effective risk data aggregation.

3 Comprehensive risk reporting.

4 Accurate and complete data.

5 Timely delivery.

6 Adaptable posture.

This can be seen in Table 5.5.

Each outcome had been clearly defined and associated to required business processes, tools and artefacts, which in turn were assessed in terms of their 'maturity' with a qualitative measure of their current and target performance, expressed on a scale from 1 to 5 (1 = lowest / 5 = highest). As a result, the binary question of compliance had been transformed into a profile

TABLE 5.5 BCBS 239 readiness

BCBS 239 readiness		
Outcome	Current maturity	Target maturity
Adequate governance and infrastructure	2	4
Effective risk data aggregation	1	3
Comprehensive risk reporting	3	3
Accurate and complete data	2	3
Timely delivery	4	4
Adaptable posture	1	3

with a 'current' level of maturity and, crucially, a target. From now on I am going to use interchangeably the terms 'maturity' and 'fitness', as the former is what you find more widely used in the industry, and the latter, of course, suits my analogy of the data personal trainer.

The data fitness assessment

As per the beginning of the previous section, the internal yardstick is the one upon which our data athlete profile should be built upon, by grading the expectations articulated in all the disciplines and sub-disciplines, with operational definitions describing, in ascending order, the level of proficiency with which a business process is performed or an outcome is produced.

For instance, from the data management discipline, one of the sub-disciplines is data quality management, which prescribes the drafting of an artefact called 'root cause analysis', which, as the name suggests, is supposed to determine the root cause of a quality issue detected during the monitoring of data quality. Table 5.6 would be used to assess the data fitness for this specific aspect of managing data quality.

In building the assessment template you might be tempted to lean on creativity or common sense, with the usual underlying feeling that your company is unique, and thus you might customize the fitness statements to the existing specificities (e.g. grading how widely adopted an existing a

TABLE 5.6 Assessing data fitness for data quality management

Data disciplines	Data sub-discipline	Definition	Fitness statements	Assessed fitness
Data management	Data quality management	All data quality issues should have a root cause analysis (RCA) document	1. No data quality issue has got RCA 2. The RCA is completed sometimes in different formats 3. The RCA process is standardized and controlled 4. The RCA process is fully digitized and 'low touch' 5. The RCA process, through artificial intelligence, is seamlessly connected to design change system	2

home-grown data quality tool is or how well complied with a specific standard is). Instead, this is the moment to try to align with the external world and adopt an industry standard model. In doing so, not only are you more likely to cover the entire spectrum of elements needed to form an opinion of the data athlete's potential, but you also gain an indispensable carrot to dangle in front of the data athlete's eye: comparison with their most respected competitors, and that's a very powerful psychological trick.

In an industry where notions of the DPT and data excellence are far from being mainstream yet, instead of data fitness you will need to search for data maturity models. There are multiple models to choose from, the most useful and best structured of which are – in my opinion – the Enterprise Data Management Council's Data Management Capability Assessment Model (DCAM),[2] DAMA's Data Management Body of Knowledge (DMBOK)[3] and the CMMI's Data Management Maturity (DMM).[4] As a data officer with 10 years' experience adopting DCAM in three different workplaces, I might be biased. However, I would still maintain that every DPT should spend quality time analysing a good sample of the available frameworks and then should pick the one that best fits their training methodology and organization.

It is also important to note that these instruments are not supposed to be an exact science. In fact, as per the example above, they are an attempt to translate into quantifiable information a qualitative assessment, so the DPT should also be wary of potential abuses. I am aware of organizations where the data fitness was measured in figures with two decimal digits, or others where an entire 'secondary market' of fitness points had been created with people committing to collaborate on improvement exercises just to gain a share of the improvement points. Imagine if we were assessing the above-mentioned example with a score of 3.27, meaning that the fitness of the RCA process would be almost a third better than 'The RCA process is standardized and controlled'! Of course this is nonsensical, and usually happens when we force the model and calculate averages across multiple areas or different disciplines to make mathematical equivalences.

Notwithstanding their potential flaws, they are still negligible in comparison with the benefits of data maturity models: at the end of the first assessment, for the first time you will be able to draw a causal link between wanting to achieve a result and improving certain data disciplines or sub-discipline, business process, or even making it part of an investment request for an IT tool. Secondly, and more importantly, replacing the conjectures and anecdotes on how good one unit or the whole organization is at data with a number, though prone to abuse, creates a strong psychological bond that fosters motivation and focuses minds. I would not understate the instant effect on team members when such numbers are plotted for each of the functions or business units for the first time in front of senior management. Endorphins, testosterone and cortisol are all powerful hormones released in response to competitive settings, focusing the commitment to reach better performances.

PERFORMING THE FIRST DATA FITNESS ASSESSMENT

Assessing demands effort, so the more thorough the assessment, the more intense the effort. The best assessments necessitate the assessors gauging whether the level of data fitness declared by the assessor is matched by the evidence. If an athlete maintains that they can run a marathon in under three hours, there should be, somewhere, an official record of that performance. These types of assessments are called 'evidence based', and to execute a complete check-up of the organization data fitness evaluated on the evidence will need to be treated as a proper project, whereby monetary and personnel resources are committed. If your organization has a similar process established in another areas like cybersecurity, data privacy or, for manufacturing companies, safety, it would be wise to leverage those examples to gain the buy-in from the management for such an extensive exercise. However, in my experience, the DPT will rarely be given *carte blanche* to perform a company-wide assessment, as the key resources (the subject matter experts (SMEs) already mentioned in the data domain owner section) would have already been employed on other priorities. Also, in an operationally focused organization, there is never a good time for an assessment. To overcome such obstacles, the DPT's contingency position should be to offer to execute instead a pilot, an assessment with a reduced scope in terms of disciplines and narrower coverage in terms of business operations. A possible outline of the pilot assessment project for the zealous DPT's perusal is outlined in Table 5.7.

POSITIVE REINFORCEMENT FOR PROGRESS

Now that the first assessment is done, whether in full or in its pilot form, it is crucial to utilize its results with maximum and lasting effect. The gym goer would be reminded to measure themselves at least once a year and, as we said, data excellence is all about establishing the right rituals, so the easiest route would be to iterate the measure and focus the data athletes on

TABLE 5.7 Assessment project outline

Project name	\<Company\> data fitness assessment
Project team	1 project leader (internal full time) / 3 analysts (external full time)
Project goal	To perform a minimally viable data fitness assessment of the areas in scope through interviews of relevant SMEs and analysis of existing artifacts (e.g. policies, glossaries, data quality issue logs, data control charts). The objective is to prove that the data fitness assessment (DFA) is a useful instrument in identifying areas where data practices should be improved and allows the creation of an initial heatmap, pointing to the areas of higher strategic dependence, where improvement should be prioritized.
Timeline	5–6 weeks: • 1 week preparatory work • 2–3 weeks for interviews (depending on SMEs' availability) • 2 weeks for completion of DFA deliverables
Data charter scope	Data management discipline and data management sub-disciplines
Approach	Max. 30 interviews with SMEs from the following areas: • sales • finance • HR • market – Germany • market – Canada • market – UAE
Success criteria	• **Control**: The data fitness assessment identifies known thematic weaknesses and risks across the organization • **Effort**: The time committed by the SMEs is limited to the duration of the meeting, and to the time of collection of the evidence, plus a 30% contingency to provide explanations to the assessment team and to validate the interview read-out • **Scoring**: Given the statistical nature of the pilot, the fitness ratings for each subdiscipline will be given
Deliverables	• Data fitness assessment questionnaire • List of interviewees • Artifact list request • Schedule of interviews • Interviews transcripts and summaries • Data fitness assessment scoring • High level comparison with industry peers • SWOT analysis • Recommended action plan

improving their score. However, over time that might create a focus on the assessment just for the assessment's sake, for example over-exercising and only taking care about dieting in the proximity of the assessment's date. In business terms, that would translate into data athletes trying to hype or over-emphasizing some actions just to improve their annual assessment, in the absence of a true adoption of what the data discipline really entails.

Instead, the DPT should now pitch the data fitness assessment to the data international Olympic committee, as defined in the 'Toning the top' section in Chapter 3, and show them how the portfolio of strategic initiatives they take care of could be better assured in its outcome, making data fitness improvement a part of each initiative execution. Translating the strategic initiative into an expected improvement to data disciplines that the initiative is dependent on, and making such improvement part of the initiative's goal, would create a strong positive reinforcement loop in which the positive outcome of an initiative is upheld by the increased fitness, and the increased fitness is evidenced by the positive outcome. The role of the DPT in the above is, of course, to understand the business' ambition enough to identify which area's fitness level is going to be of highest dependency in the execution of the initiative and so assign the target fitness score. Figure 5.3 summarizes the positive reinforcement loop that, with the help of the data international Olympic committee, you should aim to activate.

FIGURE 5.3 Positive reinforcement loop

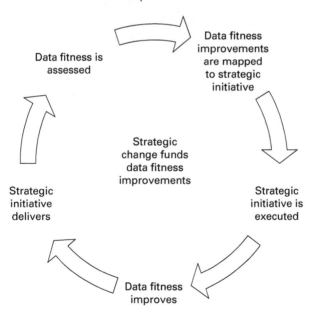

Data Workout 1 at the end of this part will show practically how to start visualizing the interlock between change and data fitness. Then we will be ready to really take on the wider challenge of 'change' and how data excellence must be embedded in it.

COOLING DOWN

- The data charter is a simple manifesto of data excellence.

- The data excellence documental backbone includes the data charter, data disciplines, data sub-disciplines and implementation documents.

- Five disciplines are recommended as foundational: data management, data science, data security, data privacy and record management.

- Based on the disciplines, a data fitness assessment can be performed.

- The data fitness assessment should be linked to the strategic change of the company to positively reinforce the progress in data excellence.

Notes

1 DAMA. DAMA Data Management Body of Knowledge, nd. www.dama.org/ cpages/body-of-knowledge (archived at https://perma.cc/KFK8-WZ25)

2 EDM Council. DCAM framework, nd. edmcouncil.org/frameworks/dcam/ (archived at https://perma.cc/6YKL-KD35)

3 DAMA. DAMA Data Management Body of Knowledge, nd. www.dama.org/ cpages/body-of-knowledge (archived at https://perma.cc/V59H-2VYG)

4 CMMI Institute. CMMI data, nd. cmmiinstitute.com/cmmi/data (archived at https://perma.cc/R6J4-ZFUF)(continued)(continued)(continued)

06

The coxswain's megaphone

Communications and data

WARMING UP

- Why communication is key to performance.
- How data excellence is reinforced by excellent communication.
- What the components of a data excellence communication plan looks like.

The importance of communication for achieving data excellence

I have always loved listening to stories, historical documentaries and stand-up comedy; I am in awe of the powerful connection that is created by understanding your past or being taken through a whimsical journey that ends in surprise and laughter. *Castigat ridendo mores* (one corrects customs by laughing at them), they used to say, endorsing the educational worth of satire, or, as we would say now: stories create a bond that inspires change.

In the last decade, storytelling has emerged as an essential weapon in the DPT arsenal, as cultural change needs a strong narrative to be sustained. One of the best stories I heard in the past was told to me by Rowley Douglas, coxswain for the British eight at the 2000 Sydney Olympics, who won the first British gold medal in the discipline since Stockholm in 1912. In the lead up to the London Olympic games of 2012, Rowley was a colleague working at GE Capital in London, and I was in attendance at an internal event to which he was invited as a guest to tell a story of sport and leadership. His story was centred around the days leading up to the Olympic final, and the role that the cox played in having the crew go beyond just the sum of the strength of the eight rowers. The 'voice from the stern' is not just there to communicate the rhythm but he can feel the imperfections in the thrust applied and, most importantly, is the only one able to follow the route. His description of the way the feeling of the athletes had to be understood and funnelled created an inspiring parallel with the life of leaders at work, and was only topped by the surprise of him producing his real Olympiad gold medal. That story heard in the lead-up to my first role of chief data officer still resonates, and that's why the last section of Pillar I, dedicated to communication, has this title.

Having toned the top, assembled a team, identified the data domain owner, issued a data charter, promoted data discipline and assessed the data fitness in respect to the athlete's ambitions, what is the missing binding action that pushes forward and propagates the data excellence culture?

When I started my first role in data 10 years ago, I had to rely a lot on external input, as data was still an obscure subject in my then company. One of the sources that I was allowed to tap in was the advisory firm, Gartner. One of the best sessions I had was with one of its analysts, Joe Bugajski, CDO at Visa, 2001–08, at a time when the data officer job title was regarded by many as a bit of a joke. Back then, Joe spent considerable time advising me and my newbie colleagues. I clearly remember a conference call in which Joe told me something that I can recall verbatim to this day. 'Roberto,' he said, 'Get yourself a communication expert! And what I mean by that is not someone who can do nice PowerPoint presentations, but someone who can help you put together a professional communication plan for data!' Joe was quite clear that a simple push from the top would never be enough and that it had to be sustained. In his view, too many data officers were relying on top-down communication and deluded themselves that just because the CEO had said in one of their communications that 'Data is the new oil' everyone would instantly agree to do anything the newly appointed CDO had recommended. I was impressed by his boldness and clarity, and understood exactly what he meant: pristine communication must be an essential part of the journey of data, so that it reverberates beyond the top-down push and goes viral. The importance of communication originates from the realization that data demands a change of processes. If it were IT or AI then, as I firmly postulated at the start of this book, a task, a project, a programme would suffice and, maybe, 'simple' change management would suffice. But because we are dealing with ingrained habits that determine the data outcome, they are not easily changed. One does not change one's habits simply because one is asked to. And to say 'one' would be misleading, as any single organization is made up of many tribes, as we have said, with many layers, and all of them have to make the emotional switch to change. This means the message has to be tailored and pushed in different ways. This is where the DPT must fathom the inner mechanism of psychology and sociology to effectively play to the right emotions (such as willingness and positivity) of a community and ensure change.

REAL-WORLD EXAMPLE
Project inception

My friend Emiliano Pimpinella once shared with me a post over LinkedIn about him giving a speech about the independence wars in Italy and the epic of Garibaldi during the country's unification in the 19th century. In watching it I was struck by a quote by a Swiss philosopher, Henry-Frederic Amiel (1821–81), 'Pure truth cannot be assimilated by the crowd; it must be communicated by contagion.' This man two hundred years ago was in fact describing how complex, top-down narratives are seldom embraced by the masses. Instead 'simplified truths' delivered by a trusted channel, someone seen as a peer, are accepted and spread much more easily. Amiel, I maintain, was explaining the social media viral effect.

At the time I was dealing with a tough corporate environment and I immediately drew a parallel with First-Line Joe, the person who sits in the workplace with their hands in the processes that I am trying to change. First-Line Joe is much more likely to change his behaviour and perform like a proper data athlete because his or her office mate or desk neighbour had once recommended becoming a data athlete over a coffee, rather than because of all the emails, videos or training sessions I could have ever produced. Short of befriending everyone in the company, I decided to use the internal collaboration platform as my way of making the contagion happen, and so Project Inception was born. If you are not familiar with the movie, it is a classic Christopher Nolan movie from 2010, in which Leonardo DiCaprio is part of a group of people who are paid to plant an idea into the mind of a target tycoon, infiltrating his dreams by a process of 'inception'. My idea was simple and by no means unethical. I asked a contractor to look into all the collaboration groups on the platform and find the ones with discussions containing references to 'data'. I then had them listed in order based on the number of members, the topics discussed and the level of the interaction. In the top 10 we found members close to our data group who we asked in the following week to repost messages related to the activities of the data team, such as the launch of one of our policies, the appointment of data domain owners or the successful closure of a project. The post was duly followed up by a like or a comment of mine or one of my team members to reinforce the impact, as the 'inceptor' was also receiving a direct endorsement from a senior leader. The experiment didn't last long enough to close the loop with a 'payback measurement' assessing how many more people had, for example, read the mentioned policy in the weeks following the post. However, given the steep rise of invites to staff and townhall meetings in the following weeks, Project Inception did succeed in raising the profile of my team within, at least, the other pre-existing data teams.

Why there is no data excellence without excellent communication

The beginning of Pillar I was dedicated to breaking data tribalism within (and to a certain extent even outside) the boundary of an organization, in order to establish the mindset that will foster data excellence. To this end I quoted an anthropologist's definition of culture, in which the most important word was 'acquired'. Culture is 'that complex whole which includes knowledge, belief, art, morals, law, custom... acquired by man as a member of society'.[1] I hope you can now agree that Joe Bugajsky's recommendation dovetails in its significance, combining together the emotional shift required to motivate someone to change with the concept of acquisition. The conclusion is that the enabling ingredient to make the needed cultural transition is the same that makes someone purchase a product: excellent engagement achieved with excellent communication! The DPT has to be able to sell a need that might not be perceived yet, to excel in data, together with his or her services, as the conduit to achieve the fulfilment of that need; however the willingness to buy the DPT's services, together with the commitment to put the necessary work in, is proportional to the perception of that need, and that is where things can go sour.

At the beginning of one of my engagements, I was professing my credo, evangelizing the management around 'definitional ambiguity' and how that was the number one enemy of their company's data maturity. My intention was to quickly gain buy-in to the new role of data domain owners, with the standards and everything discussed above. Time was going by, and traction was missing – yes, data was believed to be the most important asset, and yes, 'definitional ambiguity' was agreed as something to avoid, but I could feel that the spark was not there. Then one day in an executive meeting it hit me: there was a belief that enterprise analytics could be achieved with the issuance of a request to multiple units in multiple places and the receipt of multiple Excel spreadsheets, that a team of analysts would have stitched together in a data rhapsody on which to perform analysis of forecasts. In that instant I realized that my 'Fight definitional ambiguity!' slogan had been completely misunderstood, and my cardinal sin had been to fail to check for their understanding.

So, I changed tack and asked three different units, recipients of the Excel request, to send me their operational definitions of one of the fields requested in the spreadsheet, and I intentionally asked for a pretty banal and blinding obvious one, such as customer order date. I was not surprised when three completely different definitions came back, and I won't deny that I felt a bit smug when reporting the result of my test to that very audience of executives. The reaction I received was very different from what I had expected – apart from a slight raise of eyebrows they were almost unfazed. But you would be wrong in assuming that they were in denial – the chieftain cannot admit in front of their tribe that they were wrong, but it became clear in the months to come that the penny had dropped, even if the Excel procedure was not immediately phased out. It was reinforced in its controls and over time replaced by a proper data supply chain. In this simple example my attempt at communicating clearly had failed the most basic of the tests: understanding your audience.

Benefits of excellent communication

When improving the company's value generation performance through use of data – and that is the mission that the data personal trainer has been asked to complete – then excellent communication delivers the same as it delivers Olympic performances when employed in sport.

An athlete needs to understand the instructions of the trainer but also needs to provide feedback on his or her physical and emotional state. Motivation and support must be conveyed at the right time with appropriate words and transparency, as honest communication is the key to creating a trust environment that propels the relationship further and make it resilient to the many bumps that will be encountered on the journey. Lastly, celebration of successes is often underrated in business, but it would never be in sport, and celebration that creates a lasting legend amongst the tribes captures the imagination of the new data athlete and pushes them toward virtuous behaviours. As an example, the already mentioned data charter is not only supposed to be a cold articulation of the principles to be good at data, but it should include as a preamble a targeted and succinct message of the meaningfulness of it, something that the data athletes could relate to and feel was important to them in their life at work, something that would create an emotion that would foster an action, a change of behaviour.

Defining the structure of the communication plan

The role the DPT plays

Just as our data athletes should not assume that they can compete in the world of data, it would be advisable for the DPT not to assume that they are master at communication. Joe's message implicitly advised that the role of the DPT would be to become the customer of the communication expert and let them guide the construction and execution of a plan. So, the first action is to assess existing resources that are able to support the design of the communication plan and to gain some capacity out of their busy schedule. I have been successful in recycling existing plans from functions that were ahead of the game, like risk or sales, or the above-mentioned portfolio of strategic initiatives could also be a useful repository to identify activities that would have a communication team committed for the change management part. If the DPT were successful in linking themselves to the programme they could be leveraging those communication resources to build part of the plan as a deliverable of the initiative.

What makes an effective communication plan

Having worked over the years with various communication experts, I have tried and tested many shapes and guises of such plans. Although in their final format they are normally presented as a schedule of events with various features, the ones that worked the best had the features described below as a minimum set.

AUDIENCE SEGMENTATION

This is the leading factor to make communication effective. It identifies and groups the intended targets of the message in clusters which share a common trait, need or affinity. It forms the foundation of the plan, and the subsequent features are tailored on the segmentation (e.g. delivery methodology for the CEO and staff is always in-person). I segment my audiences based on their hierarchical position or degree of influence. My data athletes are divided into a minimum of three groups: executives, mid management (aka the 'chieftains') and 'mass market', i.e. everyone else in the company, including contractors and third-party staff having access to company data. Obviously, the CEO needs a different communication strategy to the teams that are performing data stewardship. However, as the understanding of the data athletes furthers, and the capabilities of the data personal trainer evolve, the segmentation should become more granular, to include more audiences that potentially cut across existing groups. For instance, one of my favourite groups is the 'data influencers', made up of leaders who, adopting the new vernacular of data, have the potential to influence a vast group of people. Influencers can include a well-known and admired sales person, a programme leader of a significant transformation initiative or a popular business unit leader.

CHANNEL

This is an inventory of any platform or media that can be used to deliver a message, such as an email, a social media post and a virtual or in-person training session, available within the organization for the DPT to use. Each channel in the list should be accompanied by its capabilities. For example, a collaboration suite (e.g. Teams, Google Meet, Webex, etc.) has the ability to hold video conferences for group and/or mass audiences, screen share and chat. The attributes of the channels are important when we match them with the audience segmentation, but such association would be dependent on factors like organization make up, geographical spread and company culture. A global email about data excellence to the 'mass market' would have the maximum reach and could potentially motivate a substantial number of people to action in a single task, but the abuse of mass emails could diminish the effectiveness of the message. Often people automatically bin them, and there are companies that completely ban the ability to 'send to all'. Instead, the DPT should opt for webinar series or posts on the company collaboration platforms, like Viva or Slack. For top management, outside of the statutory framework of communication like staff meetings and committees, the toning of the top should be performed preferably face-to-face. However, if there is no prospect of an in-person meeting in the foreseeable future, indirect contact via email or messages could still help make progress on their training.

CADENCE

Cadence is the frequency at which the communication touch points are calendarized and carried out, with a careful balance between too often and too little, and following the typical seasonality of the audience (e.g. prioritization meetings, budgeting sessions, townhalls). At the inception it will be wise for the DPT to make the instances of the comms plan coincide with existing meetings, to avoid adding calendar burden to the audiences. Knowing and segmenting the audiences correctly is important to dose the communication correctly to avoid fatigue.

While the profile of data personal trainer is established across the organization, it would be ideal to get to know the executive or personal assistants of the various functions and ask them very nicely to reserve for you a 10–15 minute slot at the next townhall meeting or gathering. These would be exceptionally important customer touch points that should be carefully curated, during which the DPT should present a simple and attractive teaser to their data excellence plans.

PAYLOAD, A.K.A. CONTENT

The 'what' is of course the vital part to curate, as it is the message that will hopefully generate the action. I cannot overemphasize the care that must be taken in both form and substance. I am particularly fond of metaphors (as my readers may have already noticed) and I certainly believe that using pictures helps to anchor the concept. It might take a while to establish the right format, and I am definitely more in favour of evolving a good concept step-by-step rather than exposing the audience to continuously new and seemingly disconnected stories. The DPT should aim to form rapidly a 'brand identity' that will make the audiences at ease when they tune into the 'data channels'. This could be a logo, a pattern of colours, a slogan or a tagline at the end of the communication collateral, e.g. a presentation. I would err on the side of caution and repeat these features in the communication unceasingly, as they help to form the mantra that should accompany the data athletes in their practices. As the most successful content is the content people can relate to, the DPT should gain as much intelligence as possible of existing styles that can be adopted. For example, if the finance team has 'accounting golden rules' that are well known, understood and followed, you should probably create the 'data golden rules'.

PAYBACK OR OUTCOME

Describing the tangible outcome that I want to happen by virtue of a communication action helps to measure the efficacy of the communication. For different audiences, the desired outcome could be different, and may change in time with the increase of the data excellence prowess, as I have detailed in Chapter 4 about data domain owners' engagement. However, in general the outcome should be a change in behaviour, an augmentation of data athlete knowledge or a more tactical action that the audience is supposed to take. In the section about risk and controls in the next part, I will propose examples of behaviours that our communication should prevent, mitigating data risks, or encourage, improving data value. Finally, the outcome must be measured and so a feedback loop can be established,

FIGURE 6.1 Data personal trainer communication plan

Audience	Channel	Cadence	Content	Outcome
Executive committee	One-to-one meeting	Twice a year	Conversation about data excellence, supported by maximum 5 slides	Awareness of data excellence championship of DPT role
	In person meeting	Yearly	Presentation on data excellence plan and yearly resourcing requirements	Ratification of plan and funding approval
	In person meeting	Yearly	Data risks and control heatmap and mitigation plans	Data risk appetite statement and control plan approval
Data influencers	In person meeting	One off	Personal introduction and introduction to the three pillars	Establishing personal rapport and basic understanding of data excellence
	In person or online meeting	Once a month for the first 6 months	Six slide decks of data excellence engagement plan	Increased data fluency and fitness as per plan evaluation
	Webinar	Quarterly	Online presentation about data excellence 'state of the nation' type	Awareness and buy-in on progress
Middle management	Online meeting	Monthly	Open format like lunch'n'learn, or 'any questions'	Taking the pulse on unspoken/lurking data issues, and providing tips and tricks
	Collaboration suite	Ad hoc	Post about data excellence and DPT tips and tricks	Awareness of specific dos and don'ts on data
All data athletes (aka mass market)	Online training	Yearly	Data excellence basic training on key concepts	Proficiency on data charter and data disciplines
	Email	Ad hoc	Data excellence newsletter and sharing of successes (e.g. completion of milestones)	Feeling as part of a data tribe and positive reinforcement of virtuous behaviours

whether with a simple online form or with focus groups, as constant measurement of the communication's impact is essential. Figure 6.1 shows an example of a DPT communication plan.

COOLING DOWN

- A good DPT must be also a good communicator.
- Good communication uses stories to anchor messages.
- Data excellence needs a structured communication plan.
- The structure of a good communication plan provides audience segmentation, channels, cadence, content and outcome.

Note

1   E B Tylor (1871) *Primitive Culture: Research into the development of mythology, philosophy, religion, art, and custom*, J P Putnam's Sons, New York

Data Workout 1

The first prioritized data excellence initiatives portfolio

This exercise shows you how to put into practice an important and concrete first step of the data excellence journey: the creation of a prioritized portfolio of data excellence initiatives. This exercise is priming the DPT for the full fledging of the change rituals of Pillar II, as, starting with a business portfolio of programmes, its outcome should be the basis for the first 'serious' conversation with our data athletes – where we test their resolve to implement their strategy, acknowledging that, this time, data will not be an afterthought. However, at the very beginning, the DPT might have very few resources to influence all the changes that are in motion. Therefore, this simple exercise goes beyond an inventory of the changes that are data sensitive and is an effective segmentation of the ones that should be the initial focus of the DPT's resources.

Preparation

The exercise requires two pieces of work to have either been completed or be near completion:

1 A list of all the strategic initiatives, each with a minimum description that should including name, high-level description, team or business unit, forecast duration, forecast spend, geographical scope, product line scope and the intended beneficiary.

2 A data fitness assessment, as per Chapter 5, or any high-level data maturity assessment (i.e. non evidence basis) performed on at least the business units of the organization which are mostly represented in the list.

The list of strategic initiatives (1) can be quite sensitive, and it might require a bit of insistence to gain access to them – if necessary, a 'sanitized' version would do. If such a list doesn't exist yet, it would be a good move for the DPT to work with the DA to create a first version as a first data excellence exercise. In terms of timeliness, the third or fourth quarter of the year, depending on the organization's rituals, are budgetary and strategic prioritization windows of opportunity not to be missed.

Once the list is obtained, it is very probable if data is still an afterthought that it would contain mainly organizational and financial information, as the main aim of this lists is to allocate a finite amount of investment to programmes that are deemed strategic priorities. If that's the case, it is important to collect from the portfolio or programme leads information around the data reliance of each programme. I suggest the following additional attributes to complement the existing ones: data dependency, data investment, data consumer type, data domain affected, data service, data classification, system of source. For an ideal though not exhaustive list, see Table DW1.1.

TABLE DW1.1 List of portfolio attributes, with data dependencies in grey

Name	Description
Identifier	Unique reference of the business initiative
Programme name	Name of the initiative
Lead entity (programme level)	Organizational entity which will lead the initiative
Entity DCAM maturity	Data maturity measured on DCAM model
Programme type	Carry over, i.e. rolling execution, from previous period or new initiative in the incoming period
Project budget in (k euro)	Cash amount to be invested in thousands of euros
Project length (months)	Expected duration of the initiative in months
Data dependency	Whether a dependency from data has been flagged
Data budget (k euro)	Cash amount dedicated to the data
Data service	Type of data specific activity/outcome carried out during the project

(continued)

TABLE DW1.1 (Continued)

Name	Description
Type of data	Data sets involved in the project
Sources	IT systems that would be involved as source of the data outcome
Domain	Data domains, based on the logical data model, involved in the change
Available data objects	Is there an existing data product/object that can be leveraged to accomplish this initiative?
Customer	Main category of data consumers who will benefit from the initiative
Classification	Data sensitivity categorization based on risk posed by the data
Impacted areas	Organizational entity which is contributing or dependent on the initiative

Completing task 1 could yield a list of tens if not hundreds of elements. The objective now is to narrow down where one must focus first, embedding resources from the data team to train the data athletes on their job of delivering value for the business. The prioritized initiatives should show reduced execution issues (overspend and delays) and, thus, a higher return on investment. This promotes the adoption of this practice annually or even more frequently, which would support the DPT's case for a larger number of resources to train more athletes.

Approach

The approach is to highlight areas where the 'health' hazard or the reward is the highest – a risk/reward approach. The graph I would suggest you build would have three components (see Figure DW1.1). On the X axis we plot the data maturity of the group/unit that is going to execute the initiative. Ideally, we should have performed this for all of the units the data fitness assessment described in Chapter 5, but if it is very early on in the data excellence journey, that data might still be incomplete, so any proxy data linking to the capability of the unit could be used instead. It could be as simple as a flag that accounts for the existence of a team taking care of data in the leading unit.

On the Y axis we will need to come up with a risk factor inherent to the initiative and, depending on the data available, we could create a compound index based on the size of the budget, the number of countries involved, the duration of the initiative or the number of data domains involved. In this case I have used a combination of budget assigned, numbers of data domains involved and sensitivity of the data consumed. So, the higher the budget, the higher the numbers of data domains; and the more sensitive the classification of data, the higher the risk to data execution. Finally, for additional visualization effectiveness, I have plotted each single project with a circle of a radius proportional to the requested budget.

The graph plotted is not to be taken too scientifically but rather it delivers a view of where to apply limited DPT resources: the area that is indicated as 'fit to execute' identifies a cluster of lower risk initiatives proposed by units demonstrating (or claiming) a reasonably high data maturity. Elsewhere, the area delimited by the line 'need more data muscle' encircles the programmes on which I really want to focus my DPT time, as these are the ones likely to create an issue for the organization, given that their strategic importance, and dependence on data is not matched by the required data fitness. Depending on the data that is easier to collect and the nature of the strategic initiatives, you could experiment with different definitions of the Y axis, but I would recommend that data maturity is used as the X axis. Whatever the axis definitions, it would now become essential to start to track what the outcome of the execution of all the project is, especially for those deemed 'fit

FIGURE DW1.1 Data excellence portfolio health profile

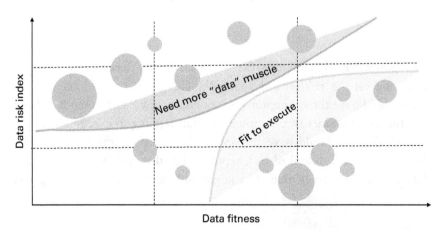

to execute' or left in the middle as effectively 'execution risk accepted' because we could not allocate resources to support them. Such a lesson learnt would calibrate the health profile to optimize the allocation of resources at the next cycle.

The initiatives in the 'need more data muscle' group are named 'data excellence initiatives', the first portfolio of the DPT and the training ground for their data athletes. Once the training gains pace it will be found that the data excellence initiatives show a certain overlap of data requirements across a finite group of data domains. Such an intersection of data dependency across the organization's strategic change ambitions forms the basis for another speciality I am going to describe later in Pillar III: data productization.

How to change the way change is done

07

The nature of change

WARMING UP

- If change is the only constant, why are our brains built to resist it?
- Why does good change that increases performance degrade over time?
- What is the organizational 'lactic acid' and how does the DPT tackle it?
- What is Six Sigma and how can it help the DPT?
- How do you tame bad change with controls?

Why do we resist change?

Change is a powerful agent that, intricately connected to the physics of time, constantly affects the world around us, from the microscopic to the galactic level, meaning the universe is in constant motion. Yet the feeling of change is deceptive. Our brain is not able to process this continuous flow, and instead gives us the sensation of a static world. This conflicted sense of change is best captured by the lyric from the song 'Time' by Pink Floyd: 'And then one day you find ten years have got behind you'. This overlay of stasis applied to change stems from a primordial need for certainty that the ancient Hominids had to develop to survive. The human brain evolved to reward habit and routine as guarantees of safety: to be able to repeat the safe path to a watering hole or to replicate a sequence of actions that provide food is rewarded by a discharge of endorphins. The learnt concept, which has a beneficial return, must be recalled and re-used if the situation requires, so the brain tends to find a known pattern to which it applies a known concept. This instinct is so important that, as learning a new concept requires the rewiring of neuropathways, this action is accompanied by discomfort and unease: it is our brain's way of effectively refusing to believe that things have changed and protecting what we already know.

When I moved to the UK I had already been driving for almost two decades, so driving was something that I was doing very comfortably, in all situations, so much that I was enjoying drives through Italy and even across Europe, whenever I could . Suddenly in 2001 a very well-honed skill was put to the test by a dramatic change: driving on the 'wrong' side of the road, while sitting on the 'wrong' side of the car. I distinctly remember the day I was given the keys of my new company car in the GE office car park. It was a blue Ford Mondeo, whose heated seats I learnt to love, and the last thing I would have wished for was to have an accident on the first day. The moment I fastened my seat belt my heart started racing, I was perspiring profusely and my brain literally ached while trying to cope with the completely new version of a well-known task. Along those few miles that I drove back to my new house in Didsbury, I was talking incessantly to myself, reminding myself to focus my eyes on the road and to use extreme caution at every traffic light or pedestrian crossing. Negotiating the first roundabout took a considerable time and the kind people behind me must have thought I'd never driven before, as they didn't beep once. They were right and wrong at the same time, because I have been driving for a long time and yet that was the first day of a different kind of driving. For several weeks I tried to minimize my driving time, because I was not enjoying it. It was, pardon the alliteration, a taxing task, but my wife-to-be lived 226 miles away, so forego-ing driving was not an option. Roll forward to 2003, we had a long road trip across Scotland and the week after I was in Naples. I was able to switch from left-handed drive to right-handed drive almost instantly and effort-lessly. How many times in our working lives do we ask someone metaphorically to change the driver side?

The connection between data and organizational change

Change, especially in recent years, has been targeted as the beast to tame. Why? Because in a world dominated by a constant drive for innovation and transformation, businesses must understand how to prepare for and imple-ment change effectively. There is an expectation that an organization delivers innovation because innovation drives growth, but there is not always the appreciation that to innovate products, change must happen within the innovator first. A manufacturing company wishing to offer profitable digital services by embedding software in its physical products must first become a software company, or at the very least start to behave like one. So, change management has become an area of vast academic study and organizational dynamic.

What is the takeaway for the DPT? Data is a digital representation of reality, so as the business context and the environment change, so does the data. A time element enters disruptively in all that the DPT supports, as there is no guarantee that yesterday's data is still a faithful representation of today's reality.

An external source that is feeding foreign exchange values to the finance team increases its precision and changes its figures from a three decimal digits to a four decimal digits format, but the change is not picked up and the feed is loaded without inspection into the financial systems. Suddenly the next financial monthly closure becomes a nightmare made up of numbers that don't match to the penny.

The sales administration team decides to save time and eliminates from their system application the field for the telephone number of the customer's legal office, and now the collection team has not got the contact details of who to call for an overdue invoice.

The above highlights two clear cases where data was an afterthought, demonstrating that not only does data have to be embedded in any relevant change, but the new status quo, the outcome of a change, must be secured against the external and internal forces that will try to disrupt it. 'Securing' does not mean rigidly locking; rather, the new status is to be appropriately responsive in order to maintain that faithful representation of the reality, which is essential to enable accurate decisions. You might think that most of the disruption to the data athlete's performance would come from massive regulatory change, market disruption and geopolitical instability. Those are clearly high impact, but I am about to demonstrate that the internal forces create a craftier more corrosive effect that must be kept in check.

The organizational lactic acid

Six Sigma is a quality methodology developed in the 1980s by Motorola that I was initiated in when I joined General Electric. It is a data-driven process that seeks to reduce process defects and to minimize the variability of its performance, as the numerical measurement of the said output (e.g. the diameter of a hole drilled in a part manufactured in series, the duration of a filament of a light bulb, the figures on a renewal contract). In synthesis, Six Sigma is a discipline that studies processes with statistical and numerical tools and implements good change to improve them. In its more widespread format the Six Sigma approach is represented with the DMAIC acronym, where the letters stand for:

- *Define:* Define the problem and performance goals.
- *Measure:* Collect data about the current performance of the process.
- *Analyse:* Investigate historical data and evaluate dependencies.
- *Improve:* Design and implement improvement actions.
- *Control:* Monitor the process performance to maintain gains.

By this short introduction you would have understood why in my first CDO role I found a lot of sympathizers in the Six Sigma teams.

The target for the performance level in Six Sigma is measured as the number of defects per opportunity, where a defect is the chance of the outcome of a process (product or service) not meeting the expectations of its customer, while an opportunity is the cumulative sum of the possible chance for a defect to arise. This could be, for example:

- Opportunity: The number of welding points on an assembled circuit board.
  - Defect: A missed welding point.
- Opportunity: The number of plastic bottle tops produced by a mould.
  - Defect: The number of bottle tops exceeding +/-1mm in diameter versus the design specifications.
- Opportunity: The customer details on an invoice template.
  - Defect: The number of customer details being blank fields.

Sigma (σ) as a representative measure of a process capability is numerically tabled based on the number of defects per million opportunities (DPMO). So, for a process to be at '6σ', the process can only be affected by 3.4 defects per million opportunities, which means a quality of 99.9997 per cent. In the manufacturing example of the bottle top, with a 6σ performance I would only discard a bit fewer than four bottle tops per one million moulded!

This apparently incredible high bar is not the point I am trying to make here, as there are processes that are reportedly at 7 or 8σ. Instead, the interesting finding over many years of improvement projects is that time degrades performance, even in the absence of any known observable causes. Over time, the process left alone inexorably deteriorates by a factor between 1.4 and 1.6, between the *short-term sigma* (quality at the end of the improvement phase) and *long-term sigma* (trending quality levels over the long-term period)

Six Sigma practitioners are thus recommended to adopt a standard 1.5 shift to take into account in the maintenance phase.[1] It might not seem much, but, given the exponential nature of the scale, taking again as example the bottle top making process, let's imagine that the process had just gone through an improvement action. Either we found out that the type of plastic was not melting correctly in the mould or that the mould metal was expanding too much when heated, exceeding the tolerance of the bottle top diameter. Let's assume that we replaced the old metal with a better alloy, and that the improvement achieved 5σ, so now 'only' 233 bottle tops would be discarded per million produced. If we apply the recommended 1.5 'shift' long term that performance would degrade to 3.50σ, which is a more worrying 22,750 bottle tops discarded!

What is happening? The answer is time! Time changes the world, and change is affecting the performance of the improved process. 'Causes of variation', i.e. unintended and, often, undetected changes, are affecting the ticking clockwork of our process and drifting its sharpness. The more the process and the variables that affect its quality are known, ideally in the form of a transfer function between all the Ys, the dependent variable or the output, and the Xs, the independent variables or the input, the more we could avoid the decrease of performance, but in the real world such models are never a perfect approximation of reality, and hence the process is always going to be ultimately impacted by the 'unknown unknowns'. My view is that in the world of data, a good portion of that 1.5 shift should be ascribed to people involved in the process going back to their old habits!

So the attentive data personal trainer would know that the work done to deliver the right data for a strategic business initiative will not only need to establish the data supply chain and improve the data to match consumer expectations, but there will also be additional work to factor in the data transformation to deliver robust guardrails and controls that will provide assurance that the performance achieved will not be affected by the human tendency to use established neurological patterns, i.e. old habits.

To cite a simple example, in the example given when I described the role of the data domain owner in Chapter 4, we learnt how to classify customers properly across the organization. The DDO introduced a list of values to be propagated to all the systems managing customer data. The opportunity management system, the system that records and manages potential commercial opportunities that could become customer orders, was a key asset to align to that data standard. Such an endeavour would have cost a substantial amount of money and labour, relative to the size of the organization, and of course there would be an expectation set to have every customer, previously identified only by certain attributes like name, address, telephone number, etc., to also be assigned another attribute, important to the company strategy. Let's hypothesize now that the classification recommended by the data domain owner is to assign each customer with their market segment based on the customer's industry, i.e. manufacturing, consulting, financial services, etc. The data domain owner is in fact supporting the finance team who have devised, together with the pricing team, a discount policy based on customer industry that should increase penetration in key segments. The systems change is launched, a new field is designed and created in the opportunity management database and a new object called 'customer market segment' is added to customer input form in the user interface. The field has been assigned with an alphabetically organized, drop-down list of 50 market segments, approved by the data domain owner. Unfortunately, so far nobody has asked the DPT their views and the field has not been made mandatory, so notwithstanding the sales team training, after a few months of usage only 50 per cent of the new opportunities are showing customers with market segment different from an empty value.

Asked to intervene, the DPT prescribes that a data quality rule checks whether the field is unassigned and prevents an opportunity being saved unless a choice in the drop-down list is made, effectively making the choice of a market segment mandatory. The new control is designed and implemented, there is even a monthly dashboard that controls that there is in fact a valid value in the 'market segment' field, and it scores consistently in the high 90s. However, a few weeks after, the finance team raises an alert that the revenue from new sales is not performing as expected. Something has gone wrong, a disproportionate number of orders have been discounted with the discount granted to the 'aerospace' segment, which happened to be a target segment that the company wanted to penetrate and hence the discount was substantial. What has happened? Did some of the sales team find out the discount was higher and decided to circumvent the system to book more orders? Possibly, but the explanation is simpler: for the most part, the same team members that were previously accounting for 50 per cent of the blank market segment, when obliged to choose one, picked the first in the alphabetically ordered list. This is called the 'Afghanistan effect' which happened to a data friend when the customer country list he was managing was made mandatory; the old habit of not caring about the field was perpetuated by the shortcut of picking the first available one.

In competition terms, our data athlete, who in the case above was the business leader wanting to provide discounts based on market segment, should be made aware by the DPT that by resting on their laurels their performance will steadily deteriorate, as more and more of this organizational 'lactic acid' accumulates. Instead, they should keep on training, so that a given level of performance achieved is not perceived as the finish line but rather as one step on an upward journey. As mentioned at the onset, data is a never-ending journey of permanent augmentation. Alas, the feeling that there is always some headwind slowing us down, psychologically, can be hard to push against, but in this case the trick is to have the new exercise regime to go live together with the new status. What I mean by the 'new exercise regime' is the additional feature in the change (making the input mandatory) that will counteract the bad change (picking the first value). The athletes will go through 'maintenance exercises', which are a diverse set of training and workouts to maintain their peak performance, to make resilient what they have achieved. In data, and in Six Sigma, the diverse set of measures to maintain a certain status at nominal performance are called *controls*. How do you avoid gaining unwanted weight? You control your nutrition, and you adjust it continuously as a lighter body will need fewer calories. How do you prevent accumulation of lactic acid? You adopt a controlled regime of training and resting. It is the same for data: how do you make sure the market segment is as accurate as possible? You check it is complete, it is within the range, etc. Controls are required to sustain value generation, i.e. performance.

Learning to tame change

The Data Excellence Operating Model (DeXOM) you will be introduced to in Chapter 9 is going to establish that any change must have embedded the ability to control its output over time (sustain phase). If the goal of the DPT is to support the data athlete to establish (or improve) a data supply chain and deliver value in economic terms, such value creation must be assured over an appropriate length of time to realize the return on investment.

In the previous section, I expressed how I adopted this tenet from Six Sigma theory, which, for that very reason, prescribes clearly that a control phase follows the improvement phase, often assumed incorrectly to be the end of a project. In the control phase the knowledge of the process acquired through the other phases, especially measure and analyse, comes to fruition in the causal understanding of what can go wrong in the process, allowing an optimal design and implementation of controls.

In Figure 7.1, using Six Sigma terminology I give a very simplified view of how the performance of a given process evolves when we try to improve it and where the control phase is operating. Applying the schematic to the customer market segment case, the performance we wanted to achieve was to be able to provide an appropriate discount to customers when quoting for a product, based on an accurate market segment.

Let's overlay the example on the graph. Our starting performance ($\sigma 0$) would be proportional to the 50 per cent of customer records holding a customer segment value measured before the improvement, with the other 50 per cent of records missing the attribute. The 'improve effort', the project to finalize the list of market segment values and to make the field mandatory, inclusive of training for the sales team, lasts until a time Tf, and pushes the performance up to its theoretical maximum – this is the sigma short term (σs). In the absence of any countermeasures, the 'Afghanistan effect' occurs and the performance degrades over time to its long-term value (σl), which is higher than the original performance, but much lower than the result the improve phase had achieved, as although we have all the data, we know that is polluted by the users' old behaviour. Instead, the DPT might have noticed from the analysis of the change that a simple control could be added to prevent the operator misbehaving.

Then, using the activity code, a list that is given to companies when they register their activity with the commerce authorities, which is available from an external source and is in direct relationship with the market segment, the DPT builds a control that checks the consistency of the market segment chosen with the activity code. It rejects the operator's input, challenging the

FIGURE 7.1 Sustaining performance improvement with controls

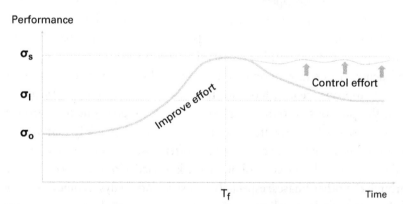

'aerospace' choice and thus pushing the performance curve as close as possible to the one at the time Tf.

Ideally such action should be part of the initial design and implemented in the improvement phase so that there is no dip in performance when an issue is found, and a corrective action is prepared and deployed. DeXOM will stress that it is important to factor the effort of implementation and monitoring of controls together with the improvement effort as early as possible in the change, so our data athlete will not be surprised or upset to find out that their toils are not over and will recognize that the upkeep is part of the improvement.

NB: For the more attentive readers I am aware that I have been circumnavigating the 'accuracy' problem, i.e. how do I certify that the market segment chosen is not just valid but also accurate? Well, in Chapter 10, establishing foundational capabilities, we will also delve into the techniques to move closer to the data quality Holy Grail: accuracy.

Three types of data controls

Having agreed that controls are key to maintain performance of a good change and to combat bad change, control theory is a vast branch of science which I am very fond of, but I would not want my fondness to let me digress too much into it. Still, it is beneficial for the appreciation of following sections of this book (e.g. data quality and data risks) to list below the three different macro categories in which all controls, including data controls are generally classified: preventative, detecting and corrective.

PREVENTATIVE CONTROLS

These are controls that are supposed to avoid the occurrence of an issue with the data. A typical example is a validation gate when ingesting data to prevent ingestion of 'bad data'. Data encryption would also be a preventative control in case of a data breach, to minimize the likelihood that the data could be illicitly exploited.

DETECTING CONTROLS

This type of control is probably the most common, as it measures an aspect of data to detect potential problems. The most common data quality controls are usually of this type as they perform as ex-post controls. In our example, the monthly dashboard controlling the completion of the field was detecting whether the information had properly been populated as an indication of a process still in control.

CORRECTIVE CONTROLS

These controls instigate an action after the occurrence of an issue to prevent a larger impact. They include actions such as cleansing of corrupted data, or the standardization of the data in a data set, like the format of a post code or a phone number.

It would be incorrect to think of these classes as independent. In data excellence the primary objective for controls should be to maintain the minimum gap between reality and its digital representation, and for that objective these three types of controls must be seen as nested mechanisms minimizing the risk that the gap becomes significant and affects business decisions. If an issue with critical data could not be prevented, it should be detected; and when it is detected, it should be corrected.

Over time, the environment in which the data supply chain operates might change so dramatically that a new improvement phase with revisited controls could be required, but this is the essence of how you help your data athlete to tame change!

COOLING DOWN

- Change happens over time, and cannot be stopped, but humans are creatures of habit and don't cope well with it.
- Businesses are trying to disrupt with innovation, but they might be themselves disrupted by uncontrolled change.
- The DPT must help the data athlete to maintain their improved performance through change.
- Six Sigma is a data-driven methodology to measure the quality of a process.
- Six Sigma helps us to explain the 'organizational lactic acid' that slows the data athlete down.
- Preventive, detective and corrective are the three types of control that help us to fight old habits and sustain good change.

Note

1   M H Schroeder (1999) *Six Sigma: The breakthrough management strategy revolutionizing the world's top corporations*, Doubleday Business, New York.

08

The data domain model

WARMING UP

- What is data intelligence and how is it related to tribal knowledge?
- How do we sketch our first data domain model as the repository of data intelligence?
- What are the three phases of a data excellence journey?
- How do we train our data domain owners?

Data intelligence, data debt and data value

In Data Workout 1, the exercise about creating the first prioritized data excellence initiatives portfolio, I showed how the DPT can influence the organization by identifying priorities in its *change* agenda that will need attention to data. Following on from the previous chapter on the importance of taming change, in this part of the book I will explore how the DPT changes the way the organization changes (Pillar II of data excellence). I will demonstrate how to use those priority initiatives as 'training' sessions to improve and sustain the data athlete's data fitness (or maturity, and from now on I am going to use these terms interchangeably), through the appropriate embedding of the aforementioned data disciplines. I will then illustrate the link between reduction of the data debt and the increase of the data intelligence as indicators of the improved data fitness and enablers of the value creation that we will explore in the last part, on Pillar III.

What is data intelligence?

What do I mean by data intelligence? In simple terms, data intelligence is an organization's awareness of its own data. In data terms, this is the equivalent of Socrates' axiom 'know thyself', because clear consciousness of oneself leads to ambitions and limitations owed to what is not known. In essence, a faithful and comprehensive 'as is' of the organization is the ground on which any performance can be built and thus, as has been my conviction since my early days as a data officer, it is the most important aspect of our data fitness that we want to improve. Since my brief adventure in Lloyds, I have been saying that if in my role as data officer I am allowed to be successful only in one discipline, let it be data intelligence. Data intelligence, or the structured knowledge of a business, refers to what data is managed, how it is used, by whom and for what purpose at any point in time and space in the business dynamic, and how those concepts that a business represents and uses are in a logical relationship. Companies are usually born from an idea of how to do or make something, and they operate, grow, transform and engage with third parties (employees, investors, customers). All these actions are driven by the need to communicate, buy, make, sell, train, engage and any other verb we come up with to describe what a company does. All these actions require data intelligence.

The impact of tribalism on data intelligence

The more digital the company becomes, the more the concepts associated with the company have to be digitally modelled. For example, to provide a real-time stock check and delivery date on the application installed on a customer's smart phone, the customer application needs the supply chain and logistic process to be digitally modelled and associated to the data that measures a product's availability. It then compares its (digitized) geographical location to the customer address to eventually display the expected delivery time on the application. In fact, the pandedomenistic trend discussed in earlier chapters requires that an exhaustively accurate digital model of the reality becomes the norm in the near future, as the key to greater and more tangible value creation from digital processes. Here the issue is that data intelligence is highly scattered and asynchronously modified across the length and breadth of the organization. Frequently it is locked up in tribal or tacit knowledge[1] whereby only the expert knows the how and not just the what, and the crucial questions that would allow that faithful model to be produced can be answered only if the expert is present or willing. Whoever has been trying to map a new application or a new process or has been asked to create an 'as is' knows what I mean. Thus, the highly sought-after SME is an irreplaceable asset for the company and at the same time its biggest risk to digital ambitions, but although irreplaceable, the expert tends to leave companies, abruptly or naturally (e.g. retirement), and that is usually the moment when the existence of tacit knowledge is truly felt, by the disruption deriving from its loss.

I was told a story of a manufacturing company that used in its processes very wide sheets of metal, and an old timer who was the only one able to operate the magnetic plate used to lift the sheets in the moulding machine. His expertise was required as applying the magnet in the wrong spot would have had the sheet warping under its own weight, thus rendering the metal sheet unusable for moulding. There were no particular measurements or guideline, and asked how he could determine whether it was safe to lift the metal sheet, the expert answered that when he activated the electromagnet, he could judge whether it was in the right position from the type of 't-clunk' sound it made. I am sure that one day we will be able to train an AI to repli-cate the same feat, but the short-term problem for the company was how long it would take a young apprentice to replicate it, and how many sheets would need to be thrown away in the process.

Scattered, unstructured and therefore inaccessible knowledge impairs good decision making, and we will see at the end of this part how it affects operational resilience with suboptimal risk management. Therefore, data intelligence, as the connecting tissue between the building blocks of knowl-edge, metadata and data, provides the basic scaffolding for building a reliable decision-making process. If we scan across the widest spectrum of business management theories, from the most ardent admirers of Henry Ford ('any color that he wants so long as it is black') to the biggest supporter of the lean start-up, all would agree that leaders need trusted data in order to make the right decisions.

What is data debt?

To tackle the next sections, it is important to recall the important notion of data debt and to introduce a second important factor that will be at the centre of Pillar III: data value.

I define data debt as the cost to make 'all data fit for all purposes'. It represents, theoretically, how much money the business should invest to satisfy all the requirements of all the data consumers combined, so that their expected value from data could be achieved. In the example used in the previous chapter on the customer market segment, the data consumer, who wished to produce customer quotations based on that attribute, experienced the gap between their need and the status quo. Only 50 per cent of the customer records had a market segment, previous bad habits *de facto* having accumulated a debt of data, because collecting new and incomplete or inaccurate data is like signing a future 'I owe you' on behalf of the company. Sooner or later, someone else will need to spend time and money to fill the gap. The statement is valid, I maintain, even in a future of AI-driven super-efficient data quality issues remediation.

Back to the market segment initiative. To achieve their goals, our pricing team data athletes were forced to invest in closing the gap between the current level of quality (50 per cent) and their acceptance level (100 per cent). In data fitness terms, they had to work out to improve their vigour, and in order to avoid lactic acid accumulation (data debt) they set in place a new regime (data controls).

What is data value?

Data value, or indeed value from data, is a very wide topic and a somewhat controversial area of discussion. From our preamble we know that the third reason data officer careers are cut short is the inability to translate data use cases into value, and so in the third part, relating to Pillar III, I will deepen the analysis and set out a more detailed structure to tackle that challenge. As for our data athletes, value from data is all about measuring performance increments, but for the sake of the following chapters I would like us to agree that data value is *the measure of the (positive) impact data makes on key performance indicators of the organization.*

The quantification of data value could be subjective and, given the cross-functional nature of data, difficult to attribute, as the correlation – or, better, the causation – between the provision of data at a certain level of standards and the creation of more or less value is a complex endeavour. In other words, it is very arduous to create a function that relates better data with more value, but it is clear that data value is dependent on data debt, as data that is not matching the expectation of an agent would impair their ability to take the decision or action that provides the intended positive outcome. That is also the reason why the closure of all the data debts is a necessary but not sufficient condition for the creation of value. This is because the 'last mile' of value creation is somehow not deterministic, but rather is literally in the hands of the agent, i.e. the data athlete.

To continue taking advantage of the market segment example, by achieving 100 per cent of the market segment populated in the customer market segment, this matches the expectation of our data consumer, and even assuming all the segments were accurate, would that mean the forecast value is fully realized? The answer is almost certainly no. It is important to keep in mind that our DPT will prepare the best ground and provide the best preparation for our data athlete, but the value is ultimately a business-driven (i.e. human-driven) outcome.

More data intelligence and less data debt equals more data value

We have already ascertained that data value is affected by data debt, but value is also correlated to knowledge: to produce an outcome a cause has to be put in relation to an effect, and these two operands of a data value equation are indeed knowledge. To be able to produce a quote that is based on the market segment, I need to know what the market segment is, where I can find it, and put it into a relationship with the customer. Then I have to calculate a price and produce a quote that I will present to a customer who may or may not accept it. All those steps, bar the last one, require established data intelligence (spatial and temporal). The higher the data intelligence, the more precise and predictable the outcome is. It should come as no surprise that in the course of our evolution, the more knowledgeable humans became about their environment and its regulating laws, the more their utensils developed in sophistication and usefulness. And eventually the maximization of the data value would only be possible when the level of data debt is minimal. With that in mind, we can now identify several phases of our data fitness journey based on the relative levels of the measures of data intelligence, data debt and data value.

Three phases on the journey to data excellence

I like to define three different phases delineating the journey to data excellence: data-reactive organization, data-training organization and data-driven organization. Figure 8.1 represents this spectrum of increasing data intelligence and decreasing data debt in organizations.

FIGURE 8.1 Classification of an organization's data fitness based on data debt and data intelligence

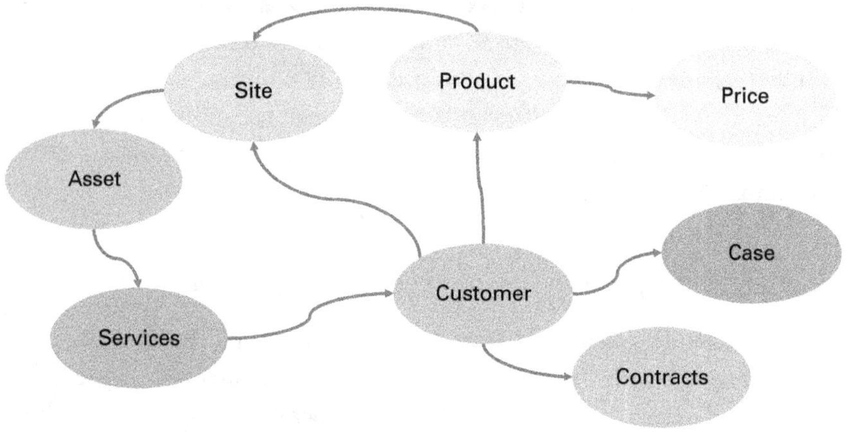

Data-reactive organization

The lowest data intelligence phase is one where questions reign and every attempt to use data is plagued by uncertainty. This is the data-reactive organization: decisions and actions are hard to make because nobody really knows, or the ones that know only know in their own way (i.e. they disagree). In that phase the data debt is not only high but the true extent of the debt is also likely to be unknown, which creates further nasty surprises when attempting to use data. You will be mistaken in thinking that this state is equivalent to an early stage or infancy of the company; this can be a permanent state of the data multiverse mentioned in the data domain owner role description, whereby the need for standard data is never felt, because it is assumed to be normal to have complex rhapsodic processes to combine data from multiple sources and multiple places just to measure, for instance, customer profitability. In the absence of attention to the resilience principle of the data charter, this can be a state in which the company regresses post a material crisis like a large merger and acquisition deal. Overall, a clear symptom of being in a data-reactive company is when, in an executive meeting discussing data, the most common question is 'Whose data is right?', as, in the absence of established and accredited sources of authority, all attendees bring their own view to the table.

Data-training organization

On the journey from a data-reactive organization to a data-driven organization sits the data-training organization. The mantra of the data charter introduced by the DPT is pushing the data athletes to deliver value with better data as they move away from the data-reactive status, transforming their change agenda in a series of 'data excellence initiatives'. In Data Workout 1, Figure DW1.1 showed the strategic initiatives as dots enveloped by two distinct areas depending on the organization data fitness and data risk to execute them. Each one of those in the upper area labelled as 'Need more data muscle' is an opportunity to inch farther from left to right on our journey. The length of the journey is not predictable and there will be setbacks, but if the DPT has been religiously practising the tenets of Pillar I, a healthy level of resilient commitment would have been accumulated with the top and a well-dosed celebration of the initial successes will reinforce the resolution to pursue the goal. In this phase, the data fitness assessment becomes a GPS tracker connecting those successes that created tangible value with the specific increase in data fitness, and so reinforcing the belief that the training pays dividends. In a data-training organization there should be also room for experimentation with potential accelerators (aka AI), but it is imperative that a healthy balance is kept between experimentation and operationalization, because an excessive number of trials risks depleting the available energies in too many directions, without real advancement on the data fitness.

A clear example of moving from the data-reactive into the data-training phase I can recall from my past is GE Capital Project Consistency. It was in the middle of the 2000s and the risk team in GE Capital sat on a multi-billion dollars unit made of hundreds of legal entities selling dozens if not hundreds of different products (from credit cards to factoring and leverage finance) exposed to more regulations every day in tens of countries. Capital was all about taking risks, risks that needed to be precisely measured, and data was then essential. But data was everywhere and obtaining an enterprise risk view at the top of the house was a very lengthy and frustrating process, not to mention the many hundreds of models (aka AI algorithms) supporting risk decisions that were in dire need of good (and interoperable) data to function properly. In true GE style, a massive programme of work was spun, but, unlike on other occasions, the solution was not 'just' to put in place another data warehouse in which to pour and to cook technically all the data feeds coming from all the systems around the globe and endlessly trying to stitch together report after report. Together with the IT solution delivery, another team I have been part of undertook a very diligent exercise of delivering also *standardized data*, a single dictionary of risk terms to be adopted and cascaded to all the entities, with validation tests enforced between the terminology agreed and the data received.

Data-driven organization

At the other end of the scale, my definition of the data-driven organization is one where questions have been replaced by answers through a conscious and resilient process of filling the data intelligence gap. Further, the organization has digitized the majority of the scattered information about the data and structured it into a corporate memory, available for everyone to use and contribute to. There is nothing in this view that means all 'statements' will need to be standard, i.e. there is only one answer to who the customer is or does. Rather, all the differences are enumerated and validated, so that variations are known and accounted for; there is finally one language for the data tribe, but the language recognizes and appreciates the richness that dialects might bring. Like the extinguishing of all data debts, this status is somewhat theoretical, as per our reflection on the meaning of change in the previous chapter. Nevertheless, the balance posture provided by the increased data fitness is able to detect and control potential perturbations. Equally, the opportunities that come from the advancement of the science of data (e.g. AI) or from any other angle are adopted in a faster and cheaper fashion with the lowest level of risk.

The data domain model

All types of intelligence have as a prerequisite a certain structure to manage information, as intelligence is effectively a machine that transforms information into a particular outcome. Data intelligence, as mentioned above, is no different in this respect and the first structure we can use to store and grow our data intelligence is called an 'information data model', i.e. the data domain model (DDM).

Managing data intelligence through the DDM

Let's imagine all the words used by the business in all its processes. Now let's use these to tell a story about what the business does, a very detailed and descriptive story, going very deep into all the necessary minutiae. Once the story has been completed, we should be able to list all the nouns in the story that have been used and all the verbs employed to connect those nouns and to describe the actions being performed. This would make a very long list, but it might also lead to the immediate realization that the same words are associated with different concepts and vice versa, different nouns with the same one, thus identifying the mother of 99 per cent of all the issues facing data – definitional integrity. For example:

- 'Order', as the formal document detailing what the buyer requires the seller to provide, could be either a customer order or a supplier order.

- 'Delivery date' can be the date that is committed to at order date, the date at which the goods are effectively delivered to the customer, or the delivery date to one of our plants.

- 'Account' could be the customer account, as the record list of all business transaction between customer and supplier, but it could also be the customer bank account or the personal account, as the credential of an employee needed to access to company systems.

I could even mention examples of two words identically spelled in different languages but with very different meanings (the word 'actual' means 'real' in English, but it means 'present' in Spanish). Suffice to say that words need context and good descriptions to become a defined 'concept' that can be additive of data intelligence.

Humanity has been 'storing' knowledge in context and, for millennia, made it accessible in the format of encyclopaedia, listing items identified by words in alphabetical order (for languages not using pictograms) and organized in volumes. However, simple alphabetical order is not practical when organizing data intelligence, for the not-so-hidden agenda here is to assign to the already defined data domain owner a data domain to own, standardize and govern, as per their role defined in Chapter 4. Thus, to build an information data model is to define the volumes of the data encyclopaedia of the firm, with each volume representing a data domain, containing a set of terms based on their 'affinity', for example customer or procurement. And here the first real ontological problem presents itself to our data athletes, (though let's shy away from the 'o' word for now): how to organize the domains.

How to create the first version of the DDM

The following is an instructive game I once played with a group of colleagues. At the time we were building the first information model of a company wanting to jump-start its data-training phase. This consisted of a table with an assortment of 50 randomly selected objects, ranging from a hairbrush to a tablet, toy or pair of gloves. The players were split in groups of four to five people and asked independently to come up with a series of sets *logically* grouping all the objects. Exactly as expected, each group came up with different sets. Logic has to be based on a rationale, but there is not a unique rationale, i.e. the objects could be grouped by any of their features, function, shape, colour, texture, etc. So, to each group their classification was logical, and when, as part of the game, every group had to explain to the other groups its logic, all the others understood and agree that was another possible way of aggregating the items. Finally, the question that emerged was, 'Which one is the right classification?' and the play master answered, of course, 'It depends!'

The learning from the game is that logic alone could not determine the best information model, represented by the classification of the items; a guideline is required to converge to a common classification and define the first version of the data domain structure. Here the emphasis goes on 'first' because, moving up the data intelligence curve, the story will become progressively more enriched and so the model will continuously be developed and adjusted to tailor the current needs. In fact, a distinctive trait of companies that are in the data-driven phase is the ability to seamlessly adapt their information models to the company circumstances. This is Pillar II of data excellence, which is all about imbuing data in the change (see Chapter 2). A strategic change in the business will, nine times out of ten, mean an addition to the nouns and verbs already identified previously, ergo an addition or amendment, a change in the data domain model, as for example necessitated by a company deciding to launch a completely new product line, or venture into the Internet of Things (IoT). So, to finalize the first pass of the model, it is useful at this point to recall the verbs that we used in the story, as the verbs would put the nouns into relationships. Then using a simple mind map, it should not take long for certain words to emerge as clusters of inbound and outbound arrows, connecting the usual suspects (customer, supplier, employee, account, order, opportunity) and their descriptive elements would surely be potential candidates for a first pass.

Simple domain model starter

Our customer signs a contract for the provision of products at a certain price. The customer receives our product at their site where the product is installed as an asset for which the customer is entitled to our service. If there is a problem with the asset the customer raises a case with us.

As seen in Figure 8.2, already with such a simple story we can identify eight *concepts* in a logical relation that we could select to be the first atoms of our proto-data domain and, very quickly, we could start to add items to it. For example, in the customer bubble, which we provisionally call customer data domain, we could start to include all the customer identification details like address, country, market segment, website, etc. Similarly, in the contract data domain we could start to add contract types, contract terms, amount, payment schedule, etc.

The effort of building the first version of the DDM can be accelerated if a process framework is already available (see Figure 8.3). This process framework should be in effect another narration of our story above describing what the company does and, in that case, the DPT should propose to model

FIGURE 8.2 Proto data domain model: An information model based on business reality

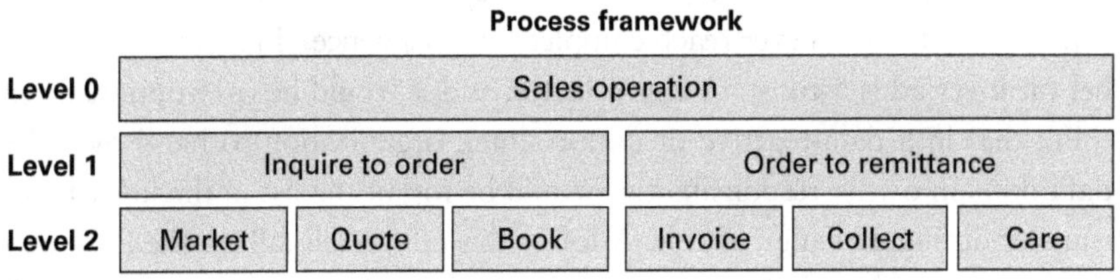

Process framework

Level 0	Sales operation					
Level 1	Inquire to order			Order to remittance		
Level 2	Market	Quote	Book	Invoice	Collect	Care

FIGURE 8.3 Process framework example

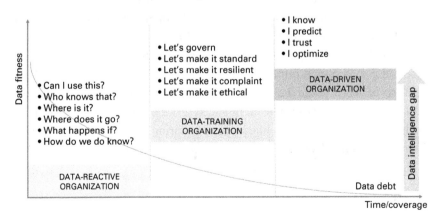

the first data domain model by taking the process framework as a first template. An example of the process framework can be seen in Figure 8.3.

Note to all the aspiring data personal trainers: it is always advisable to check whether the framework is properly maintained and kept in sync with the actuality of the company.

DDM best practices

I have said that the data domain model is a living document, to evolve and expand in accordance with the dynamicity of a changing business. However, that does not mean we should review it every month; most importantly, we should try to evolve it following certain continuity, in order not to dramatically impact all the capabilities and rituals that we are going to associate to it. To achieve the best results, I would recommend following the criteria below.

KEEP THE DOMAINS TO A MANAGEABLE NUMBER

Each domain should have at least one data domain owner assigned, and for certain complex domains (like third parties, i.e. organizations and individuals) it might be necessary to have a leading data domain owner and one or more deputies. As we will see in the section below about the data domain owner regime, each of them will need to be followed closely, to be trained and continuously guided for a sustained period until they become self-sufficient (although some of them might never reach complete independence). In addition, personnel turnover adds a constant churn factor, and it would be over-optimistic to think that in a data-reactive or data-training organization to hand over the data domain owner responsibilities would be top of the list in the knowledge transfer during a change of role. A lot of this effort will fall on the DPT and their team, who hopefully by that time will be fully able to train the next DDO.

In order to keep the number of counterparties to train in the low double digits, an optimal number of data domains would be between 10 and 20: though the data domains model would vary from industry to industry, in my experience you would expect to have circa 40 per cent of them as a common layer of data domains related to enabling activities like finance, human resources, compliance, information technology, sales, etc. The other 60 per cent, so between 8 and 12 data domains, would be more pertinent to the specific industry. For example, in financial services those would be domains such assets, risk, portfolio, while in manufacturing you would define specific industry grouping like supply chain, engineering, logistics, etc.

SPLIT BIG DOMAINS INTO SUB-DOMAINS

Back to the encyclopaedia example: the number of items beginning with the same letter varies and so there are sections with a lot of words. These words are usually broken down in one or more volumes of standard size, splitting, for example, the letter A in two volumes: A–AM and AN–AZ. Likewise, for 'large' domains, it is a good practice to have sub-domains (domains that are a subset of a larger one), reflecting the reality that it would be improbable to have an effective data domain owner assigned to a very large scope of knowledge, especially if that body of affine data spans many processes and organizational constituencies. For example, 'third parties' is defined as the domain of the data concerning all the parties external to the company that are bound to it by a formal or informal interaction. It is an essential domain to manage yet a very wide one as practically every process of the company would involve a third party. For ease of assignment of ownership, one could break down the domain into four sub-domains of investor, customer, supplier and employee, as they all are third parties to the organization.

To reduce potential inconsistencies, I recommend following the rule that the *root* data domain should contain the maximum number of common terms while the sub-domains would have only specific terms. In the aforementioned example: the definition of address as two lines of address information plus the city, postcode and country code should be the common part held at the third party level. Leaving that information at the discretion of the various sub-domain data owners would run the risk of the address of a supplier being defined in a different way from the address of a customer. By the same token, the employment contract duration should be a specific term to be kept at the employee sub-domain level. Such an arrangement could resolve jurisdictional issues arising from the ownership of a large domain not being exerted from just one part of the organization, as the data domain owner for third party could be still in charge of the full domain, while the data sub-domain owners belong to a different part of the organization, in the employee case human relationships. Be mindful of abusing the model; it should not be more than two layers deep, i.e. domain–sub-domain, third party–supplier. And the sub-domain should be a meaningful grouping, to avoid a fragmentation under the banner that John is more expert in supplier contract durations, while Jane is the one who knows everything about supplier contract clauses, and hence creating two distinct sub-domains made of one term each.

AVOID TOO MUCH VARIATION IN THE MODEL

Organizations are in continuous flux, so the names of teams and functions that make up a firm change continuously. Less frequently, these changes affect *what* the organization does and consequently the terms the organization uses in its processes, i.e. the data. Here it is crucial to avoid domains becoming merely a reflection of the organizational chart, as it would introduce into the model (already in constant development) unnecessary non-value-add tasks and possibly confusion in the organization. Imagine a data domain that has been named global marketing, the domain collecting the concepts and terms to interpret market tendencies and to establish a strategy to place our product on said market. Though there is not an issue with the expectation of its content, the global marketing team, who has been appointed as the data domain owner, has insisted on the name. While the adjective 'global' in the context of the domain management does not significantly change the footprint of the domain, the name matters, as when in the next months a reorganization of the global marketing team concludes with the creation of a new team called strategy and marketing, which merged the former strategy team into marketing. The effect on the domain model would be either to leave the domain as is, giving the impression that that domain reflects a legacy organization, or to change it to become 'strategy and marketing' but in this case we would need to merge the strategy and marketing domains. And in Chapter 10 we will see that there is more behind just changing a name to the domain in the matter of metadata management, which is the sub-discipline that takes care of the DDM.

MANAGE DATA DOMAIN REQUESTS

Over time, if the DPT has done their job correctly there is going to be a 'surge' of data domain requests, as more acquire the taste for being an owner. Here the temptation to create an 'empty section' in the encyclopaedia, just to make a statement of power, is definitely within the realms of possibility. However, the DPT needs to stand firm and mandate that the willing data domain owner first demonstrates the case for a new logical grouping, coming up with a story made up of words and actions that have not already been told.

REAL-WORLD EXAMPLE

I once had someone asking me to set up a key account management (KAM) data domain for a subset of accounts, i.e. customers, that were larger in nature and important to the company's growth, and thus treated as VIPs. To my question of why it was necessary to create such a domain, they replied plainly that the KAM team had now been created under their leadership, and so it was important for them to govern all the data related to the key accounts. I pointed out that the data of the key accounts, from an operational definition point of view, were practically the same as the accounts. So, my recommendation was to define only the term *key account* – to which they were visibly disappointed. It took a few iterations, including a thorough workshop on how to 'tick and tie' each attribute, to demonstrate that the metadata, i.e. all the data descriptors, of the key account was essentially the same as the 'normal' accounts.

The data domain owner's regime

Once the first pass of the data domain model has been agreed, the DPT's attention should be focused on the data intelligence's most important contributors: the data domain owners. Their identification might be eased by the previously mentioned identikit in Chapter 4, which suggested that an established and respected leader, with tenure in the company and passion and expertise in the area they command, could be a good candidate to become a data domain owner. I want to stress again that this should always be presented as a 'data task' within their existing role, and not as an attempt to turn them into data people.

Nonetheless, acting as a data domain owner gives the individual a pivotal role in growing the data intelligence. It is also very different to the other tasks on the actual list of these leaders. So far in their careers, they might not have needed to extend their authority beyond the realm of their own area, as they have been very much chieftains of their own tribes. As in the examples mentioned above, once given the responsibility of 'owning a concept' for the whole company, they might become reluctant and insecure as there is a perception of over-extended responsibility outside their scope of work. Their data domain ownership muscle might have never voluntarily flexed before, therefore most of the data domain owners will need a very structured regime that gradually nurtures them into the desired shape.

Over the years I have come up with a regime based on five sessions, though some of them might require a bit of repetition. The plan is to work together with the candidate data domain owner in their own environment, using existing use cases and examples from their domain to demystify the word 'ownership' and to create for them a new ritual: using their expertise and lending their time to increase the data intelligence of the company. In each of the five sessions below I describe the (data) fitness goals and the desired achievements at the end of the session, inclusive of recommendations for the DPT to successfully complete it.

Session I: Warm up

FITNESS GOAL

Initial interaction between the DPT and the DDOs to present what the role entails and the rationale of defining a domain under their ownership.

DPT RECOMMENDATIONS

This is a critical make-or-break session, in which I suggest going the extra mile to make the DDO feel at ease and conclude that being a DDO is the natural extension of what they already do. Even in the most command-and-control type companies, I would not present this as a must-do with the DPT being just the messenger of a top-down directive. Instead, I would ask them to give an overview of their current challenges and important projects on the table, and I would latch on to examples that illustrate how higher data intelligence could support them. It is unavoidable that with the DPT having 'data' in their title there is going to be a challenge relating to finding the right data for the project/report/investigation in weeks rather than months, which is the hook!

DESIRED ACHIEVEMENTS

- The candidate DDO understands the importance of the role.
- The candidate DDO is willing to explore their candidacy to be a DDO, continuing to the next session.
- A list of possible data domain names is created.

Session II: Spatial awareness

FITNESS GOAL

A session to determine the nature and purpose of data domains, introduction to the organization's data domain model and a deeper dive into the role of the DDO.

DPT RECOMMENDATIONS

This should be a group session, to which the DDO also invites experts and key members of their team. In the pre-session, the DPT should recommend that the DDO themselves explain the aim of the session and gains their team's collaboration to the challenge, mentioning examples for which the ownership of the domain will support the tackling of longstanding team issues. The DPT should talk them through the data domain model thus far defined and have ready options for the domain name and a draft of the description.

DESIRED ACHIEVEMENTS

- Affirmation of the role: A formal communication is sent to the DDO team and relevant stakeholders.
- Agreement on name and description of the data domain: An entry in the data domain model is officially made.
- Domain insertion: Feedback or amendment suggestions collected during the meeting on adjacent or connected domains are raised with relevant data domain owners.

Session III: Extension

FITNESS GOAL

Map the organizational and technical boundaries of the data domain. Gain familiarity with the conceptual modelling.

DPT RECOMMENDATION

In preparation for the session the DPT should work with the DDO and the experts in the team, including the IT supporting function, in order to landscape the processes and systems potentially encompassed by the domain. As a first intermediate outcome the DDO team should be able to itemize the processes in input and output data sets, hence deriving data sets that are uniquely produced in their domain, inferring data they should own. The DPT should at this stage explain the linkage between the ownership, data intelligence and application of data intelligence to the management and governance of data. It would be key to motivate the athletes, reminding them of the higher purpose of augmenting the standardization and structure of data for faster and more precise insights.

DESIRED ACHIEVEMENTS

- First draft of candidate business terms: Based on the analysis of data sets, some terms would quickly emerge as critical, e.g. the customer's name, address or bank account. An exercise to write down a good operational definition should be completed.

- Increased familiarity with data modelling: The understanding of the difference in conceptual modelling versus the physical modelling of a software application is desirable to reinforce that the task is a business and not an IT task.

- Optional: Agree the structure of the sub-domains, based on the DPT's judgement of the complexity of the domain. It could be the right time to introduce further segmentation of the domain, especially if some specific areas seem to require a more urgent need.

Session IV: Data cardio

FITNESS GOAL

A series of workshops to evaluate the processing of business term review and approval, followed by an introduction to data standards.

DPT RECOMMENDATION

The rhythm of this series of session should prepare the DDO to become independent as much as possible. However, there might be a sense of tediousness in going through long lists of terms and defining for each one of them rules and sources and classification. The DPT should immediately remove from the exercise the technicality of punching the result in the chosen data intelligence repository, i.e. metadata management or data catalogue tool, as that would be perceived as a non-value-add task. Instead, any effort should be made to concentrate the DDO and the team in the effort of articulating from their experience what good looks like for the data they own, so facilitation, scribing and data uploading support is a must have presence in the session. At the start of a new session, if the system allows, a pictorial representation of what had been achieved in the previous session would be a strong reinforcement to inspire more progress.

DESIRED ACHIEVEMENTS

- First draft of data standards: For each of the candidate terms, the session should output data validation rules, classification, authorized users and usage, source of authority, etc.

- Nomination of data stewards to support data intelligence: Whether existing already or not, there should be a formal appointment of a group(s) across the organization with the duty to elevate the data identified to the DDO standards. The choice of having a centralized or federated group of stewards should be in line with the organizational models reviewed in Chapter 3.

Session V: Establish rituals to continuously improve performance

FITNESS GOAL

The DDO achieves independence and creates their governance structure while establishing proactive engagement with the DPT and other governance bodies for continuous improvement of their domains.

DPT RECOMMENDATION

The session marks the end of the training, with deep involvement from the DPT. For the future, the DPT should act more in an oversight and support capacity rather than as an involved lead. The DDO might have dissimilar experience in running governance meetings, so the DPT's last training objective should be establishing the data domain council as the focal point for the formal enactment of domain ownership. While the DPT or one of their team members should be a permanent member of the data domain council, the DDO should be encouraged to set up and manage their own backlog of domain issues, with the DPT still taking responsibility for the technical management of the data. The majority of the interaction would now be happening during the requirement phase of data excellence initiatives, as per the Data Excellence Operating Model that we will examine in the next chapter.

DESIRED ACHIEVEMENTS

- Launch and facilitate the data domain council: Chaired by the DDO and comprising key subject matter experts, and open to ad hoc attendees, it should be a forum run at least monthly where the standards of the domain are kept up and socialized.

- Proactive update or creation of new data standards: Through their established network but more simply through their normal business operation, the DDO captures instances of improvement for the domain they own.

- Engage with other data domain councils: The visibility of the data domain model and the organization of DDO boards naturally creates a network of collaboration between different domains, which DeXOM will help to cement further!

COOLING DOWN

- Data intelligence is a company's awareness of its own data.

- Tribal knowledge is non-usable data intelligence.

- Data value is what you harness from data.

- Data debt is the difference between status quo and desired status to harness value.

- The data domain model supports the structuring of data intelligence.

- To become data (fit and) driven you need to increase data intelligence and reduce data debt.

- To train your data domain owner there is a five-session training plan.

Note

1   E Fenoglio et al. Tacit knowledge elicitation process for industry 4.0, *Discover Artificial Intelligence*, 2 (6). link.springer.com/article/10.1007/s44163-022-00020-w (archived at https://perma.cc/G3SW-JMMJ)

09

The Data Excellence
Operating Model

WARMING UP

- Where does the Data Excellence Operating Model originate?
- What is a data consumer story?
- How does the data domain architect translate the story into design?
- Why is data design a reality check for the data athlete's ambition?
- What is the Sustain phase?

Introducing the Data Excellence Operating Model

A key feature of an athlete is agility – the ability to quickly adapt to the physical demands of the sport they are practising. We could characterize this as the speed at which an athlete can change direction or velocity, or simply vary their body posture to perform better. Thus, comparing an athlete's agility with that of a data athlete, I believe, is another fitting analogy: data requires agility because, as discussed, change affects data, and data must influence change, so both rapid reactive and proactive responses are key. Such responses must be coded in the moment of change with a structure that increases the likelihood of a positive outcome and builds on the achieved agility with a continuous improvement approach.

Before becoming a CDO, I held an IT governance role, during which I had to build and run a portfolio management office (PMO), for the IT function. This was towards the end of the noughties and a massive push to agility was emerging in IT, with the concept of DevOps (develop and operate) becoming the new buzz word. The established paradigm of how a company could execute a change prescribed that once the requirement had been clarified with the requestor (or customer), a project team would be assigned to work through design, build and test phases until the completion of the deliverables. Upon a successful acceptance test from the requestor, the delivered change would be promoted into the production environment. Once in production, the operation team would take over the maintenance of the change as part the management of the live environment. However, analysis of a litany of high-profile and multi-year IT projects that completely failed to deliver on the benefit case suggested that, aside from other causes of failure, the length of the development phase, during which the design of the change is assumed to be immutable, was a material contributing factor to the failure. Over a long period, change happened and requestors change their minds or needs. In addition, the knowledge about what was delivered was not always properly transferred to the operation team, and in association with the discharge of responsibility from the development team, it created customer dissatisfaction with the turnaround time to fix bugs and the overall reliability of the production environments.

Thus, DevOps is an attempt to minimize the risk of divergence between the requirement and the deliverables, and to maximize the availability and reliability of the production environment. This involves fusing the two teams into one to create a continuous loop of development and operations, and shortening the delivery time by breaking the project down into successive short bursts of change, in which the requestor is continuously involved and allowed to directly influence the next cycle. It is what we all experience now with our digital devices and the applications we use. At the beginning of the century, you would have still bought a cardboard box with a CD inside and installed that on your PC; say it was Microsoft Windows XP, and the application features didn't change for many months if not years. During those years, Microsoft worked to try to come up with a better product and you would have then bought Microsoft Vista, whether your needs were better satisfied or not. Nowadays every time you switch on your PC something might have change, a screen has been optimized, a new feature has been added, and bugs are continuously reported and fixed in 'releases' or 'patches'; thanks to DevOps the product evolves continuously. Looking back now, it seems natural to me that, placed with the question of connecting change to data, the agile development practices that are at the foundation of DevOps would have inspired my own Data Excellence Operating Model (DeXOM).

The founding principle of the Agile methodology is that development is made of a rigorous series of cycles prioritized according to a stack of intended outcomes (backlog), each described by a script (user stories) and performed in a very short burst of three to four weeks (a sprint). Data is inherently agile: a dashboard or a report can always be broken down into its constituent parts and each part put through the same process of being sourced, cleaned, processed and visualized. The difference is that data can be reused and, if the proper methodology is in place, the effort reduces over time and the *velocity*, as data delivered in the given unit of time, significantly increases. This methodology, which changes the way we change and deliver a continuous enrichment of the company's data intelligence, minimizes over time the levels of data debt and hence provides the best posture to deliver value at speed and at scale, is the Data Excellence Operating Model (DeXOM).

The premise is still that, to give their best, every data athlete needs their own tailored regime of exercises, but all successful personal trainers have a *modus operandi* that they adapt and customize to their trainees. Over the years I have been developing my own framework, based on the original intent of embedding data in the change. DeXOM articulates the expectation of an ever-present set of operating tasks, a sort of data circuit training, that is triggered in sync with certain phases of change. At each change, going through the DeXOM exercise, the data that is involved in the change is strengthened in integrity and quality, all the while imprinting in the organization's muscle memory something that, alien at the beginning, becomes an unconscious reflex. For instance, the identification of the authoritative sources is one demonstrable benefit. The process that maps each piece of information required by our data athlete or data consumer to the sources inside (or outside) the company with the highest level of trust might have been a completely unheard of task at the beginning of our journey. Any data leader would still maintain it as a crucial initial step in undertaking a data project, but I have been in workplaces where the concept was completely foreign. It took only a few change cycles with high-profile projects before the 'authoritative data source' became a 'badge of honour' that everyone was asking for, sometimes in the wrong context. But that viral spreading of an idea, albeit not 100 per cent pure, provided some comfort that, in all the ongoing conversations, a certain level of data muscular stimulation was happening even in my absence.

As mentioned, by virtue of its derivation from agile methodologies, the DeXOM approach does not need a minimum quantum of data to be effective. Rather, it works for one small report or for the multi-year programme of digital transformation involving multiple domains of data. The emphasis is on the scope that the data consumer is going to identify. As you will learn going through this chapter, DeXOM is also where the new roles introduced in Pillar I of data domain owner and data domain architect will play their central part in helping the data athlete to complete the circuit measuring lower data debt and higher data intelligence.

On the other hand, as I have often repeated, the DPT has to be adaptive to their data athletes' needs and that is valid for DeXOM too. The one proposed in this book has to be considered, like the data charter, the discipline, the data fitness assessment or the names of the roles, as an initial stencil that the DPT should assimilate and strive to improve. This should include a retrospective check point to refine, adapt and model to their environment, with the addition or modification of steps and artefacts. Those adjustments would be essential to incorporate the local lingo and to amalgamate DeXOM with other pre-existing change management processes, such as the Enterprise Program Management Methodology, Business Process Redesign Framework, Merger Integration Process or, indeed, IT Development Lifecycle. In fact, DeXOM presumes that a common methodology is prescribed and enforced, and so beware of the *missing shelf effect*.

The missing shelf effect is something that I have experienced in several work environments, whereby I was figuratively bringing to my new place a lot of new data fitness equipment to outfit their metaphorical gymnasium for data workouts, but a backbone change management process was not present or it was very fragmented and/or not properly controlled, i.e. at best there was a guideline with an ineffective ask to follow and no controlled enforcement. The *shelf* from which to pick tools and best practices to increase the likelihood that data was not an afterthought was missing, nobody was prescribed to use them as part of their workout, in fact in the worst case no one was even going to the gym. Data must be a payload of the whole change, so the only real prerequisite for DeXOM is that an existing process of change management (business or IT) is performed and followed to an acceptable level. The risk is that data change is perceived to be an exercise divorced from the business realities, data change for data change's sake, which would negate the overall ambition of the undertaking. Aside from the difficulty of obtaining buy-in, and therefore commitment of resources, to target efforts to improve data in areas that are not perceived as a priority by the business, the introduction of a disciplined framework in an unruly environment for all the reasons enunciated so far would be near to impossible. Looking back again to the example in Chapter 7 about the customer market segment, would the DPT be able to be relevant if the exercise had been completely unstructured or happened completely under the governance radar? Hence in Chapter 10 I will examine what the DPT can do to stand up or be a catalyst for the *enabling capabilities* DeXOM relies on.

The structure of DeXOM

The basic four-part structure of DeXOM shown in Figure 9.1 naturally mimics the phases of any change. They are:

- *Requirement:* The request from the change beneficiary (or their delegate) enunciates what they expect.
- *Design:* The requirement is translated into a set of instruction or documentation that describes the change in all its aspects, business and technical, exhaustively enough to be implemented.
- *Build:* The design is carried out to produce a deliverable (e.g. software change, artefact) and tested by the requestor for acceptance.
- *Sustain:* The outcome of the change, digital or physical, is operated and maintained within its nominal operational performances.

Each phase of the model is intended to produce one or more specific artefacts, which are the complementary ones to artefacts in other streams of the change process. For example, in phase I, the data requirement, even in the absence of the abovementioned shelf, it is likely that someone has already listed the creation of a business requirement as a to-do, which then leads to a functional and technical requirement. If these already include all the necessary points related to data, then all the better. However, in my experience, the exercise frequently overlooks the need to tone the data muscle. This is often the case with report requests that are supposed to analyse the marketing investment performance of a company. These are intended as the correlation between the amount spent in promoting the brand and the return realized in increased sales. Huge process analysis and a copious number of pages are drafted to define the business process around the analysis and technical definition of the extraction procedures and the calculation, completed by a meticulous description of the user interface. Sadly, there is no stated expectation about the completeness or the validity of data and as a result, during the test phase, the data consumer realizes that the report is not very useful, as most of the necessary data is not present or valid. Data has been treated as an afterthought. Let us analyse each phase of DeXOM in detail.

FIGURE 9.1 The four-part structure of DeXOM and content example

Requirement	Design	Build	Sustain

Requirement

→ What outcome is to be achieved?

→ What value will be generated?

→ What data is needed?

→ Where is the data located?

→ How is it used and by who?

→ What are the applicable standards?

→ What are the compliance needs?

→ What is the current level of DQ?

→ What are the risks?

Design

Data design
→ Identification of auth. source
→ Identification of consumption point
→ Identification of referential
→ As is/to be data model design
→ As is/to be data flow design
→ Data quality rules design
→ Data risk and control design

Data plan
→ As is/to be gap assessment
→ Data debt evaluation

DDA go/no go
→ Resources are adequate to address data gaps

Build

Build
→ To be conceptual model
→ To be logical model
→ To be data flow

Data debt remediation
→ Reduction of data non-conformities

Data monitoring and controls
→ Build DQ rules
→ Build monitoring controls

Sustain

Delivery
→ Build completion is signed off
→ Data acceptance is signed off
→ Monitoring plan is signed off

DQ monitoring and issue management
→ Issue management is activated
→ Data quality rules are monitored

Data controls
→ Controls are executed
→ Test of effectiveness is performed regularly

Phase I: Data requirement

The data requirement phase is one in which the intent to change something existing or produce something anew is assessed. As far as DeXOM is concerned, the intent from the data athlete is funnelled through the DPT, as somewhere upstream it has been detected that the fulfilment of intent requires an act of consumption of data. Thus, data requirement is a phase in which a set of questions must be answered by the data consumer to state unequivocally what they want.

What's the story?

The elicitation of a data requirement is the trickiest phase to secure, because this is where we really convert the goal of the data athlete into the exact data exercises that will provide assurance about the desired performance. Unfortunately, this effort, like the elicitation of a requirement in general, depends on human-to-human communication. This is where the DPT has to exceed their emotional intelligence, where a word or a nuanced expression can make the difference between the acceptance or rejection of a proposal shaped by many hours of work. I personally enjoy working with the data athletes to listen to their ambitions and capture that in a formalized manner to help them turn their intent into a winning performance – as long as I am not the one transcribing (luckily nowadays there are plenty of tools that can perform that chore). As much as possible, I prefer to make the session an interactive one, and no matter how outlandish the intent might seem, as a real personal trainer I will maintain composure and signal empathically to the data athlete that I believe their intention to be worthwhile for the sake of the company. It is important to reinforce the bond between data athlete and data personal trainer, as in the next phases it is going to be required, so the DPT should be able to display some specific knowledge of the DA's area, inserting key words or expressions that will make them feel the DPT is part to their tribe. If they are from sales we should be conversant in leads management, pipeline, upselling and conversion rates. Likewise, if our data athlete is from finance we should punctuate the conversation with asset, capital, equity and leverage, and so on.

Socrates had a word for the exercise of extracting the truth from a fellow human being and climbing the ladder of metaphysical understanding: *maieutica* (from the Greek for 'midwifery'). Why am I referencing a philosopher dead for more than two millennia, and whose words have only come down to us via Plato? Chiefly because human beings haven't changed much in 2,000 years and the Socratic method still has merit in creating self-awareness of one's real intent.

How to build a data consumer story

My 21st century interpretation of the Socratic method is a dialogue that fosters the data athlete's self-discovery of their intents. The DPT asks thought-provoking questions to expose the real complexity of the endeavour, often revealing biases and contradictions that need to be curated for the desired outcome to be achieved. Applying this method to collecting the data requirement is what generates a data consumer story.

In my line of work, when I ask for requirements, I am more likely to receive the following haiku-style Post-it note, or an equally laconic email: '(Please) Build me a dashboard that has got all the logistics data with a green drop-down to select all the filters I need and… don't forget the "download to xls" button!'

At the risk of appearing facetious, with data there is a common perception that there is no need to explain things in too much detail – until, that is, the delivery turns out to be below the expected results, the consumer is not satisfied, company resources have been squandered and data is the culprit. At the same time, I must be mindful of finding a balance between a Post-it and the old fashioned, never-ending requirement phase involving months of preparation and filling out incredibly long templates. For this reason, the key questions that the data consumer stories (DCS) need to address are around what our data athlete wants to do with data or what they expect from data. My goal as the DPT is to extract the next intended action (NIA) as an essential first step of the journey and validation of the process we have agreed to undertake. The trick here is to help the data athlete to verbalize their intent. Nine times out of ten, that verbalization stimulates questions never asked before, which ultimately describes, at the best level of detail, what action be triggered or enabled by the data being provided. Let's say that the story being developed should produce a quarterly sales report, a dialogue such as the one below could happen:

DPT: 'When you receive the quarterly report what is the first thing you do?'

DA: 'I check that all the units have met their target.'

DPT: 'How would you do that?'

DA: 'I compare the figures on the dashboard with what the units' lead committed to me at the beginning of the year.'

DPT: 'Where are those commitments kept?'

DA: 'I have them in emails in my email inbox.'

DPT: 'What happens if one unit leader has not met their target?'

DA: 'I call them to understand why they haven't.'

DPT: 'Can the targets be adjusted during the year?'

DA: 'Yes.'

DPT: 'What happens if their targets and the ones you have got on emails are no longer the same?'

DA: 'Oh… it shouldn't happen, but if it does it might create a disagreement.'

I could proceed longer, but, as you would have noticed a couple of important points have emerged already from this one-minute-long exchange: we need to have 'targets' as part of the data that we standardize and visualize, and we should have the units included as audiences for our report. In the world of haiku requirements and where data is taught to be IT, this level of thinking is a muscle that our DA has rarely been forced to flex. The *full* story is inside them somewhere and I need to help them to visualize it in its entirety.

A useful tool to help structure the dialogue is to follow a simplified value chain mapping, applied to information flow, as shown in Figure 9.2.

The idea is to stimulate deeper introspection in the DA's walking their story in steps going, unusually for Western cultures, from right to left:

- What is the *outcome* we want to achieve?
- What are the *actions* that will achieve the *outcome*?
- Who are the *agents* that will perform those *actions*?
- What is the *knowledge* that the agent needs to perform those *actions*?
- What are the best *sources* for that *knowledge*?

The DCS is then built describing one or multiple outcomes, generated by certain actions, which involve agents. These might not be necessarily all humans, as we already have automated and intelligent agents, and will have more in the future, but it is good practice to associate the ultimate accountable data consumer to all agreed actions. The agent would need the necessary knowledge to perform the action, and such knowledge would come from a source.

So, by keeping to the chain described above, the following DCS extracted from the aforementioned Post-it note is not far from a real-life example:

As a logistics manager (*agent*), I would like to understand whether all my shipping is happening on time (*outcome*). To do that I need to make sure that, at the time of creation of the daily shipping schedule, I have included all the goods that have a planned issue date of today (*action*). To do that I compare the logistic system delivery list (*knowledge*) with all the items in the enterprise resource planning (ERP) (*source*) that have the planned good issue date of today. Once I have that data, for each anomaly or inconsistency I must communicate with the delivery centre team to investigate and remediate within a service level agreement (SLA) that allows me to make the afternoon slot, in case I have missed the one in the morning.

FIGURE 9.2 Data consumer story value chain

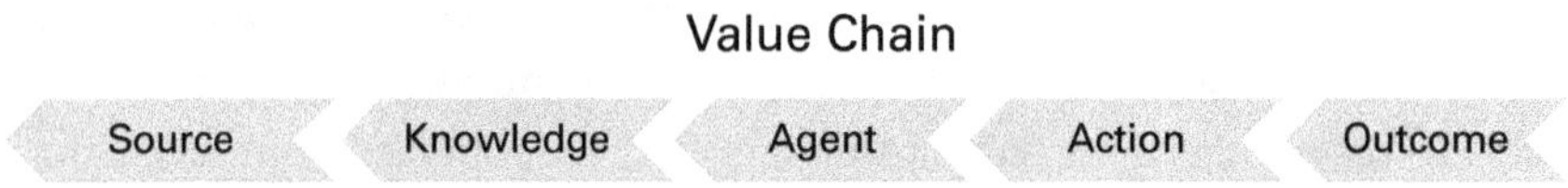

Value Chain

| Source | Knowledge | Agent | Action | Outcome |

Structurally, in a story I would also expect to clarify the following elements: the persona from whose perspective the story is seen ('As a...'); the need and the level of satisfaction associated with that need; and, as mentioned, the end of the story, which should be a 'mean to' (this is effectively the next intended action (NIA)). And even in this extremely simple story a few pieces of our data intelligence puzzle start to emerge:

- *Business terms:* Deliveries, daily delivery schedules, planned issue dates, etc. These words are essential to the success of the endeavour and need to be clarified, i.e. associated with a uniquely identifying description or definition.

- *Outcome:* The 'new' item that the story would deliver, the translation of the need into a measurable and quantifiable deliverable (further on, this will be broken up into its constituent parts).

- *Sources:* ERP, logistic systems. These are the places where the data are located in the story and need to be *certified* as appropriate places.

- *Expectations:* On time, SLA, anomaly, inconsistency. Here the data consumer specifies or at least gives some idea of the criteria they would use to judge whether the story is realized.

Socrates might have hesitated to put the subject of his analysis under so much scrutiny, but here the DPT has no choice, as they have to go deeper, dissect and question every aspect. Just as a personal trainer observes how their trainee moves a limb or lifts a weight, every movement a tell-tale of an existing weakness or an acquired bad posture, so the DPT weighs every word for potential ambiguity or looks for a fatal flaw to defuse. The story is there to lay the basis of a beneficial exercise on data.

The structure of a data consumer story

Although the conversation with the data athlete should flow as freely as possible, based on the expectation set out above, it would be good to have a template to capture the story in a defined structure. Thus, beyond the story itself, a data consumer story template should aim to capture these supplementary items.

THE CRITICAL SUCCESS FACTORS

Expressed as critical to quality (CTQs), these are positive statements that define the conditions and assumptions necessary for the success of the story. It is also the part where dependencies and interlocks with other programmes, teams or events are highlighted.

Some examples are as follows:

- Another project that must deliver an essential component of the story should be successfully completed on time.
- The availability of expert resources in another team must be secured.
- A third-party contract for the provision of a service must be executed before the start or the end of the story.

A LIST OF PRODUCTS THAT DELIVERS THE STORY'S OUTCOME

These are the functional outputs that will deliver the outcome, easily recognizable in the story as the ones subjected to a measure or related to an action of knowledge creation. Given that the lineage of the data consumer story is traced back to the agile product development methodologies, I am starting to use interchangeably the words outcome and product, more specifically *data product*. As we will explore in the final part of the book, data productization is key for the value creation, and the story is extracting from the DA the features of the data product they will utilize to create value. So, in this part of the story we will enumerate and describe the artefacts and deliverables that the story requires. A report, a set of metrics, a new data set and/or a new system dedicated to curate or to manage data (e.g. master data management) – from now on I will classify these as data products.

THE INFORMATION FLOW THAT SUPPORTS THE STORY

Easily confused with the 'data flow mapping', at this stage we want just to describe a high-level flow of information, or knowledge, from the one or many sources identified and the target consumption point. Not necessarily systems or applications, in cases where the data fitness is low, the steps in the flow can also be people and their tacitly knowledgeable spreadsheets. This part is needed to overlay the story in the organizational space, and identify places, dependencies and expectations. For example, we have just found from the story above that the source of information for the units' sales targets is only in the sales director's email inbox and not in our data warehouse (the assumed consumption point).

THE STANDARDS THAT MAKE THE STORY ACCEPTABLE

Quality is in the eye of the consumer; although subjective, the story must capture what the 'good enough' expectation by the agent (data athlete) is. Here the more quantifiable items and dimensions are captured the better, and the cheaper it is going to be to deliver, for iterations due to misunderstanding are inefficient usage of money and resources. The objective is to add to the story not just the 'traditional' levels of quality (e.g. completeness or coverage), but also other standards that would complete the story, such as accessibility (i.e. who can access the data), or retention (for how long the data is to be maintained as relevant), as well as classification or certification of compliance to regulations (e.g. privacy, localization).

THE RISKS THAT THE STORY DRIVES

In physics, for every action there is always an opposite reaction. Using data to generate value creates the same risk. Further, the newer or more sophisticated the manner in which the data is used (see generative AI), the higher the risk this might trigger an unforeseen issue. So, a moment of reflection must be spent with the DA scanning the horizon and asking what can go wrong. Is the story risking the breach of existing regulations? Or are the actions that the agent is going to perform likely to be, or to be interpreted as, noxious from an ethical point of view? In the past I have successfully used reverse brainstorming techniques to landscape risks, whereby instead of brainstorming improvements, as a group you set out to 'break' the process or try to negate the benefit from the outcome.

Example of a complete data consumer story

To illustrate the above in practice, below is a complete, albeit simple, specimen of a data consumer story based on the logistics manager story.

DATA CONSUMER STORY
On-time delivery improvement

As a logistics manager, I have been informed that our customer's satisfaction index has been impacted negatively by the timeliness of the delivery of our goods.

We have worked with our shipping company and have secured an optimal performance of their delivery process. However, we realized that our delivery centre is failing to include in the shipping list sent to the shipping company a complete list of all the goods that should be shipped on the day. This is impacting the delivery date that was provided to the customer.

Therefore, I would like to ensure that our shipping list is as accurate as possible, and to do so I would like to be sure that at the daily shipping schedule's time of creation, all the goods that have a planned shipping date of today are included in the list.

I think I need a report that compares the shipping dates coming from the ERPs (our factory systems) with the daily shipping schedule produced by the delivery centre system with all the items in the ERP that have the planned goods issue date of today. My assumptions are based on the 'as is' information flow I have been provided (Figure 9.3) by our technical team.

Once I have that data, I would communicate every inconsistency with the delivery centre team to investigate and remediate within an SLA of two hours that allows me to make the evening shipping company's pick-up, as I would have missed the morning slot by then.

Critical success factors

- Delivery centre team are informed of the new process and can be supportive.
- All systems involved are adequately maintained and reliable.
- Shipping company performance is monitored and kept nominal.

FIGURE 9.3 'As is' information flow

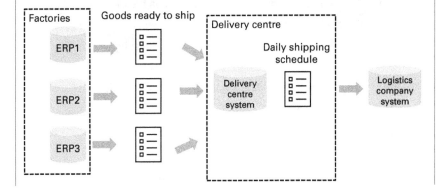

Data product(s) description

Shipping list anomaly report

The shipping list anomaly report compares the list of all goods appearing in the goods ready to ship (GRS) extracts from all ERPs and the daily shipping schedule (DSS).

An anomaly is defined as follows:

- an item on the GRS combined list is not appearing on the DSS
- an item that appears on the DSS but not on the GRS
- an item that is on the GRS but with a shipping date different from current day date
- an item that is missing or has a incomplete product ID or customer ID

The anomaly report should have the following dimensions to provide the deliver centre team with supporting information for their analysis and troubleshooting:

- by product family
- by customer geography
- by plant

Data quality standards

- *Timeliness:* The anomaly report should be produced every morning by 0800 local time.
- *Coverage:* The anomaly report must be performed on the GRS consolidated data including all the plants.
- *Completeness:* The shipping date in the GRS reports must be 100 per cent complete.
- *Validity:* The product ID should be a valid entry in the product ID list; the customer ID should be a valid entry in the customer ID list.

Data risk/ data protection and privacy

- *Data minimization:* Customer address and other details that are shared with the shipping company should not be included in the anomaly report.
- *Data security:* The anomaly report should only be available to the logistics manager.
- *Data retention:* The anomaly report should be retained for one month and then be disposed of.

If, reading this seemingly simple story, you have come up with loads of questions or ideas then I have achieved my objective: I have shown that there is room for adding depth and breadth in the voyage from Post-it note to dashboard. If the objective of correlating the outcome to the value is kept as the north star, the DPT must stimulate the incorporation in the data consumer stories of more details and finer expectations or risks.

The data requirement document

If the data consumer story is the outline of the outcome the DA wants to achieve, the *data requirement document* is the detailed list of what is required to achieve it. Unlike other types of requirement documents, the data requirement document must address any potential ambiguity of meanings, and in doing so uniquely identify all the business terms needed to complete the story.

The team involved in the story should have assembled a list of terms and for each of them should have identified a suitable data domain of pertinence. This is when the data domain owners are called into action. I deliberately didn't start the story with a list of *fields*, which, as per my stated idiosyncrasy, would perpetuate the 'data is IT' misnomer. However, I have been careful to indicate them as business terms because that's what they are: words that are a part of a business language and therefore in need of a clear and unambiguous standard definition. The data domain owner's task at this point is to go through the list of terms that are likely belonging to their domain and to standardize them. The amount of support needed, and the time taken to complete the data requirement document, is somewhat proportional not only to the quantity but also to where the different data domain owners are in the training cycle, and in the transition from a data-reactive organization to a data-training organization you are likely to find domains with no data domain owner in place yet. This is one more reason to insist that DeXOM is followed, as discovering more domains and providing them with proper ownership is the direction in which data intelligence is increased.

In practical terms, a completed data requirement document should achieve the data domain owner's validation of at least the following characteristics for each entry (business term):

Term name and synonyms (NB: this includes derived terms, i.e. metrics or calculated indexes):

- operational definition
- business process affiliation

- sensitivity classification (e.g. public, restricted, confidential)
- type (e.g. alphanumeric, date, currency)
- data domain and, if necessary, data sub-domain
- source of authority and authorized provisioning point (could be in *candidate* status)
- data quality acceptance levels (could be expressed in multiple quality dimensions)
- tolerances level (expressed by the data consumer, but deemed acceptable by the DDO)
- applicable geographical jurisdiction
- subject to external regulation or standards (e.g. GDPR, BCBS 239 or UNSPC)[1]

The data requirement is the moment the DDO's time is used to review and normalize the requirement and to augment the company data intelligence repository, as the new terms are memorialized and existing ones might be amended.

Methodologically, completing the data requirement should be performed during session IV 'data cardio' types of workouts as described in Chapter 8. Additional stamina might be necessary to overcome a likely hurdle occurring during data requirement sessions: a data consumer unwilling to align their requirement to the DDO standards. Data consumers are biased towards what they want in the way they wanted; in their view a different meaning or measure might jeopardize the outcome. People find it tedious to attend workshops that become bogged down by disagreements over definitions with seemingly no options to break the stalemate. And parting ways with an 'Ok, do it the way you want it!' is the worst-case scenario that, instead of progressing on the curve of higher data intelligence, expands the data multiverse of inconsistencies that generates more data debt. This is once again the moment for the DPT to shine, as we saw with the CEO dashboard story in Chapter 4. The reluctance to accept someone else's view or definition, apart from being deeply rooted in the brain's egocentric bias, can be simply down to one of these three root causes:

- Genuine misunderstanding: Communication between human beings is tricky, as we discussed at length in Chapter 6, but in this instance it is the easiest of the issues to resolve. Arranging a workshop where practical examples are examined and simulated with real data should quickly pave the way to an agreement, or worst-case scenario broker an agreement to disagree, that could be stipulated in the requirement as an exception for a given context (e.g. a special arrangement for a customer, or a specific geographical or regulatory driven meaning).

- Goal misalignment: This is the case in my CEO dashboard example. The two parties are not coming to an agreement as they perceive that agreeing would come at the detriment of either their reputation (e.g. customer or management commitment retraction) or their remuneration (e.g. bonus decrease). The DPT approach would be helping to articulate potential options available and to bridge the existing positions, making as explicit as possible the reason for the disagreement. When senior leaders are involved, objectifying the problem helps focus minds as an escalation to higher power would not be seen as a sign of seniority after all. It usually unties the knot and facilitates a deal.

- Hidden agenda: Next in the increasing gradient of difficulty, once the field has been cleared of misunderstanding and misalignment, the obstacle we are left with can be called politics, or Machiavellian *modus operandi*. Even if most people working together wish to do the right thing, that statistic ought to contemplate that from time to time someone has got ulterior motives. This is the worst-case scenario for working together towards a good team performance, let alone to come to an agreement on business terminology and requirements. Assuming that they are still acting with integrity, and are just unreasonably difficult to work with because of pre-existing bias or personal dislikes, I would recommend outmanoeuvring them, seeking collaboration from more amenable team members or a person of influence, and one or more firm escalations should be tried as well. As a very last resort the DDO could accept an exception or a derogation to their standards, but it should be justified by a very well-defined business need.

NB: The more trained and established the data domain owners involved in the requirement are, the smaller should be the involvement of the DPT to solve the matter. Besides, being the authority and the guardian of the standardized data intelligence is their core data duty.

Phase II: Data design

Data design is the translation of the data requirement into a blueprint of conceptual, logical and physical flows, inclusive of transformations and data flow controls, that delivers the requested data product(s) with the desired characteristics from the sources to the target consumption point. As such, design is work that requires the skills found in architects, in the sense that an intimate knowledge of the business and technical fabric of the organization is needed. Not surprisingly, there are as many architectural roles as there are layers woven into the said fabric.

The role of the data domain architect

I have already introduced the data domain architect as part of the DPT triumvirate, a member of the team with specialized expertise around setting the appropriate tracks and fields, that allows information to be delivered in an unobstructed and faithful manner from A to B. Recently there has been great attention to 'security by design' or, with the enforcement of regulations such as GDPR, 'privacy by design' as methodologies to guarantee that certain features are present in the final product so the likelihood of an undesired effect (a cyber-attack or a data breach) is minimized. The reason I came up with DeXOM is to respond to the issue of data being an afterthought, which we examined at the very beginning of this book. What DeXOM does for data is to 'shift it left', and to move all the required 'by design' elements upstream, e.g. quality by design, retention by design, accessibility by design.

The expectation is that our data athlete would realize their ambition to use data that is fit for purpose by design and not after a long period of fixing the data after the change is over. The data domain architect is therefore the translator of every explicit or, as much as possible, implicit expectation from the data into a corresponding design feature, features which they will align to the data standards enunciated by the relevant data domains. In fact, in most cases there will be multiple data domain architects working together on the same data consumer story, as it is unusual to have a story consuming data from just one domain. The artefact that they deliver is the data design document and in Data Workout 2 at the end of this part we will also be creating a full specimen of such document for the 'On-time delivery improvement' data consumer story introduced above. Nevertheless, a well-structured data design document should be inclusive of at least the following parts.

STANDARDIZED DATA REQUIREMENT
Based on a preliminary data requirement artefact extracted from the story, its standardized version, still in a tabular format, is achieved by the data domain architect(s) working together with the data domain owner(s). They corroborate the list of terms with all the required ancillary information that

would make the design effective such as clear operational definitions, sources of authority, critical data element classification and quality expectations. Scanning the data intelligence repository, the data domain architect should also identify each term in the list, and all entries in the document should be clearly marked as existing and confirmed terms, new terms or existing terms to be amended, that would have new or amended features in the 'to be' state (e.g. amended operational definition, new referential set, new source). Finally, based on the stated expectations of quality, the data domain architect should perform a data quality assessment to quantify the existing gaps versus the demand.

DATA MODELS

These are the description of the conceptual, logical and physical models associated with the data consumer story. In Chapter 8 I introduced a simple mind map as a starting point of the data domain model: any new data consumer story is an opportunity for the data domain architect(s) to expand and enrich the model. They are simultaneously providing the data athlete with new concepts to interpret their reality and win their data competition, and at the same completing the puzzle of the company's data intelligence. Furthermore, their modelling is connecting the concepts, i.e. the business language of data, to the physicality of the world of data, i.e. the digital architecture made of systems, interface and databases that instantiate, as the architect say, the information, the actual representation made of bits and bytes. The connection between the different model types is called *vertical lineage*, as opposed to the horizontal lineage, which instead is the depiction of the journey of data from the sources to the target point of consumption. The concept is connected to the physical layer via a system agnostic structure, the logical model, that bridges the human concept with the information technology way of representing information.

As Figure 9.4 shows, the concept that we would have encountered in the story as the compact term *customer address* is in effect a composition of attributes that the architect models logically in a data structure represented effectively as a generic table. The structure is then used to map the components of the logical structure to the various physical places (i.e. systems or data sets) which are processing the various attributes. Finally, as part of the design the architect will translate the quality and integrity expectations, normalized in the data requirement document with the data domain owners, into a data standard model that is practically executing rules and calculating metrics to control the data. It is demonstrable that this approach, although

FIGURE 9.4 Vertical lineage: conceptual, logical and physical model

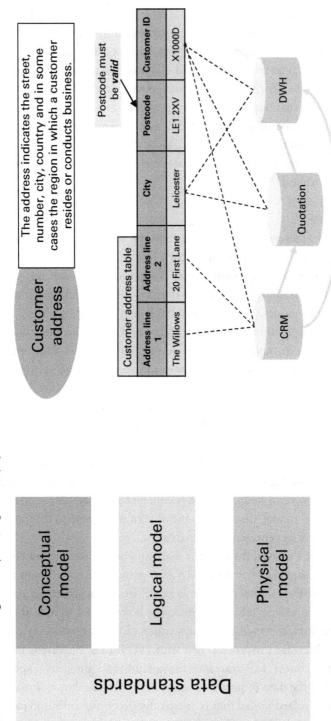

requiring heavier lifting in an organization with low data intelligence, is significantly more scalable and efficient in comparison to an approach where there is no vertical lineage and delivering data is achieved through repetitive mapping of physical structures of system tables and columns. In a rapidly changing information architecture, the system-to-system mapping would grow permutationally in its complexity.

DATA FLOW DIAGRAM

This is the formalization of the initial diagram presented in the data consumer story. The diagram is the bridge between the two worlds of the 'business' and the 'IT'. As such, it should represent the requirement in a way that the data consumer gleans that their request is fully included, but it should contain enough information for the IT team to realize the flow in their infrastructure. It should be essentially a drawing, possibly produced using an appropriate design tool, so as to have it available, if required, as a structured format (e.g. JSON or XML). It should clearly show the 'as is' versus the 'to be' versions. As per the previous sections the data flow diagram (DFD) should provide assurance that consumption is happening from the appropriate source of authority and it should describe the location and design of data flow monitoring controls and operational controls, like ETL validation, data quality check points, access controls, encryption or intrusion detection.

DATA DEBT EVALUATION

As part of the design 'as is' assessment, using the gap assessment in the standardize data requirement, the data design document should include a monetary evaluation of the gaps between the data consumer expectations and the level of the conformity of the required data, in terms of data quality, access, retention, etc. This should be translated into actual effort or amount, though the precision of that calculation is proportional to the overall data intelligence status, as it requires a detailed knowledge of the overall business model.

DATA CONTROLS

Finally, as a guarantor of the stability of the 'to be' data flow, based on the data standard model, the architect defines the data control plan. It is in fact an overlay to the data flow locating the position, the design and the effectiveness of the controls that should maintain a satisfactory level of the consumption after the change; in Six Sigma terms, upholding the short-term sigma. Examples of controls are data quality cockpits, monitoring of extraction, transformation and loading (ETL) tasks, data retention schedules and disposal, encryption at rest and in motion.

A moment of truth for the data athlete

The data design provides the opportunity to enforce an important check point that should reduce the likelihood of failure – it is a 'moment of truth'. At this stage in the Data Excellence Operating Model, the DA is still free to withdraw from the challenge as there is now enough information to pose the question 'Is this worth the effort?' The design includes in its data debt assessment the additional cost, or at least its approximation made with a reasonable level of confidence, that it will be required to achieve the story. The combination of the data consumer story with its acceptance levels and the data requirement document, together with the blueprint for the data flow with the gaps in data sources and controls, all point to a level of data debt that wasn't appreciated at the beginning. This in turn allows a reality check on the data athlete's willingness to commit the necessary people, time and budget to deliver. This is clearly the case in the abovementioned example of the marketing investment performance report. Instead of waiting until the test phase to find out that the report is of no beneficial use given the lack of data, at the end of the design phase the data debt assessment would have detailed that, for example, 35 per cent of the critical data elements, the ones on which the performance measurement relied the most, were not present, i.e. their physical fields were empty. Either based on the pre-existing experience in the team or with some simple business process modelling or, even, activity base costing approaches, the architect and the data athlete should then be able to calculate the amount needed to remove the data debt to a portion of the 35 per cent gap. That amount will need to be added to the initial project business case to recalculate the cost–benefit analysis, and a more informed go ahead should be provided.

When the time comes to shake hands on the data design document and a gap in resources to deliver the best solution is known, if the initiative is to be progressed without repaying the data debt adding to the project resources, the DA should be made aware that they *de facto* accept the risk of delivering a suboptimal solution. A 'surprise' at test phase is transposed into risk acceptance at design. However, that is not easy, as risk-taking, especially outside of financial services, is not exactly a well-toned muscle. We will find out more about data risks and risk-taking in Chapter 11.

The data design authority and its role

Given the sensitivity of the requirement and design phases, it is good to introduce an additional guarantee for officiality and soundness of the exercise being undertaken. The data design authority (DDeA) is a guarantor that the practices adopted are safe for all the data athletes and appropriately followed. I might be pushing the metaphor a little too far by likening the DDeA to the body in charge of administering anti-doping tests, but – just like sporting cheats – in data there is sometimes a tendency to believe that the end justifies the means.

As the denomination would suggest, the DDeA is the governance body that oversees the design and consequently the implementation of a change that affects data. It is a body whose members are usually a mixture of architects and data leaders, and, as such, it should have in its terms of reference ample assurance of independence from the teams that are involved in the execution of data excellence initiatives. It should be present and officially providing approval at two stages, at a minimum: the end of the design and the end of the build. The remit of the DDeA is to keep the change leader true to their intent. If at any point the DPT loses their grip on their trainee, the DDeA should have been invested with sufficient authority for them to be listened to and complied with. Of course, if there is an existing design authority in other functions like IT, the extension to data of their authority could shorten the timeframe to have a fully functional data design authority in place. Yet the organization might not be ready for such types of controls, especially if most programmes have been happening under a devolved authority, maybe under the overused 'agile' banner, so some *phasing in* might be in order.

A lighter warm-up exercise that could accustom the organization to the DDeA would be a portfolio assessment like that in Data Workout 1 at the end of the first part (Pillar I). The DDeA could be introduced as support for the projects that were in need of more data fitness to increase the likelihood of success. From the set of projects that scored higher than the red line on the Y axis of data risk, the DPT could select a sub-set of vitally important initiatives, based on materiality or investment, and introduce them to the DDeA as a factor of extra care to ensure that the risks highlighted for the execution are mitigated. If the organization is planning to consolidate their customer managements system in one platform, for example, this is the kind of project that would be very expensive and have material repercussion across the many constituencies should data be forgotten, and, in a data-reactive organization (i.e. low data fitness), it would make an ideal candidate for the data design authority to demonstrate its worth.

Support would come in the form of a specialized trainer, who could be an architect from another domain, assigned to the project to perform a peer review of the work done by the data domain architects. At first, the support could entail the co-editing, rewriting or creating from scratch the data design if missed altogether, but that should be seen as an investment of time with the higher return of properly embedding data in change. For the projects selected it would be advisable to formalize the sign-off of the design phase in a proper DDeA session, with the aim of reviewing formally at the end of the build phase, when the ticking and tying of every highlighted risk and the respective mitigation actions would be officially recognized. As with any other foundational capability, the first circuits will be the toughest; the DPT and their DDeA allies will need to gain enough senior management support to be allowed to ignore the fair amount of huffing and puffing, agitation and annoyance that will happen at all the levels. There may be allegations of slowing down execution, excessive bureaucracy, adding no value and all the typical cursing that accompanies the stretching and flexing of a muscle that has never been exercised before. But, just like the athlete reeling from the pain and fatigue induced by lactic acid, the message must be clear: no pain, no gain.

Surely you can prepare for that moment in advance. How? As part of toning the top, this is the moment to uncover past performance data show-ing, for example, how many projects have been completed to schedule and within budget, and if they weren't, what the main reasons have been. Together with the fitness assessment, it is adding to the baseline of our DA performance and can be used to motivate improvement. Similar to the port-folio mapping of initiatives, this type of data should be the bread-and-butter of a portfolio or change team – their role is to oversee how the company investment is translated into the desired outcome.

The portfolio team's data could provide the DPT with a case for the DDeA when armed with simple problem statements like 'Only 50 per cent of our projects are on time and to budget: missed data dependencies account for almost half of the root causes.' Even in the absence of a change team or portfolio team, there should be a basic process that helps to create such a baseline. Any reputable organization should have in place an issue management or incident process. So, it should be easy enough to access that data and to perform, if not done yet, a rapid investigation to connect some of the most materially impacting incidents to something that went wrong at the time of change, as 99 per cent of the issues are usually owing to badly managed change. Of course, here the additional step would be to connect those material issues that happened because of a change, to some of the risks that the DDeA is committing to reduce. In the age of interconnected data supply chains and fast AI-driven data propagation, any company could have had a data breach, a customer data blunder or a very near miss that could be connected to a data risk that was not taken properly discovered, controlled and mitigated. Armed with such 'truth', it would be sage for the DPT to measure performance during a couple of circuits (i.e. new projects) to demonstrate the abatement of post-roll-out issues, the increase in on-time delivery, and the increase, of course, of overall data fitness.

Phase III: Build

Once the data design authority has given its approval and the data design document has been finalized, the actual build phase can take place. This is the construction of the flows and the controls that we should presume the technology, or IT, or digital team, whatever its denomination, is capable of implementing through the necessary infrastructural and applicative changes, following an effective methodology. At a point in time, the story is accomplished in all its components, and it is accepted by the data consumer. I am not going to go into detail about the above type of build, I would just like to emphasize that *this* is the phase in which the effort so far employed to increase data intelligence and reduce data debt must come to fruition, otherwise our promise to the data athlete will be broken. Thus, at the time the new flows go live, and the data products are delivered, three goals must be accomplished:

1 The *to be* conceptual and logical models must be available and live in the data intelligence application or data catalogue, and properly connected to the physical model.

2 The data controls and data monitoring checks are not only part of the catalogue too, but have been tested and are ready to be operated.

3 Most importantly, the level of data debt in the underlined data has been brought below the stated tolerances.

In the last part of the book, we will examine an approach to optimize the reduction of data debt in relation to the agile approach for the development of data product, which could see an iteration of build and sustain phases. However, we assume for now that the build phase closes when the data consumer requirements are met.

Phase IV: Sustain

The sustain phase covers the period from the acceptance of the deliverables to the next change that would affect the newly implemented operating mode. This is a future point in time when a change would modify the existing source to target flow. Until the moment at which a new data consumer story will modify the same data supply chain or part of it, the sustain phase is in place to control the achieved performance, as per our little excursion into Six Sigma. We have activated controls to reduce the likelihood that the achieved improvement deteriorates over time, and consequently the value generated might be eroded.

It starts with the critical step of accepting the deliverables completed and tested in the build phase. The acceptance needs three parties to be secured: the original requestor, namely the data consumer that told us the story; the provider or the maker of the deliverable, who both are hopefully data athletes now showing improved data fitness and the data design authority. The data consumer verifies that the story has been accomplished through the change, while the data design authority authenticates with the provider that the outcome has been achieved as per design, and that any gaps have either been closed or accepted as is or logged with a plan to close. The sign-off documentation will also list any accepted deviation from the original requirement. In the case of a deviation from the conceptual model, the DPT would have worked with the data domain owner and the data domain architect to ratify this.

Finally, as part of the 'to be', the sign-off must include the data control environment, which is made by all the controls that have been implemented to guarantee that all the agreed data standards are, for the data in scope, kept within expected tolerances. Needless to say, for the sustain phase to be the phase in which the DA has been given the new rituals to follow and such rituals provide assurance that our outcome is still valid, and that the NIA is still achievable and beneficial, an augmented or strengthened organization might be needed to not only operate new processes but also to monitor and respond to the new controls.

COOLING DOWN

- Data is inherently agile.
- The Data Excellence Operating Model provides assurance that data is done by design and stops being an afterthought.
- Understanding the data athlete's next intended action is key to build the data consumer story.
- Requirement, design, build and sustain are the four phases of the DeXOM.
- Conceptual, logical and physical modelling are the bricks of data intelligence.
- It is better to admit the data debt gap is too big and stop, rather than to deliver an unusable data product.
- The data design authority is like the anti-doping agency for data.
- The sustain phase is often the most expensive part of the change, and the data athlete must budget for it.

Note

1 UNSPC. United Nations Standard Products and Services Code, nd. www.undp. org/unspsc (archived at https://perma.cc/92HF-UPC3)

10

Establishing the enabling capabilities

WARMING UP

- What else does DeXOM need beyond the 'missing shelf'?

- What are the enabling capabilities?

- What can the DPT do to support them?

- What are the first disciplines to focus on?

- Why is it never too early to talk about data ethics?

- Why am I not focusing on data visualization?

Beyond the 'missing shelf'

I am sure you are keen to practise the Data Excellence Operating Model and later, in Data Workout 2, I will give ample space for you to have a full tour of DeXOM. However, it should have become even clearer how its successful adoption cannot depend solely on the zeal of the DPT's ability to gently encourage their data athletes to exercise. Indeed, there are some crucial dependencies that must be acknowledged and facilitated. I am of course referring again to the 'missing shelf' effect – the lack of an effective and consistently adopted change methodology that would make the mission of tackling data forgetfulness, even with full adoption of DeXOM, harder. Of course, the missing shelf would not only impact data: organizations that cannot properly orchestrate change would experience other symptoms, such as a struggle to transform and simplify processes, a lack of critical skills, an unpredictable realization of financial return and, of course, an accumulation of technical debt. Furthermore, if we look closer, beyond facilitating the payload of data, a good change management process cannot stand alone. It requires other building blocks to be established across the company, which together are also necessary foundations and bricks for the data excellence gymnasium. Based on my experience I have identified eight of these building blocks, which I call foundational capabilities, whose solidity the data personal trainer must be acutely aware of, as they have a direct impact on the overall performance of the data athletes.

The eight foundational capabilities

To pinpoint the foundational capabilities, let us consider the macro process of change that goes from the gathering of the strategic intent and the management of the portfolio to the execution of change and to the control of the new direction that then generates change. With this end-to-end view in mind, I have identified the group of critical capabilities necessary to support the Data Excellence Operating Model (see Figure 10.1).

The capabilities' names might differ slightly from organization to organization, so for better identification and action I provide a succinct operational definition of each, followed by how they are necessary to DeXOM, and examples of how the DPT could support their mutual development and integration. I must stress that the complete absence of any of those would severely harm the mission of the DPT, so this list should also be used as a potential due diligence to perform at the very beginning as part of our inception

FIGURE 10.1 Foundational capabilities: Building blocks of the data excellence gym

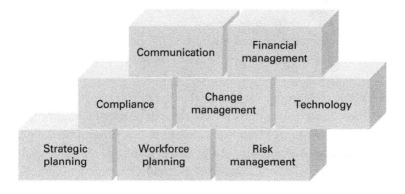

planning with the top executive and the data international Olympic committee (mentioned in Chapter 3, the control functions such as compliance, governance, audit, etc.), so boundary conditions for the success of data excellence would be set.

Strategic planning

This is the process by which the long-term vision from the top is articulated in a strategic sequence of ambitions to be met to gain market share, increase revenue and generate value. It is usually achieved through a combination of top-down strategic vision and bottom-up resource planning, and it is delivered as a long-term strategic plan and a more detailed short–medium term one written into the former.

DeXOM DEPENDENCY
Any weakness in strategic planning would deprive the methodology of a frame of reference for measuring fitness (in this case intended as 'suitability') of the various stories and epics presented by the data athletes. In other words, the DPT would not be able to interpret and, if necessary, adjust the data athlete's ask without reference to what is important for the company.

HOW THE DPT CAN HELP
As these processes are very data-hungry, the DPT could use their skills to treat the strategic planning itself as a data consumer story, offering to the management a stronger trustable data backbone for the strategic direction being ratified and for implementing the ongoing tracking.

Financial management

Whether for profit or not-for-profit, any organization should have in place sound financial practices to guarantee that cash flows are feeding business activities and allowing growth and financial resilience and stability.

DeXOM DEPENDENCY
Data excellence is a new endeavour that must be supported financially, and in the specific form of DeXOM stories need funding commitment. Equally, the financial management is supporting the harvesting of the value declared by the data athlete, with a third-party certification by a finance controller. It is crucial to the challenge of delivering better business cases, which, incidentally, is not just a problem for the DPT.

HOW THE DPT CAN HELP
Thinking about the data excellence gym as a 'data business' with sound accounting is a must, as anything that is done under DeXOM should be costed and continuously scrutinized for efficiency gains. Also, financial acumen should be stimulated in the collection of the data consumer story with clear articulation of the value by the data athlete. Beyond that, in Chapter 13 we will go through an approach to fund data across the organization.

Communication

The reputation, agility and resilience of a company relies on effective and authentic communication. Internal versus external is nowadays a fictitious segregation, as all the third-party recipients of corporate messaging ought to be addressed professionally and reliably, be they employees, customers, regulators or investors.

DeXOM DEPENDENCY
Unsurprisingly, the 'change in the way we change' that DeXOM represents travels through effective communication, from the engagement and acceptance of new ways of working to the celebration of successes.

HOW THE DPT CAN HELP
Beyond what has been described at length in Chapter 6, and following Joe Bugajsky's advice ('Get yourself a communication expert!'), I would reiterate that this is so important that I would fund a resource in the communications team if they were struggling to support my team.

Compliance

In a complex and interconnected world, where corporate impact grows, the public's attention to such impact is satisfied by increased regulatory pressure. All companies are now regulated, all companies are permanently exposed to potential penalties and severe reputational damage if internal by-laws are not properly administered and controlled. A compliance process that is watchful and authorized to respond in a timely manner is a must, as is partnering the organization, designing clear policy and standards, and advocating ethical behaviours.

DeXOM DEPENDENCY

No change is viable if it breaches compliance, so a compliance capability that duly enunciates and curates the compliance envelope with policies and standards allows DeXOM to translate them into effective guardrails to embed during (i.e. standards) and after the change (i.e. controls).

HOW THE DPT CAN HELP

The best the DPT can do is to provide assurance that compliance is as upstream as possible in the operating model and that it is *delivered by outcome*. The compliance requirements should be considered during the design phase and not retrofitted on the solution once completed. If the requirements don't exist, the DPT could do a quick analytic exercise and, given the company profile, plot a heatmap of regulatory landscape that, once signed off by the compliance team, could be used to bring their counselling in, when data consumer stories are narrating a possible compliance impact.

Technology or digital

It is difficult to underestimate the importance of a good technology capability. I said at the very beginning that data is not IT, but data lives in the technological substrate of the company, and so the whole technological architecture is a crucial enabler for everything that the data athletes are attempting to achieve. The right balance of standards and controls versus agility and innovation is a tricky one to strike but digital is surely the core.

DeXOM DEPENDENCY

In the previous chapter we didn't go deep into the 'build' phase because that relies on technology, but it is clear that without the proper build the story cannot be delivered.

HOW THE DPT CAN HELP

The relationship between tech or digital teams and data teams can sometimes be tense and detrimental to the overall result. Its root is usually around the perceived power held by managing data, particularly now with AI, but it is frequently caused by data teams not sitting hierarchically with technology and seen as second-guessing tech choices around infrastructure, even in some cases creating 'shadow IT'-like organizations. Therefore, establishing clear competency and jurisdictional boundaries is a worthwhile exercise.

My recommendation would be to interlace the capabilities exactly as DeXOM suggests: to elicit from the data athlete the best requirement for the technology capability to deliver its outcome, with minimal influence on the 'how' and maximum clarity on the 'what'. To exemplify this point, facing a story asking for real time supply of encrypted data to an existing set of analytics that is currently only fed weekly and unencrypted, the DPT should be openly delegating to the tech capability the technical solution (ingestion tooling and encryption application) and focus on the payload and the controls.

Risk management

The enterprise's ability to define an organized taxonomy of potential threats to its strategy, operations and finances is an essential muscle. Risks so defined are further broken down into types and drivers so that mitigation plans are put in place to reduce the potential impact to a tolerable threshold. A corresponding set of controls is implemented to provide assurance that the risk profile is maintained.

DeXOM DEPENDENCY

The design and sustain phases are very susceptible to the absence of risk management. If you have a good understanding in place of risks existing in the environment that is impacted by the story, the solution implemented could include mitigation actions. Equally, if the new solution might trigger new risks, the sustain phase would require additional controls. The lack of the appreciation of risk management would undoubtedly affect the sustainability of the outcome.

HOW THE DPT CAN HELP

This is so important that Chapter 11 is dedicated to it! Suffice to say that the DPT should be contributing to the augmentation of the risk lingo in the company in two ways: introducing data risks in the existing risks nomenclature, and augmenting the assurance of the other risks with adequate data. Risk data athletes are go!

Workforce planning

Contrary to common preconceptions, this capability does not coincide fully with human resource or personnel. Rather, it is a continuous activity of matching strategy and operation with an adequate level of skills, through forecasting, developing and acquiring the right talent for the organization. As already mentioned in Chapter 4, skills employed in critical processes, depending on the company lifecycle, might be sourced from consultancy, internal upskilling or outsourcing services, so an integrated skill and capacity fulfilling capability is essential.

DeXOM DEPENDENCY

One of the integral layers of the operating model is the skills of the people involved. A well-thought-out and executed workforce plan is essential to create the minimum mass of expertise and talent to sustain the methodology, e.g. data domain architects.

HOW THE DPT CAN HELP

The DPT can bring to bear their conceptual modelling skills and help the HR team to model the required competency, job codes and name structures that are the foundation of such capability. It is a sensitive area, but it would offer the data domain owner for the employee data domain an excellent use case to train on.

Change management

Last but not least, our missing shelf is often seen as the ability, post-change, to foster new behaviours in people involved in the change. I prefer the definition which describes change management as a truly organization-wide ability to change all the constituent parts of the organization. These capabilities are of course all connected, but in the case of change, a stronger connection exists with strategic planning and financial management, with the strategic planning to outline the vision to be realized, and the financial management to provide the resourcing to achieve it. Here, change management is the vehicle that using efficiently the resources orchestrates the displacement from the 'as is' to the 'to be'.

DeXOM DEPENDENCY

As discussed, if DeXOM operates in the absence of structure and method, it will have a very limited scalability and sustainability.

HOW THE DPT CAN HELP

Beyond the actions illustrated in Chapter 9 and the practical exercise in Data Workout 1, the DPT should become the best ally of any change or portfolio management team, using data to identify and manage cross-programme or cross-project dependencies, in order to provide assurance that delivery will be on-target and on-time.

Naturally, the scope and nature of the capabilities might vary depending on the size and the complexity of the host organization. Nevertheless, the DPT should stimulate all the parties involved to operate as an ecosystem to provide DeXOM with the best chance of success. This in turn will accelerate the adoption of data excellence practices and the trajectory towards a data-driven organization.

Priority sub-disciplines

In the same vein as focusing on the enabling capabilities that undergird our data excellence gym, it would be useful now to look back at Chapter 5 and reconsider the skeleton of the disciplines and sub-disciplines the DPT should put into practice to adhere to the principles of the data charter. Just as for the enabling capabilities, it is not my intention to write a metadata management or data quality management manual, as plenty of literature is available, including the most common industry standards already referenced. However, although I proposed a data fitness assessment in Chapter 5 as a guide to prioritizing the evolution of disciplines and sub-disciplines, the framework might still be felt to be an overwhelming task for the DPT at the beginning of their mission. What should they build first? I use the word 'build' intentionally, as this is a very intense portion of the life of the DPT. Setting up the new disciplines and having them adopted at the same time can be taxing. So, if the DPT has limited resources to set up the machinery in their gym and low power to operate the model – limitations which at the beginning are very likely – I would invest time and resources in the (sub) disciplines below, as distinctive boosters for the data athletes' performances. In support of the DPT inception, I present below four subsections with additional clarification around the nature of the disciplines and a list of short- and medium-term actions, based on the practices and artefacts contained in their outline to launch them effectively.

Metadata management

In Chapter 8 I mentioned that I really fell in love with metadata while I was working at Lloyds Banking, so it is not surprising that I strongly recommend the DPT to prioritize it. If data intelligence is the 'know thyself' that ultimately powers a data-driven organization, metadata management is the sub-discipline that accumulates it, structures it and makes it available, current and crucially connected to the physical part of data, i.e. its digital representation (see Table 10.1). For instance, everything that we extract from the data domain owners during the training sessions or the Data Excellence Operating Model is translated into data intelligence with metadata management. Hence it is important that the metadata management practices are staffed, accessible and flexible.

TABLE 10.1 Metadata management

Horizon	Action	Tools and artifacts
Short term	Define first draft of data domain model using industry templates or any other existing internal process	• Digital map of data domain model with DDO names
	Leverage internal wikis or dictionaries to set up first prototype of data intelligence repository, making sure to start capturing business terms and concepts, and descriptions (pending DDO confirmation, classification, source systems, etc.)	• Shared spreadsheet or web list of existing terms
	Set up a metadata work group to design metadata management features and issue implementation document for the disciplines	• Metadata glossary • Metadata validation standards
	Agree with technology or, if existing, enterprise architecture teams the metadata target architecture, and perform a quick market intelligence to fill in the gaps	• Metadata architecture diagram • RFI for data intelligence repository and modelling tool
Medium term	Introduce metadata modelling in capturing process and produce first example of vertical lineage	• Data modelling standard • Data modelling tool • Data lineage standard
	Using the metadata validation standards, grade the content of the data intelligence repository and initiate improvement actions	• Data domain standards assessment • Metadata non-conformity log

(continued)

TABLE 10.1 (Continued)

Horizon	Action	Tools and artifacts
	Evolve metadata work group into a data intelligence council and have them steering the procurement and first implementation of the data intelligence repository	• RFP for data intelligence repository • Data intelligence repository implementation plan
	Define data intelligence repository development backlog and assign it to the data intelligence council to prioritize and manage based on data excellence portfolio of ambitions	• Data intelligence repository release plan

Data quality management

Immediately after and, as you will read in the actions, tightly interlaced with metadata management comes data quality management. Let's be clear, data quality is quintessentially about industrializing the effort of closing the gap between reality and its digital representation, and to maintain those gaps over time at an acceptable minimum (lowest data debt). Without being too philosophical about this, since Chapter 7 I have delayed the conversation about *accuracy*, defined as the Holy Grail of data quality. Now, having agreed upon enough concepts about data excellence and the relationship between the data personal trainer and data athlete, we are also ready to agree that *accuracy is a relative term*! If you agree with the premise about data quality as a measurement of a gap, then you ought to agree that 100 per cent accuracy is never achieved as that gap is never filled. Why? Because accuracy is a relative term, and it is always measured by the eyes of the data consumer.

> If in the process of approving a loan application I ask to see the passport of the applicant to confirm their identity, I scan the first page and I use it to duly lift all the details and insert these in the loan management system. I triple check it and the passport picture is crystal clear. Consequently, all the details are faithfully reproduced in the system. Do I have a 100 per cent accurate representation of that passport? The answer is no, because my colleague who deals with anti-money-laundering and anti-terrorist checks would like to have a picture of all pages to assess whether the individual has visited 'blacklisted' countries. It doesn't matter to my colleague if the data I collected is 100 per cent accurate, that is not an accurate representation of the applicant's passport.

The conclusion to draw from the above example is that accuracy is relative to the use of data, and once again what the data athlete/consumer wants to do with it drives the level of data intelligence needed through an expression of data quality expectations or controls that test whether what we have got is *good enough*. Therefore, even in its crudest form, data quality management should guarantee that the above-mentioned controls, known as data quality rules, are captured and used to assess the conformity of data to the expectations. Here is where the interlock with metadata management is the strongest, as definitional ambiguity is a derivative risk in data quality, too. Seemingly identical rules applied to the same data can derive a different measure of the same gap. Why? Because syntactically and semantically the rules were not the same. For example, a rule that counts the number of empty 'fields' in a data set and another that counts the number of empty records (i.e. all the fields in one record are empty) might both be called 'data set completeness check' and deliver very confusing results. It is, then, necessary to apply the same rigour that defines data to the rules that are measuring data, to a point that if the rule itself is not clearly defined and validated in the data intelligence repository, it should not be used to monitor data. That approach will not only guarantee effective data quality management, but it should also prevent the dangers of the uncontrolled proliferation of data quality rules that in the long term would degrade the value of the discipline. See the actions required for effective data quality management in Table 10.2.

TABLE 10.2 Data quality management

Horizon	Action	Tools and artifacts
Short term	Identify a list of highly visible quality issues and initiate remediation reviews	• Data quality issue executive report
	Assemble data quality work group and assist the release of data quality implementation documents, together with data quality engine features	• Data quality standards • Root cause analysis template • Data quality engine features list
	Collect the list of data quality rules in synchronization with data domain owner training sessions and data intelligence repository	• Data quality rule dictionary

(continued)

TABLE 10.2 (Continued)

Horizon	Action	Tools and artifacts
	Define with technology the target architecture for data quality (NB: must be integrated with metadata management)	• Data quality architecture diagram
Medium term	Set up data quality issue remediation process leveraging existing incident or issue management process	• Data quality issue ticket process • Data quality issue repository
	Use the same issue management process to establish data profiling service	• Data profiling tool
	Evolve data quality work group into a data quality council and have them steer the procurement and first implementation of the data quality engine	• RFP for data quality engine • Data quality engine implementation plan
	Define data quality tool development backlog and assign it to the data quality council to prioritize and manage based on data excellence portfolio of ambitions	• Data quality engine release plan

Data privacy and data sovereignty

When I first read the EU GDPR, I came away with two thoughts. The first was that this was just a reminder of what we should have done for personal data (and in my opinion for *all* data) a long time ago. Secondly, Recital 4 really struck me: 'The processing of personal data should be designed to serve mankind'.[1] What we do has serious consequences, and governments are watchful of where their citizens' data goes and what is done with it. Whether you are or are not part of a company that processes high-risk sensitivity data, this discipline is a must to train the data athletes to deal with sensitive data. Although nowadays we are all regulated, i.e. we owe data to third parties to attest to internal processes or practices that might pose a risk to public welfare or economic security, not all organizations have the structures in place to manage such new developments. Hence my emphasis on compliance and risk management capabilities above. If we add to the deglobalization trends we all observe, a regulatory restriction of flows of data across jurisdictions, known as data sovereignty, is a new challenge we need to train for, requiring additional context to our data. These promise to become as complex as the intricate set of custom controls in place today for the shipping of physical products between countries. Table 10.3 outlines the actions that should be taken to ensure data privacy is adhered to.

TABLE 10.3 Data privacy

Horizon	Action	Tools and artifacts
Short term	List processes that might be using personal data, at the very minimum sales and marketing and HR processes	• List of activities processing personal data • List of third-party processors of personal data
	Capture the purpose and the jurisdiction of data source and target and dependency from third parties	• List of data exposed by jurisdictions to potential sovereignty rules
	Draft process to capture data privacy issues, leveraging existing incident process or risk register, and to notify data breaches	• Data privacy incident log • Data breach notification procedure
	Draft and ratify the data privacy policy of the organization, accompanied by a training module	• Data privacy policy • Data privacy essential module
	Nominate data privacy champions	• Data privacy champion list
Medium term	Draft and negotiate insertion of data privacy clause in contracts with third party managing personal data	• Data privacy clause • List of third-party contracts in scope
	Design a data privacy deliverable to be included in DeXOM design and sustain steps	• Data privacy by design standards • DeXOM data privacy by design addendum
	Establish process to fulfil data subject access requests (aka privacy right request) and monitor compliance with timelines	• DSAR fulfilment tool
	Define data sovereignty exposure and mitigation procedures	• Data sovereignty by design standards • DeXOM data sovereignty addendum

Data ethics and culture

I have already discussed company culture, but a special place is reserved for data ethics, as, since mentioning responsible data in the data arena (Chapter 1), I hope I have shown how important it is to strike a balance between the power that data unleashes and the accountability that comes with it. This is even more critical now that the last technological challenges to exploit 'big data' fully have been overcome with the advent of the latest advancement of artificial intelligence (aka generative AI). In this new environment it is crucial to instil an attitude to doubt what is being done and to navigate to an answer, that, albeit never delivering 100 per cent certainty, would still be corroborated as the one to stand by. Bearing in mind that it would be a mistake to make a distinction between data ethics and any other ethical initiatives happening in the organization, the strength of the data excellence approach is that it is focused on integrating data with the rest of the company fabric. In data ethics such an approach is essential, as to be technology agnostic future-proofs the ability of the company to navigate the difficult questions that will come. See Table 10.4 for the actions that should be taken to implement data ethics.

TABLE 10.4 Data ethics and culture

Horizon	Action	Tools and artifacts
Short term	Engage with compliance, diversity and inclusion, corporate social responsibility and/or ESG teams and have the data charter recognized in their cadences and standards	• Data charter • Amended CSR/ESG plans • Amended code of conduct
	Leverage the exercise of assessing processes for data privacy, and identify possible areas in scope for data ethical risk	• Data ethics risk map
	Initiate a data ethics group to draft the company approach	• Data ethical standards • Data code of conduct
Medium term	Work with change teams to institutionalize projects' ethical points, as a moment in which ethical doubts are pressed and discussed	• Ethical addendum to change management methodology

(continued)

TABLE 10.4 (Continued)

Horizon	Action	Tools and artifacts
	Design and deliver data ethics training programme	• Data ethics training module
	Identify leading figures from the data ethics group and ask them to lead the creation of an ethical board, as a sounding board for ethical issues	• Ethical board terms of reference

To conclude, you might ask: why am I not prioritizing data analytics and visualization? My answer has sparked more than one robust debate at work and at data meet-ups, as many people I know feel strongly about being in control of the media that fulfils the consumption, as a tangible recognition of value created. First of all, data analytics and its most prominent part, data visualization, are of course essential, and, as mentioned in Chapter 2 describing the genesis of the data journey, they have frequently been established long before the 'need for data' is articulated company-wide, and, for our data athletes, it is always the finishing line they want to get to in the fastest, most accurate and most cost-effective manner (which is the ultimate goal of data excellence). However, maybe because I have experienced how easy it is to be pigeonholed in the marginal role of 'chief dashboard officer', whose value is measured by the number of dashboards delivered in a given unit of time, I would recommend that the DPT maintains an arm's length relationship with the world of visualization. This is a relationship whose emphasis should be taken away from the ostentatious cosmetic of the beautiful graph and focused instead on making that graph the most relevant, trustworthy and useful tool from which to derive value. A relationship that avoids situations like one when, many years ago, I was summoned to a 'priority one' issue call on a Friday night, because our web reporting tool was down, and the finance team could not complete the month-end process because the 'reconciliation engine' built on the tool was not accessible!

Thus, in the following chapters I will insist and prove that the value chain started with the capture of stories and then fed through a reliable operating model is the most important investment of time to deliver the right content that guarantees a positive return for our data athletes. The DPT gives them the moral boost, the training and the *products* they need to win in the competitive business arena, though they should never take their focus from the connection between good data and good decisions, which undoubtedly suitable visualization can be a catalyst for. However, nobody ever won a gold medal just because their shoes were the shiniest.

COOLING DOWN

- There are eight foundational capabilities that enable DeXOM' s success.
- The capabilities vary in name and scope, but their minimum viability is crucial.
- The DPT must make alliances and instil data in each one of them.
- Metadata management (aka data intelligence) is the most important sub-discipline to have the organization embrace.
- Data quality management must be kept very close to metadata and used for improving metadata too.
- Data protection and more specifically data sovereignty are not a burden but an opportunity to build a better process.
- The ethics of data is not another ethic, but rather a sub-discipline to prioritize which entails a change of lifestyle.
- Data visualization should not be the most prominent feature of the DPT's role.

Note

1 European Union. Regulation (EU) 2016/679 of the European Parliament and of the Council of 27 April 2016 on the protection of natural persons with regard to the processing of personal data and on the free movement of such data, and repealing Directive 95/46/EC (General Data Protection Regulation), 2016. eur-lex.europa.eu/eli/reg/2016/679/oj (archived at https://perma.cc/R9NK-GX88)

11

Data risks and control environment

WARMING UP

- Why is resilience important?
- What are the risks associated with data?
- How do you draw your data risk heatmap?
- What is an RCSA and how do you perform one?
- What are the three lines of defence for data risk management?
- What is control fatigue?

Introducing the concept of data risk

If you ask the best coaches to list the traits of a world-class performer, the word 'resilience' would undoubtedly make the top five. The determination to push through fatigue to keep improving, the fixation with the pursuit of an intent, and the unshakable conviction that somewhere there is still a drop of untapped energy to overcome an unbeatable adversary, are the characteristics that make champions. However, the true legends are capable of perfectly balancing their thirst for glory with the risks that they can take, an awareness of the personal limits that keep them grounded to provide assurance that nothing adverse spoils the moment they cross the finish line. Resilience is also the capacity to absorb a shock caused by unforeseen circumstances and to return as quickly as possible to optimal conditions, whether during a competition or owing to injury or accident.

This is the final lesson the DPT has to impart to their DA on changing the way change is done – that of data risk management. Here I would preface that, as in other sections, I am not going to pretend to condense the whole universe of risk management within this chapter. Instead, I would like to define or reprise the few concepts that are needed to support the specifics of data risk management that I am about to focus on.

Why define data risks? We mentioned in previous discussions that risk management is inherent to using data to create value and, as such, data risks need to be defined and mitigated. Let's remind ourselves of a few key points about risks and data:

- If digital products are made of data, exactly like any new product, there are risks connected to the raw material (sourcing of data), manufacturing (data processing), logistics (data storage) and usage (consumption of data).

- In Pillar I, I recommended that the DPT should seek alliances with the control functions – the data international Olympic committee – namely the risk or audit or safety team, depending on the industry. In the DPT's quest to prevent negative impact on the business, they should be made receptive to the potential risks coming from data.

- The data charter's principles can be read as a risk mitigation manifesto, whereby the data is potentially not governed, standardized, resilient, compliant or ethical.

- Data risk evaluations and mitigations are prescribed in the disciplines, distinct fields of data activities for the data athletes to get involved with. These include data management, data science, data protection and record management (see Chapter 5).

- The design and implementation of controls that are managing data risk is weaved stringently in the Data Excellence Operating Model 'sustain' phase.

I mentioned that the enterprise risk management (ERM) discipline is gaining ground in many industries other than just the financial services, as there is a common trend towards building resilience as a holistic ability. Operational, financial and commercial resilience are interpreted by investors, regulators and partners as a must-have strength in the conduct of a business. Understanding what the drivers of adverse events are and keeping them within a given 'acceptable tolerance' is the expectation of effective enterprise risk management, as zero risk exists only in the event of zero action, which is not exactly the mantra of a thriving business!

So, although in non-financial services organizations it is becoming more common to find risk officers, and to come across terminology like risk category, risk overseers, risk drivers and risk appetite statements and, of course, key risk indicators (KRI), we would not be properly performing our role as data personal trainers if we were not clearing the air of any possible ambiguity about the terms (see Figure 11.1). Hence, before going deeper into the field of risk management, let's consider data intelligence for a moment.

Equipped with a pill of risk knowledge, our clever DPT should make sure to leverage such an apparatus to the benefit of data excellence, and the first step is to propose to the risk officer, or their equivalent, to include a list of data risks in their taxonomy.

Different types of data risks

Similarly to the data domain model, there are many possible options available for classifying data risks and, just like the DDM, the taxonomy is destined to evolve over time as innovation and changes in data trigger new risk types. It is unlikely that the DPT will be able to instigate their own data risk framework in the absence of ERM, even in the embryonic phase; in my experience, this is an area in which the missing shelf effect is a show-stopper. However, if there is already a company risk taxonomy, it is very likely that it would be based on existing risk and control standards such as the ones from the Committee of Sponsoring Organizations or the National Institute of Standard and Technology, hence it would be good practice to map data risks accordingly.[1] Table 11.1 provides a starter-kit data risk taxonomy for the DPT to initiate their athletes to the topic. It is modelled on the definitions in Figure 11.1 and uses a common classification of risks as strategic, operational, compliance and reputational.

Data risk heat map

From our initial conversation with the risk officer, we should have managed to obtain a list of incidents (from the loss database) and we should have already used that list as a catalyst for the introduction of the data design authority in Chapter 9. If the list contains at least a couple of years of history and it reports an estimate of the losses incurred from the loss database, it is providing the basis for a further step to embed the notion of data risk. We should be able to determine the likelihood of the 'adverse event', as the probability in time that such an issue would materialize and its *impact*, the

FIGURE 11.1 Data risk nomenclature

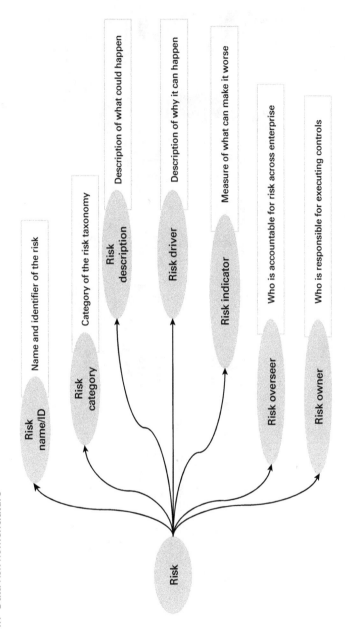

TABLE 11.1 Data risk taxonomy

Risk category	Risk name	Risk description	Risk driver	Risk indicator	Risk overseer	Risk owner(s)
Strategic risk	Insufficient value from data	The data strategy does not translate into actual value	Lack of senior management buy in	Total spend on digital transformation (including headcount)	CEO	Division lead
Operational risk	Inadequate data standards	Strategic initiatives are not completed on time or to budget, and don't deliver expected benefits	Data consumers are not considering data by design	Number of strategic initiatives requiring data	COO	Strategic initiative lead
Operational risk	Inadequate data intelligence	Decision making is clouded or impaired as data is inconsistent	Data domain owners are not in place or not effective	Number of reports or metrics created	COO	Data domain owners
Compliance risk	Breach of data regulation	Regulatory fines are imposed	Business is not aware of regulatory requirement	Number of regulations concerning data and digital	Legal counsel	Data leaders
Compliance risk	Data liability	Financial penalties are imposed	Data is over-retained or under-retained	Number of client requests	CFO	Data leaders
Reputational risk	Irresponsible usage of data	Harming individual rights or civil liberties	Data scientists use data regardless of their sensitivity	Number of digital products / AI model created	Chief AI officer	Data scientists
Reputational risk	Data loss	Leakage or corruption of sensitive data	Basic cyber hygiene is not followed	Quantity of data stored in non-enterprise grade solutions	CISO	Cybersec leaders

measurement of its negative effect on the organization and the wider ecosystem the organization is involved with (e.g. customer damage). Likelihood is usually measured in a simple discrete scale of values such as very likely, likely, possible, unlikely and rare, whilst for the impact a qualitative scale of materiality such as very low, low, medium, high and very high can be used. Likelihood and impact are then used as x and y dimensions to create a block graph with coloured areas representing a desirable or undesirable likelihood–impact combination of risk, as per Figure 11.2.

This seemingly crude graphic is actually a powerful tool in focusing the executive's attention, as once the DPT starts to plot the data risks, maybe initially just relying on his or her own professional judgement, the magnitude of the risks the company is really taking – most times unsuspectingly – is starkly revealed. Pain has a negative reinforcement in our memory as it binds to the experience that generated it to remind us not to repeat the same mistake. So, the first set of risks plotted should be linked to the history of the most damaging issues experienced so far, in the first person, by the organization or by peers in events that were 'too close to home'. A substantial data breach with potentially regulatory implications, or a publicly resounding blunder with a customer owing to poor data quality, are easily decontextualized and generalized, so should be the first ones pinned on the board. The rule is to focus on the data issue that could be linked to a defined data risk, at the beginning in its 'inherent' form, i.e. describing its risk potential if nothing is done to mitigate it. For instance, the risk of a data breach for a

FIGURE 11.2 Data risk heatmap template

		Very low	Low	Medium	High	Very high		
Very likely							Yellow	Orange
Likely							Green	Red
Possible								
Unlikely								
Rare								

company that continuously processes vast amount of data of a confidential nature using a variety of third parties should be assumed inherently 'very likely – very high'. With this example, if there is no experience of daily data incidents, then it is probably due to either effective existing controls (more about these in the following sections) or a copious amount of luck, which usually runs out at the worst possible moment!

The operational usage of Figure 11.2, the data risk heatmap, prescribes the plotting of individual *risk entries* under one of the risk names in the taxonomy above, to simplify the communication of the journey of the risk exposure mitigation. Operationally, in their data-training support and during the DeXOM circuits, the DPT should encourage their data athletes to start capturing what could go wrong in their performances and so initiating a *risk register*, recording the risk entries by risk name in the risk taxonomy, which will allow a more granular identification of responsibility and mitigation.

The data that can be captured in the risk register is ample, and its scope is proportional to the maturity of the risk management practices, so I just provide a simple example in Table 11.2 to highlight the relationship between the taxonomy above and the risk register.

Even in the absence of an exhaustive risk register, and using a 'gut feeling' approach, as early as possible I would streamline the communication for the top management by plotting the top 10 risks on the heatmap. As can be seen in Figure 11.3, the DA should be helped to identify firstly the position of the *inherent* risk (1), which, as discussed, is the gross risk; then they will project a position of the *residual* risk (2), which is the current evaluation of the risk exposure; and finally they will designate the risk appetite (3), which is the target level of acceptance of the risk. In the most mature (and usually regulated) firms, the risk appetite statement is the output of a specific process. Targeting such a level of fitness is subject to the data athlete's organization's strategic intention; however, it is still good practice for all other identified entries in the risk register for the overseeing person or function to formulate a worst-case impact hypothesis and to assess whether the materialization of that risk could pose a significant threat to the organization's resilience.

TABLE 11.2 Example of data risk register entry

Risk name	Risk entry ID	Entry title	Entry description	Affected process	Owner	Impact description	Frequency
Breach of data regulations	001	Missing access request process	Lack of a process to provide retail customers with on time response to their data access requests	Sales	Sales process owner	Customer complaints raised to regulator result in financial penalties	100 customer data access requests per month

FIGURE 11.3 Plotting inherent, residual and appetite for data risks

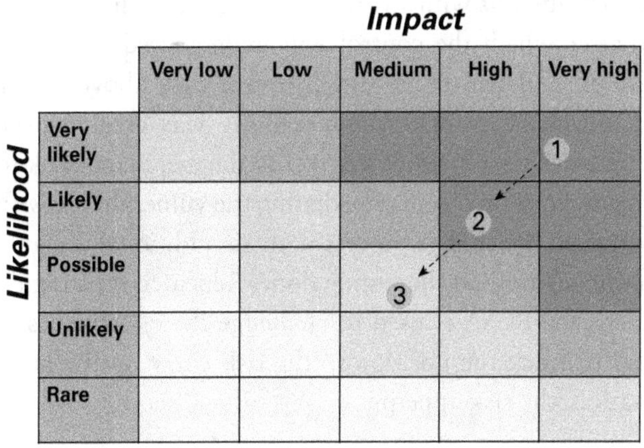

The risk and control self-assessment

In line with the nature of the Data Excellence Operating Model, practising the monitoring of risks is an organization-strengthening exercise that must be iterated cyclically in order to improve precision and effectiveness. The risk equivalent of the Data Excellence Operating Model – in its design, build and operate and maintain columns – is the risk and control self-assessment (RCSA), and the two perfectly dovetail. Assuming a pre-existing enterprise risk management approach, the RCSA should be an existing shelf already in force and that the DPT should be quickly able to adapt. We could think of it as the DevOps for risk management, as its aim is to establish a loop of risk assessment–control implementation–effectiveness measure–correction. The RCSA's ultimate outcome is for each owner of an entry in the risk register to perform an evaluation of the risk, then to assess whether the controls implemented (see control types in Chapter 7) with the mitigation plans are reducing the materialization of a risk in line with the heatmap position type 2, residual risk.

As part of the RCSA, the hypothesis that the controls are effective must be tested; the test is performed comparing the impact and likelihood assumptions with internal historical trends or market observations. For example, we assumed that the risk of a customer data breach in our web ordering system of a level serious enough to report to the regulator was once per year (likelihood = possible, impact = high). Instead, from our incident log we found out that we had two breaches (likelihood = likely). From this we can deduce that something has gone wrong. In general, whenever an issue points to a different heatmap positioning of the residual risk, we talk about control failure. As with any failure, a root cause investigation must be conducted, after which the control will undergo redesign to remove the cause of failure and will be re-tested. In our case above, we might have found that, during a change, a vulnerability was created exposing data when the customer session switched over to the merchant bank for the electronic payment. So, apart from remediating the vulnerability, we would also have strengthened the change process with an additional design review and pre-production signing off the testing done. Repeated on a regular basis, or at least yearly, the RCSA is used to challenge the effectiveness of existing controls and to track the position of the risk entry on the heatmap to its final destination, the risk appetite.

Data control effectiveness

What is the control environment for data and what is its purpose?

Control effectiveness is the measurement of the control ability to perform its nominal mission, given the distribution of eventuality the control might be subject to. From the three types of control examined in Chapter 7, preventative, detective and corrective, the effectiveness should tell us whether the controls are able to prevent, detect and correct as per the intention in the data consumer story. For instance, in the 'On-time delivery' consumer story (Chapter 9), it is clear that the anomaly report is strongly reliant on the completeness and timeliness of the ERP data extracts. So, we would expect that the controls that oversee the extraction job are effective, i.e. we have proof that the job is executed and that a checksum of the data in the extract validates the expected number of records, and crucially if the control detects missing records or invalid checksum, a corresponding action is taken by something or someone to correct the issue. The DPT can foster this effectiveness by creating an environment whereby a set of controls is continuously executed and monitored to guarantee 'stable data operations'. Following DeXOM, the DPT can help coach the data athlete during the design phase, so sufficiently 'chatty' controls are designed. A 'chatty' control is one that streams data while functioning, and that data supports the assurance of the effectiveness. Each subsequent sprint or initiative adds to the existing control set and expands the basis of control data, forming a control environment for data, that needs to be kept to a reasonable level of manageability, because as every DPT should know, the risk to contain here is *control fatigue*.

The concept of data control fatigue and its risk

Data control fatigue happens when the control degrades in its effectiveness not because of a failure of the controlling mechanism itself, but because of the failure of taking action when a control is triggered. In the case above, a failure of the control could be due to an improperly managed change: the data ERP data model has been changed, and as a consequence one of the columns is no longer appearing in the extracts, the checksum is not affected by the values in that column and the record count is still accounting for all the records, but the extract is not fit for purpose anymore. Control fatigue instead is akin to the long-term/short-term sigma shift that we learnt about in Chapter 7, but affects the controls that are supposed to prevent that very phenomenon. A typical example is the so-called 'four eyes' check, which is a two-stage set of controls when a first operator or agent would check something for its standard compliance and, given the critical nature of the item, a second check would then be performed by a second operator on the same control. Only if the two checks match, positively or negatively, is the control deemed to be successfully executed. Fatigue, in this case, would manifest with either of the operators becoming complacent with the other performing the check and banking on another set of eyes. Without particular feedback downstream, unwittingly the two operators could not only degrade the robustness of the check but also slip into a 'zero eyes' check whereby no real control is executed, and an issue would occur because there was no detection or prevention. The nature and the design of the control has not changed, but fatigue has affected it.

The following is an amusing, if thought-provoking, anecdote of an incident that happened years ago when I was still in IT. One of my peers was the IT lead for a regional division and their counterpart in the IT infrastructure team had implemented a change advisory board (CAB), a control formed by a group of people to decide whether a proposed change to one of the IT systems was properly executed. That meant that all members of the CAB group had to review the details of the change and then vote on whether to approve it, leading to the new change being implemented, hopefully without adverse consequences. After one particularly swift approval, the infrastructure lead began to suspect that my IT friend was not being sufficiently thorough in scrutinizing proposed changes before approving them, so he then decided to 'test' CAB group members. At the next change, in the form detailing the rationale for requesting the change, he sneakily added a few paragraphs detailing that at the end of implementation, all the servers be wiped of their data, the CPUs removed, the data centre wiped cleaned with bleach and the electricity switched off at the mains (or something equally flippant along those lines)! Of course, my unsuspecting friend approved the change without a single question or remark!

Another type of fatigue is connected with the 'chattiness' of the controls, as the amount of data we decided to generate has to be wisely distilled to avoid the control operators being overwhelmed or falling into analysis-paralysis. If our ERP extraction job control should produce adequate data to provide assurance about its effectiveness, such data has to be interpreted and offered in a simple digestible manner to the person that has to take an action if an issue is detected. The incorrect way of doing that would be to send a separate alert for each ERP's job with a long list of checksums and record totals with no substantial difference in format and emphasis between a 'good job completed' and an 'issue with a job'. The operator would quickly start to ignore the content and simply glance through the email, very likely missing the one that shows, buried under a lot of data, an issue has occurred. As with all interactions with our DAs, the DPT cannot rely just on good intentions. Rather, good change must be defended systemically, as the overall journey of being better is at stake.

Three lines of defence

Projecting on a wider ecosystem of data supply chains that are controlled to prevent risks, the traditional approach that is implemented to avoid control fatigue relies on an organizational structure called *three lines of defence*. Modelled like an old castle defence system, the idea is to have multiple concentric levels of defence to minimize the event of an attacker storming the castle, i.e. an issue occurring.

The first line is that level of the organization closest to the process at risk, the agent involved or overseeing the tasks being executed. In the case of data, the agent could be stewards processing customer data or a data scientist building pricing engines. The first line is responsible for the execution of the controls that have been designed specifically to mitigate one or many of the data risks, for example checking periodically that only the approved employees have access to the container of confidential data in order to avoid unwanted leaks.

The second line of defence is a systemic 'four eyes' check, which has the critical role of *assurance* and is formed by a group of people, most commonly in a control function like risk, compliance, quality or safety. Their role is to provide assurance that what is done by the first line conforms with expectations.

Finally, the third line is an independent reviewer, whether internal or external. They are a group that is not hierarchically or legally linked to the previous two lines and are effectively auditing their work.

The issue with this approach is not in its structure, but rather in its perceived cost and added bureaucracy. Money spent always weighs more painfully on your mind than the money you have avoided spending. So, no matter how loudly the risk heatmap shows the potential financial and reputational impact, an army of employees 'checking the checkers' is perceived as an affront to the lean and efficient model all companies want to emulate these days. In any industry where margins are squeezed, the former model is seen as simply unaffordable.

However, in reality there is a lot of merit in maintaining a certain segregation of duty between the processor and the controller. Allow me for a moment to intrude more in the life of the DA, though I promise it is going to be done with full attention to their privacy. As a smart DPT I need to think about how to make the DA in the first line of defence more effective without being on their back all the time. The answer from the world of health and fitness tech is to invent and deploy wearable devices, an instantaneous and effortless way of knowing whether my actions are within the parameters of my intention to stay healthy. Maybe I haven't got instantaneous feedback on what is going to happen to my weight if I eat that chocolate bar, but I can see if I have done enough exercise today or have been active or slept enough – all 'indicators' pointing to a reduction of a risk, e.g. cardiovascular disease, or performance improvement.

Data risk management and, arguably, enterprise risk management, need to undergo the same transformation. Controls should be designed in line with the process and should rely more on sensory data rather than on the operator checking a box in a parallel universe of controls. Exactly like quality controls, they need to be contextual and should have the effect of reducing the work of the second line of defence to a 'low touch' effort, based on metrics and indicators. Once again, the goal of a data-driven organization with very high data intelligence and the lowest possible data debt should yield the positive by-product of allowing exactly that. In such a *data nirvana*, the risk of unauthorized access to data is not mitigated by tediously long workflow requests with multiple levels of approval (four-eyes checked, for sure) and manual actuation of data policies that might be different by system. In a data-driven world, being authenticated to the network means that I know who my data athlete is, what their purposes are, what projects they are working on and therefore what data they need and at what level, and that is exactly what is provided to them. An effective data control environment based on high data intelligence supported by granular sensory data delivers the true democratization of data, while encoding the famous data governance in the fabric of the organization. The best data governance is the one you don't see!

COOLING DOWN

- Great athletes are resilient, and to be resilient you need to know how to take risks.

- Data risks are the risks to our data resilience.

- A taxonomy of data risk should be harmonized with the existing risk taxonomy.

- The data risk heatmap is useful to plot the journey from inherent, to residual, to appetite risk.

- RCSA and DeXOM go hand-in-hand in creating an effective data control environment.

- Data controls are subject to fatigue, especially if they are 'chatty'.
- The three lines of defence are an organizational way to minimize control fatigue, but they can be perceived as expensive.

Note

1 COSO: www.coso.org (archived at https://perma.cc/SF89-6KZP); NIST: www.nist.gov (archived at https://perma.cc/YEM5-X5C4)

Data Workout 2

DeXOM circuit workout

Having explained the different parts of the Data Excellence Operating Model, this data workout is designed for the aspiring DPT to experience a circuit workout based on the data consumer story ('On-time delivery improvement') in Chapter 9.

I have used the word 'circuit' a few times already in conjunction with DeXOM, and it was not by accident. Circuit training is a type of physical workout composed of a consecutive series of different types of exercises and resting periods. It is structured in such a way that the body is stressed in a comprehensive manner and is proven to have athletes achieving and maintaining an all-round fitness condition. That's exactly what DeXOM is intended to provide to our data athletes, with the additional benefit that the DeXOM circuit, together with improved data fitness (i.e. higher data intelligence and lower data debt), is also supposed to deliver the value associated with the data consumer story. So, this is training with a prize at the end of it.

In this workout we will use the data consumer story as training and will go step-by-step from requirement to sustain. To start, let's first jog our memory with the DeXOM structure shown in Figure DW2.1:

FIGURE DW2.1 Data Excellence Operating Model structure

Requirement

→ What outcome is to be achieved?

→ What value will be generated?

→ What data is needed?

→ Where is the data located?

→ How is it used and by who?

→ What are the applicable standards?

→ What are the compliance needs?

→ What is the current level of DQ?

→ What are the risks?

Design

Data design
→ Identification of auth. source
→ Identification of consumption point
→ Identification of referential
→ As is/to be data model design
→ As is/to be data flow design
→ Data quality rules design
→ Data risk and control design

Data plan
→ As is/to be gap assessment
→ Data debt evaluation

DDA go/no go
→ Resources are adequate to address data gaps

Build

Build
→ To be conceptual model
→ To be logical model
→ To be data flow

Data debt remediation
→ Reduction of data non-conformities

Data monitoring and controls
→ Build DQ rules
→ Build monitoring controls

Sustain

Delivery
→ Build completion is signed off
→ Data acceptance is signed off
→ Monitoring plan is signed off

DQ monitoring and issue management
→ Issue management is activated
→ Data quality rules are monitored

Data controls
→ Controls are executed
→ Test of effectiveness is performed regularly

Requirement

To start the workout, I have reproduced the data consumer story, with all the terms italicized that we should consider as important for the accomplishment of the story:

DATA CONSUMER STORY
On-time delivery improvement

As a logistics manager, I have been informed that our *customer's satisfaction index* has been impacted negatively by the timeliness for the delivery of our goods.

We have worked with our *shipping company* and have secured an optimal performance of their delivery process. However, we realized that our *delivery centre* is failing to include in the shipping list sent to the shipping company a complete list of all the goods to be shipped on the day. This is impacting the *delivery date* that was provided to the *customer*.

Therefore, I would like to ensure that our shipping list is as accurate as possible, and to do so I would like to be sure that at the daily shipping schedule's time of creation, all the goods with a *planned shipping date* of today are included in the list.

I think I need a report that compares the *shipping dates* coming from the ERPs (our factory systems) with the daily shipping schedule produced by the delivery centre system with all the items in the ERP that have the *planned good issue date* of today. Once I have that data, I would communicate every inconsistency with the *delivery centre* team to investigate and remediate within a service level agreement (SLA) of two hours that allows me to make the evening shipping company's pick up, as I would have missed the morning slot by then.

Critical success factors

- Delivery centre team are informed of the new process and supportive.
- All systems involved are adequately maintained and reliable.
- Shipping company performance is monitored and kept nominal.

An 'as is' information flow is shown in Figure DW2.2.

FIGURE DW2.2 'As is' information flow

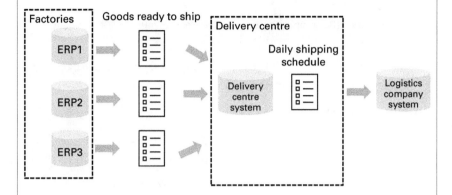

Data product(s) description

Data product: Shipping list anomaly report

The shipping list (SL) anomaly report compares the list of all goods appearing in the goods ready to ship (GRS) extracts from all ERPs and the daily shipping schedule (DSS).

A *shipping anomaly* is defined as follows:

- an item on the GRS combined list that does not appear on the DSS
- an item that appears on the DSS but not on the GRS
- an item that is on the GRS but with *a shipping date* different from present date
- an item that is missing or has an incomplete *product ID* or *customer ID*

The anomaly report should have the following dimensions to provide the delivery centre team with supporting information for their analysis and troubleshooting:

- by *product family*
- by *customer geography*
- by *plant ID*

Data quality standards

- *Timeliness:* The anomaly report should be produced every morning by 0800 local time.

- *Coverage:* The anomaly report must be performed on the GRS consolidated data including all the plants.
- *Completeness:* The shipping date in the GRS reports must be 100 per cent complete.
- *Validity:* The product ID should be a valid entry in the product ID list; the customer ID should be a valid entry in the customer ID list.

Data risk/data protection and privacy

- *Data minimization: Customer address* and other details that are shared with shipping company should not be included in the anomaly report.
- *Data security:* The anomaly report should be only available to the logistics manager.
- *Data retention:* The anomaly report should be retained for one month and then be disposed of.

Based on the above, we proceed to create a draft requirement document, i.e. a table with the details we extract from the data consumer, that we can use to engage the relevant data domain architects and data domain owners to initiate the design phase's first step in the creation of the standardized requirement document. In a real business environment, it might take a few iterations to have the data consumer finalizing their story (remember Socrates and his *maieutica*) and articulating what they really need to generate value. Although I maintain that it is good practice to have a sound understanding of the requirement coming from the story *before* engaging the data architects and domain owners, the DPT should find the right balance based on their athlete's attitude. Some of them will have an incredibly clear idea in their mind that just needs to be scribed, whereas others need whiteboarding collaboration and multiple iterations to crystallize the ambition in a story. A good DPT will adapt and support either way. However, in the latter case it may be more effective to interlace the story composition with the standardization of the requirement operated by the data domain architects and owners, though this might be perceived as less efficient for these oversubscribed experts, as it would be piecemeal instead of being dealt with in one go.

In this simulated circuit I assumed that the engagement has happened and a standardized requirement of all the elements relevant for the manufacturing of the story's data products has been finalized. Although most of the consumer story's terms do not belong to the logistic data domain, given that the anomaly report (the requested data product), is strictly pertaining to the logistic team, the logistic data domain architect has been chosen to lead the design work with the identified data domain owners. Again, as in the ontology game in Chapter 8, the absolutely right fit does not exist, and the DPT, or better still the data design authority, should monitor the exercise and potentially recommend a different lead or a co-lead if progress is not satisfactory. Nevertheless, in this simulated circuit the logistics data domain architect has swiftly confirmed or amended the initial information such as proper operational definition, criticality of the business term toward the outcome, the sources of authority and the expected versus current level of data quality. In order to contain the exercise within a manageable word count and still give you the full experience of the DeXOM circuit, I had to make some simplifying assumptions:

- I reduced the number of data requirement columns from the recommended list in Chapter 9.

- I assumed that the existing reports, e.g. goods ready to ship, have already been defined in previous stories and that as the data they contain is not explicitly mentioned in this story, this does not have any influence on the outcome.

- I excluded the possibility that current data quality levels are affected along the data flow, i.e. there no loss or gain of quality from the ERPs to the shipping company system, which, as any DPT would know, is not the typical pattern, but gives us a simplified data control plan.

- I postponed the full data debt evaluation to Data Workout 3, as we will be better equipped conceptually after having gone through Pillar III: value.

Therefore, the standardized data requirement document is as seen in Table DW2.1.

The data cardio sessions performed with the data domain owners affected some of the terms. For instance, the *committed delivery date* was chosen, as there are multiple terms that refer to a delivery date, whereas others such as *plant* have been more precisely identified as, in this case, *plant ID*. Finally, the logistics data domain owner recommended that the entry in the anomaly report itself be defined as a business term, the *shipping anomaly*, and they promoted the description provided by the data consumer as the operational definition of the term.

TABLE DW2.1 Standardized data requirement document

Data requirement document						
Data consumer story	On-time delivery improvement					
Department	Logistics					
Actor	Logistics manager					
Revision	1.0					
Date	Oct 24th, 2025					
Term name	Operational definition	Criticality	Data domain	Source of authority	DQ tolerance	DQ current
Customer ID	An alphanumeric code that uniquely identifies the customer of the company	Medium	Third party	Customer master	is complete = 100% is valid =100%	95% complete 100% valid
Customer (name)	An individual or organization engaged in a commercial transaction with a company (goods or services)	Medium	Third party	Customer master	is complete = 100%	100% complete
Customer address	The physical location of the customer, which they expect their good to be delivered to. Composed of a street address, a postcode, a city and a country name	High	Third party	Customer master	is complete = 100% is valid >95%	98% complete 96% valid
Customer satisfaction index	A measure of the customer's satisfaction with the goods or service quality rendered by the company	Low	Third party	Customer master	N/a	N/a

TABLE DW2.1 (Continued)

				Reference data system		
Customer geography	A set of groups of countries numbered from one to six which every customer is assigned for reporting and account management convenience	Low	Third party	Supplier master	is complete >90% is within [1..6] = 100%	70% complete 100% valid
Shipping company	A company that provides transport to move goods from a sending address to a delivery address	Low	Third party	Supplier master	N/a	N/a
Delivery centre (ID)	An alphanumeric code that uniquely identifies the place in which the company stores goods waiting to be shipped to customers or to other company locations	Medium	Logistics	Real estate DB	is complete = 100%	100% complete
(Committed) delivery date	The date of the delivery of goods that is communicated to the customer on confirmation of their order	High	Logistics	Logistics DB	is complete = 100% is a date in the future = 100%	95% complete 98% valid
Planned shipping date	The latest date by when a product should be shipped to the customer to arrive on or before the delivery date	High	Logistics	Logistics DB	is complete = 100% is future date = 100%	90% complete 100% valid
Product family	An entry in the taxonomy of the company products that uniquely identifies a group of products with similar functions or features	Medium	Product	Product master	is complete = 100%	50% complete

(continued)

TABLE DW2.1 (Continued)

Product ID	An alphanumeric code that uniquely identifies the product unit sold by the company	Medium	Product	Product master	is complete = 100%	95% complete
Plant (ID)	An alphanumeric code that uniquely identifies the production plant of the company	Medium	Supply chain	Real estate database	is complete = 100%	100% complete
Planned goods issue date	The date successive to the day the product manufacturing and packaging process is completed and potentially ready to be shipped	High	Supply chain	ERP system	is complete = 100%	95% complete
[New] shipping anomaly	Defined as a unit of product that is listed: – on the GRS list but not on the DSS – on the DSS but not on the GRS – on the GRS but with a planned shipping date different from present date – missing in either the GRS or the DSS or having an incomplete product ID or customer ID	High	Logistics	To be identified	is not measured yet	Not available

As expected, the data consumer had high expectations about the data and that is reflected in their stated tolerances almost invariably at 100 per cent. Where possible, a review of the current yield of the data quality has been performed, and it would be later used to gauge the viability of the story.

Design

With the standardized data requirement provided, the logistics data domain architect sets out the production of the data design document, which I report below in a mock-up form.

DATA DESIGN DOCUMENT

Data consumer story: On-time delivery improvement

Domain architect lead: Logistics DDA

Data domain architect support: Third party, supply chain, product

Date: 4/11/2024

Version: 2.1

Document structure:

1 Conceptual model.

2 Logical model.

3 Data flows.

4 Data quality rules and controls.

1. Conceptual model

(N.B. In Figure DW2.3, for ease of reading, I had to omit the relationship descriptor from each line connecting the different concepts, which would express the relationship in the typical triplet form concept–verb–concept. That descriptor is quite important when the model is physically built as it will encode the data intelligence contained in the consumer story. For example: a plant receives a customer order which has a product ID, and the customer order has a committed delivery data, etc.)

The conceptual model in Figure DW2.3 has been defined and agreed with the data domain owners of the third party, logistics, product and supply chain data domains. All the terms have been grouped in their respective domains. The terms in the grey boxes are modified or ancillary terms (i.e. not directly part of the story's requirement but necessary to the modelling) and the terms in the black boxes are the new terms. The model is being built using the company's modelling tool and, as part of the production change release, should become effective in the company's data intelligence repository.

2. Logical model

(As the logical model is the crucial step to connect the data consumer story and the physical representation of the data within the data flow, in this exercise we will model only the new concept that the story is relying on as a conduit to the next intended action: the shipping anomaly)

The logical model in Figure DW2.4 shows the structure of the new identified concept, the shipping anomaly, and its dependency on other concepts in the story.

Note: The model includes the dimensions required by the data consumer in order for the secondary consumer of the information, the delivery centre team, to triage the anomaly: by plant, by customer and by product.

For the sake of model completeness, some of the ancillary terms had to be expanded (e.g. order).

3. Data flows

The data flow diagram (Figure DW2.5) describes the systems involved in the processing and delivery of the data that allows the logistics manager to obtain a shipping anomaly report. It is a flow that physically closely follows the logical model structure. It has also identified that the best source to produce the shipping anomaly report from is the logistics DB, which is also declared as the source of authority for the shipping anomaly concept. The shipping anomaly report is the place where all the data needed to curate the anomalies is collected.

4. Data quality and controls

The data flow diagram has been used to overlay the data quality checks and controls that address the quality expectations and risk concerns raised in the story. As per the legenda in the data flows:

- An *encryption* of the data process is recommended for the customer and supplier data transferred respectively to the ERP for the processing of the order and to the delivery centre system for transacting with the shipping company.

FIGURE DW2.3 Conceptual model

Product domain
- Product ID
- Product family

Supply chain domain
- Plant ID
- Customer order
- Production time
- Planned good issue date

Logistic domain
- Delivery centre (ID)
- Shipping anomaly
- Planned shipping date
- Committed delivery date

Third party domain
- Customer (name)
- Customer satisfaction index
- Customer address
- Customer geography
- Customer ID
- Shipping company (name)

FIGURE DW2.4 Shipping anomaly logical model

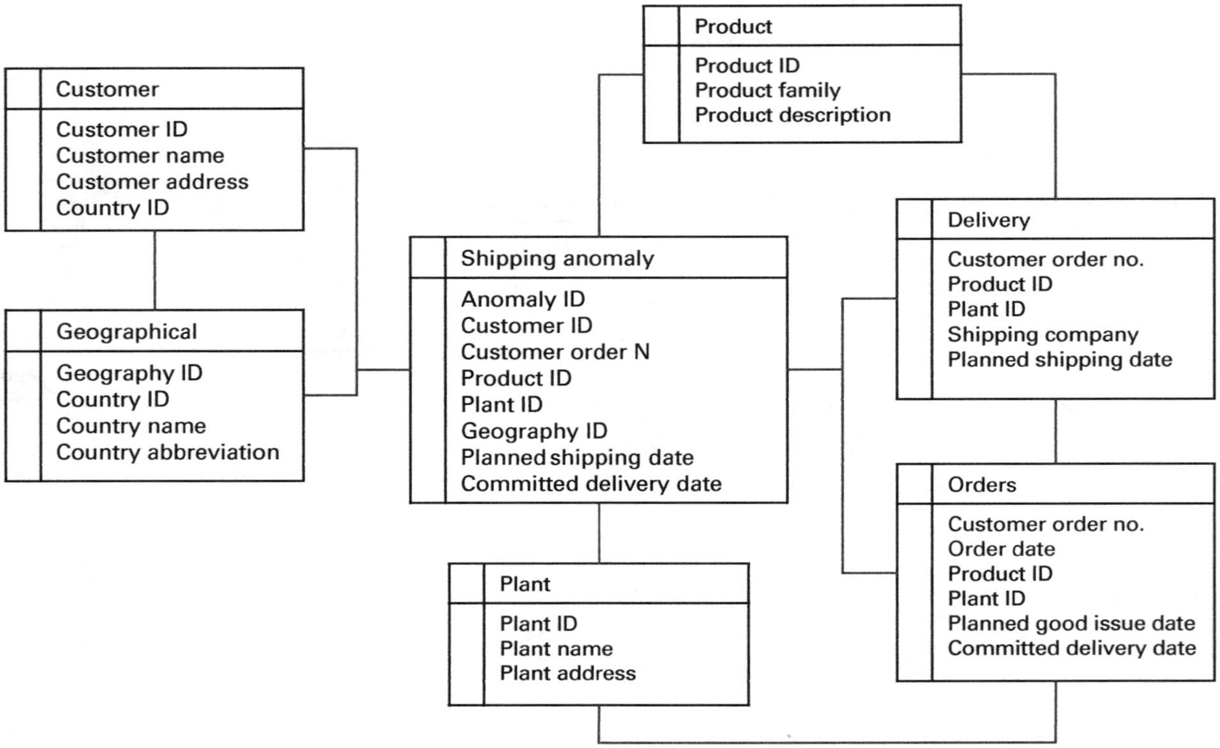

FIGURE DW2.5 Data flow

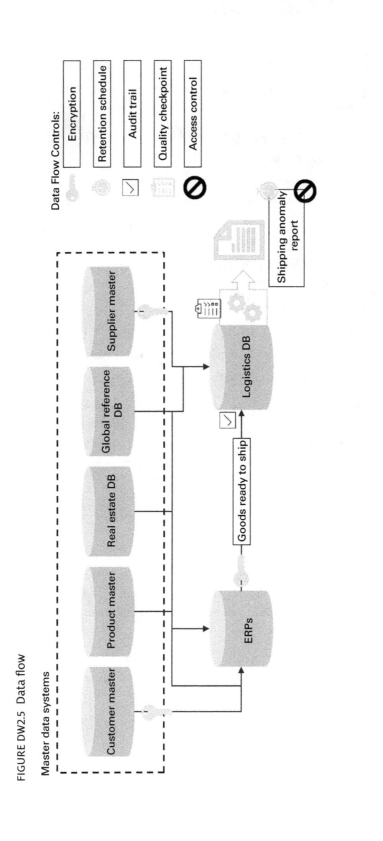

Master data systems

Data Flow Controls:
- Encryption
- Retention schedule
- Audit trail
- Quality checkpoint
- Access control

Customer master

Product master

Real estate DB

Global reference DB

Supplier master

ERPs

Logistics DB

Goods ready to ship

Shipping anomaly report

- A *retention* schedule of one month is set on the shipping anomaly report.

- An *access control* that restricts the visibility of the report to the sole logistics manager is prescribed.

Finally, as data quality pertains, the following data quality controls are defined:

- Audit trail goods ready to ship:

  o The number of files received by delivery centre systems must be one per plant, and cover all plants as per real estate DB plant list.

  o The files must be received by 0800 local time every working weekday.

  o The sum of all the ERP records of goods with planned shipping date = today() must be equal to sum of records in all goods ready to ship files delivery centre DB.

- Shipping anomaly data quality:

  o Must have geographical ID complete and between 1 and 6.

  o Must have plant ID complete and validated vs real estate DB.

  o Must have product family complete and validated vs product master.

The above controls are expected to be added to the delivery centre system operations and monitored by the delivery centre team. In the absence of other changes to the above environment, a test of effectiveness of the prescribed controls must be executed at least once a year.

Build

Depending on the inherent risk or strategic materiality of the exercise, as defined and shown in the portfolio assessment exercise (Data Workout 1), the data design document might be subject to further scrutiny before proceeding to the build phase. In fact, the DPT might want to configure three possible outcomes:

1 *Self-certified*, similar to the 'fit to execute' in Data Workout 1. Given the overall data fitness of the involved parties and the relatively low risk of the exercise, the data domain architect is empowered to proceed to build phase.

2 *Peer reviewed*, a more uncertain scenario. Maybe the matter is of high complexity, affects multiple domains with low data intelligence, or involves sensitive data in sensitive processes, so it is recommended that another architect should provide an independent assessment of the design, which will then be signed off by both architects.

3 *DDeA reviewed*. In high-risk scenarios the data design authority should perform a review and potentially suggest changes to the approach, different sourcing of data or additional controls and recommendations which will be then verified at the end of the build phase.

For our simulated circuit, there is no need for a peer review or a full data design authority assessment and the design is transferred to the delivery team for the build phase, which is the one that sees our data athlete involved the least. So, for the sake of this exercise, we assume that the build has been completed and delivered as per the design document. Notably, the delivery *must include* the data intelligence uplift, which is effectively the publishing of the data models and data flows inclusive of the representation of the data quality rules and the controls in the data intelligence repository. The other critical delivery is the reduction in data debt that, as previously mentioned, we will practise in depth with Data Workout 3.

Sustain

The closing stage of the exercise is the sustain phase, which from a pure DeXOM point of view I simplify in a workout checklist. It is in fact a moment of reflection and mindfulness that confirms what has been gained, makes us consider what has been missed and sets the data athlete up to maintain the achieved results. It is the phase in which the agents involved in the (now) active story would have been trained to use the data they require and start to measure the expected value, in this case the increase of customer satisfaction with the punctuality and precision of the delivery.

In the spirit of the data charter, we make this a moment of resilience for data, formalizing the achievement and the commitment in a simple sustain checklist for the data consumer, data domain architect and potentially the data design authority to sign off (Table DW2.2).

TABLE DW2.2 Sustain checklist

1. Have all the necessary artifacts been satisfactorily completed?	☐
Yes, the artifacts completed and signed off are: *1) Data consumer story* *2) Standardized data requirement document* *3) Data design document* *4) Data debt remediation* *5) Test plan* *6) Change approval board minutes* *7) Post release maintenance schedule*	
2. Have all the data models been completed and published?	☐
Yes, conceptual, logical and physical model changes are in production.	
3. Has the data debt been assessed and minimized?	☐
Yes, the data debt associated to data that was critical to the delivery of the story has been identified and reduced within the data consumer's tolerance.	
4. Have all data risks been identified and mitigated?	☐
Yes, no further risk than the ones identified in the data consumer story have been identified. The controls recommended in the design have been deployed and tested for effectiveness. Control owners have been assigned and trained.	
5. Have monitoring and issue management processes been defined and activated?	☐
Yes, the details of the change have been added in the issue management portal, the handover of monitoring and issue management with the delivery centre ops team has been completed. The data consumer has agreed the SLA.	
6. Was the expected value achieved?	☐
[This is the crucial question, and an accurate measure might only be obtainable after a period of observation. The good DPT will set a reminder to revisit the circuit and answer the question. In this case we assume that this question has been answered further down the line.] *After 6 months an increase from 3.3 to 4.0 (on a scale of 1 to 5) of customer satisfaction with the delivery has been measured.*	
8. Data design authority (if applicable)	☐
No DDeA review was necessary	

This concludes our DeXOM circuit training, so you can relax now.

Generating (and sustaining) value

12

The productization of data

WARMING UP

- Can data be a product?
- How can a data product make our data athlete better?
- What are the challenges in adopting data productization?
- How does portfolio management have to change in order to accommodate data products?
- How do you maintain data products?

Can data be a product?

It's all about value

The end of the beginning of your journey through the tenets of data excellence is approaching, as we enter Pillar III: value. My hope is that by now a certain anticipation has been established as to how the DPT will be able to unlock value. As data leaders, we have pored over the statistics, so we are all too aware of the dangers of flying too close to the burning sun of digital and AI. Many have met the same fate as the mythological Icarus. After trying at length to harness such vast potential energy, they have failed to create any tangible value and so reputations have taken a fall. So, this part is dedicated to overcoming the third macro challenge mentioned in Chapter 1, which concerns the general lack of robust business cases. The example of the requested dashboard delivering value by displacing a few hours of Excel work by paid employees, mentioned in Chapter 1, is more common than you might think. Weak business cases not only fail to identify the right balance between better data and more value, but are also frequently hampered by data consumers' approach to data, whereby the data is either perfect or unusable. Having gone through the mindset preparation of our data athlete and then laid the foundation of a training methodology that takes care of the data fitness, we should be ready to produce a performance that delivers value. But first I would like to further expand on the notion of the data product, as this is central to the improvement of business cases and value creation.

What is a data product?

From the Latin *producere*, to bring forth, to give rise to or, even better, to bring into being, this is undoubtedly one of the most distinctive human traits. Since the beginning of time, we have been crafting the world around us, continuously making new objects, conceiving of and creating products that we hope will make our lives better. Everything around us was once thought and then designed, manufactured (which literally means 'made by hands') and, of course, given or sold to someone for their advantage. You use kitchen implements, as opposed to picking raw food and biting it, to absorb nourishment in a more convenient form, by slicing and cooking. You have a car to get to places faster than walking, and so on – it is fair to say the entire world is made of products that are used to deliver a certain value.

Data is a product

So, can data be a product? In Table 12.1, we analyse what a product is and then check whether data fits the identikit.

TABLE 12.1 Data as a product

A product is...	And so data can...
conceived to satisfy an existing or presumed need	be defined by thinking about the type of users that could benefit from it
designed for a specific purpose	be made functional to a specific domain or usage
expected to generate an outcome	be used to generate value, informed actions or decisions
crafted out of raw materials or made of parts	be made of different elements and exists in very complex structures

(continued)

TABLE 12.1 (Continued)

A product is...	And so data can...
manufactured following a manned or unmanned process	be processed manually or automatically
certified to comply with regulations	be protected and assured to comply with regulations
bought or sold	be monetized
improved overtime	have its quality and standards improved in a continuous fashion
phased out for obsolescence	be disposed of when it has lost its value

I think we can positively conclude that data can be treated as a product, so let's understand now why that is important from a value point of view and, especially, what role the DPT plays in *data productization.*

Why it is important to treat data as a product

In the previous part, inspired by the Agile development framework, we introduced the Data Excellence Operating Model as a methodological framework to train the data athlete in taking care of data at critical moments of change, thus increasing their data fitness. However, beyond physical fitness, what distinguishes a champion from an amateur is the appropriate adoption and use of technical gear. If data and sport demand that the best decisions are made at peak levels of fitness, with a strong mindset (Pillar I) and following the right training (Pillar II), then what makes those decisions the winning ones – and therefore the guarantor of best value – is the use of a data product tailored to their needs.

It is true that the ancient Greek athletes used to race naked to prove to the Gods their physical prowess. However, the same technological advances that brought to us a myriad of new products became a vector of performance enhancement during the modern Olympiad. Very few of the best runners today would win running barefoot. One notable exception is Ethiopian athlete Abebe Bikila, who won gold at the 1960 Rome Olympics by running the marathon wearing no shoes!

We now have all the cards in our hands with which to close the chasm between business cases and true value from data: cultural transformation, an operating model for change and the productization of data.

How to develop data products

Agile product development

A product is made of features – distinct characteristics that are useful for the user and might be rated by different users with different levels of usefulness. Imagine that you are designing a new Swiss Army knife so you asked different users to list of the ten tools they would like to have in the knife. Different users will give you a different list, but each have a potential benefit in mind for each tool.

In Chapter 9 we learnt that the Agile product development approach replaces long periods of development with a series of sprints that are supposed to produce complete features and deliver the best product for the user that gave the story, including the user in the development loop, and adjusting the prioritization of features and even the story based on user feedback. In our hypothetical case of a new Swiss Army knife, the main concept of the story would be the 'multiple utensils in a pocket' nature of the product. The user could be delivered a first *prototype* in the form of a wooden mock-up with a few of the tools in the list – a knife, screwdriver and maybe a little a wrench, with a simple folding and unfolding mechanism. The user would then be able to gauge whether the dimensions are appropriate for the tool to fit in a pocket and will have a good picture of the number and type of utensils available. Of course, the prototype would not be of any practical use yet as a wooden knife can't cut many things, but it would be enough to decide whether to proceed to the next step. The next iteration delivers what is called the *minimum viable product* (MVP) and, as it suggests, this iteration is a finished good that delivers the core of the functionality that the user was interested in. Therefore, it is something that could be of value for the user, which could be traded for a price. This would be a fully finalized tool with at least one knife blade of good-quality steel that folds perfectly. So, even if the development of the product stopped there, the user would still have a viable product for use when outdoors. From here it is easy to imagine the next iterations that would add multiple tools from the list or even produce a different version of the product with a different list of utensils to satisfy multiple users.

Agile data product development: From story to product

Now let's transpose this case to data. Where do we start? From a data consumer story of course, that is where we find what our user/customer/

data athlete wants to achieve with the data, in effect providing us with the product features that we should assemble for them, thus allowing them to express their fitness to the fullest. We have already used the logistics manager story extensively in previous chapters, and focused narrowly on a simple use case on purpose because we want to demonstrate certain details of DeXOM. In that case, the product delivered was the shipping anomaly report. To demonstrate the true agility of data and how an Agile sprint would work, I am going to select a broader and more high-level story, which is called an epic. An example of this is:

> As a pricing manager I need to analyse the leads of the company to optimize my pricing strategy.

Without even going into too much detail, in the sentence above there is a clear data product identified, the *leads* of the company, as the potential commercial deals that could be closed with prospects or existing customers, and a first hint of the intended value – the optimization of the pricing strategy. In fact, at a very macro level, you could look at the concepts that helped us define the first pass of the data domain and identify the set of data corresponding to those concepts as data products. Indeed, you could perform the test 'Is data a product?' here, and for each one of the questions the answer would be a yes. Even assuming that the concept of leads is completely new and there has been no exercise to improve the data intelligence around the sales process (thus making the data debt effectively unknown), we could offer the pricing manager a first prototype of the data product as an Excel spreadsheet, provided by the laptop of one of the more knowledgeable sales representatives. The starting gun of our epic has been fired and a sequence of DeXOM cycles can be applied to successive data consumer stories in refining the data product, augmenting features like:

- authoritativeness: moving from multiple Excel spreadsheets to a proper record system
- coverage: making sure that all the leads of the company are recorded in the system
- quality: ensuring that all the leads have the minimum required data
- dimensionality: adding 'by customer type', 'by quarter', 'by region', et cetera

The quantity and quality of features developed for the data product, as with sports technology, will evolve with the increased ability of the athlete to understand their performance limits and then to push through them with proper coaching and improved training. In our data analogy, with the increased number of circuits the data athlete refines their attitude to the value that is delivered by better data intelligence and lower data debt.

If you have followed and agree so far, I am sure that whoever has tried implementing Agile behaviours in their practices will start having painful flashbacks about workplaces that overnight declared themselves as 'agile'. Such workplaces ended up implementing what I've heard described as 'frag-ile' – a half-baked practice where expectations of speedy delivery bypassing requirement and design phases are soon disappointed. I am aware that if your environment is still working in *Waterfall* (the approach using programmes of works with a start and an end data), productization of data seems like an impossible double (Agile *and* data) somersault. The fatal flaw in establishing Agile practice is very often the failure to establish resilient 'squads', the teams dedicated to the development of products. In the description of the DevOps transition above, it was already implicit that the two teams that merged become completely dedicated to the entire continuous process, so much so that the icon used to denote DevOps is usually a Moebius strip, symbolizing an infinitely recurring loop. To any leader wanting to transition to Agile, one should explain that of the three people in their operations who are managing a nice stable process, they should assume that at least one is no longer dedicated to that stable process and is instead involved in developing a product on a permanent basis. With this foreknowledge some of those leaders would probably have cold feet about the transition.

Scaling data productization

So, what should the DPT do to establish data productization? Once more it flows from the strategic intent found in the strategic portfolio, where we originally identified the subset of projects with dependency on data (though in practice if you look closer, the ones that do not depend on data are the exception). Then we assessed the fitness of the teams executing them and made a choice of which projects to focus our attention first. We would then have followed DeXOM and initiated the gathering of data consumer stories, then go to the data requirement. At this very point it is important that our acquired data intelligence serves us in performing the next step. The DPT must find the resources to build the logical network described in Figure 12.1. This network is my view of a starting seed for data productization, as from the first cluster of projects the DPT has to encourage their athlete to look

FIGURE 12.1 From data project to data products

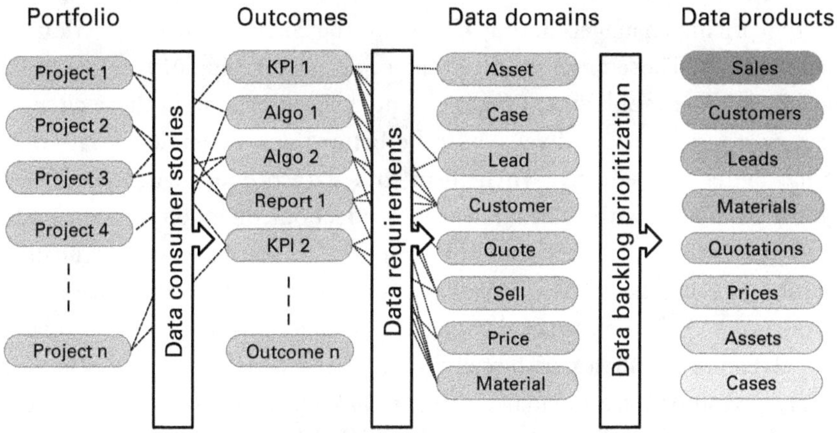

Portfolio	Outcomes	Data domains	Data products

across the set and find commonalities. These commonalities from the data consumer stories are going to be the terms and crucially the outcomes, hereby represented by reports, KPI or, even AI models (aka algorithms).

When broken down into data elements belonging to the different data domains by the requirement phase in DeXOM, it should be simple enough to start to identify structures that, properly clustered in that specific domain, would form our proto-data-products. Based on the *popularity* of a specific data product, as the data product that is more used or in demand by multiple data projects, the priority of the overall backlog of the backlogs is defined (noting that each data product should also have its own priority of backlogs).

Inception phases are hard, and at the very beginning this will be felt by all the data athletes, just like going to the gym and exercising for the first time but with the additional pain of feeling that the exercise doesn't result in a final product. Why? The DPT will need to deal with a data consumer used to specifying a report and to receiving that report after a given time. Instead, the DPT will need to explain that they will receive a first version of that same report, covering maybe only a third of their country market scope. Later, they will be delivered another version with better customer data quality, and maybe much later 95 per cent of what they are asking for. This is the time to pinpoint an MVP from the story, and to show our data athlete that it's better to make an earlier step towards their intention with a first pass of their racing gear, rather than idling and waiting for the perfect outfit. If the data consumer story is not enough, there is always some external factor that might pressure your data consumer into accepting a first version of the product, as long as it is delivered faster. Think about our logistics manager or the pricing manager during Covid or the Suez Canal obstruction of March 2021. Those crises required the rapid prototyping of measures and insight to react rapidly to an unprecedented situation, and in those circumstances a fast partial answer would be better than a completely late one. What better occasion to switch them to a data product? An issue like a global pandemic, with its dramatic shock effect on commodity prices, could help to set up the first 'raw material' data product, used to monitor the fluctuation of purchasing costs to make timely adjustments to the price of the goods sold. Or in the case of the logistics manager post the incident in Suez Canal, facing the nightmarish scenario of rerouting deliveries and cancelled or delayed shipping, a squad dedicated to making the 'delivery' data product a repository of all the deliveries with SLA hits by a different shipping company could be another seed of growth. No matter the starting point, once we have the first squads focused on providing some of our athletes with the best products for their endeavours, the DPT should drive the creation and promotion of a reusage virtuous circle.

How data productization enables value

With the DeXOM truly followed, especially for the sustain phase, our data fitness improves, and with better data intelligence and lower data debt the sports gear ready to be used in the various competitions (the data products) should grow in variety and maturity. Going forward, each new data consumer story should not be seen as an isolated exercise of increased innovation but rather analysed through the perspective of data product reuse. This is *the* best value promise we can offer to our data athlete: the pursuit of data excellence – from the data charter to the Data Excellence Operating Model – reduces time and cost to value. In our epic about leads, it is plain that the consumer will need more than leads to make their analysis – they might need to cross-check a successfully closed lead with the customer data, and perhaps analyse the time it took to produce the quote and the discount that was applied. So, being able to leverage work that was previously performed to, for example, improve the customer market segment, or consolidate all the orders that have been fulfilled in all the various systems, instead of going through multiple requirements, design and build phases, would allow the pricing leader to test their hypothesis earlier and at a lower cost.

How can that be replicated and scaled? The requirement drawn from the data consumer stories should identify a combination of different products. Some will be products reused as is, others will be products to be enhanced, while others will be products created anew. Such prescriptions are not easy for our data athlete to swallow, especially if we are pushing them to reuse. The choice of reusing a product, instead of having one custom made, is based on the trust of functional equivalence, i.e. the reused product is as good as if not better than the one the data consumer is requesting to be built. I am sure Usain Bolt would not be happy reusing someone else's running shoes. However, trust is predicated on good data, and once you have transitioned away from data-reactive organization status towards data-training status, this is when the data intelligence that we are accumulating in the central repository should start to pay dividends.

At this point, bringing in the data domain owners to opine on the requirements, a thorough search for reusage should be performed by the data domain architects to offer their data consumers opportunities for reuse. In fact, the data debt assessment step described in Chapter 9 should include the reusability assessment. The benefits of this are so significant that the DPT should mandate that the architect's assessment, which will inform the design phase, should propose reuse first, modification second, and only design for creation of a new data product when strictly necessary, as we are breaking new data intelligence ground. In this push, the data domain owners that have completed their training and are at full maturity would almost naturally slip into the shoes of the data product owner. This is the person or body that decides the overall development strategy of the product and consequently the prioritization of the backlog of each product. They choose, for example, whether to increase the coverage, add functionality or fix certain issues first.

Thus, in practical terms, when adopting a data product approach, it is no longer enough to oversee the execution of different initiatives run independently, although it is still crucial to guarantee certain expectations of the development performance, such as efficiency, delivery on time and to budget. Instead, leading a data excellence portfolio becomes a much more dynamic and holistic mechanism that aligns multiple development flows to the moment in time that certain requirements are met, as per Figure 12.2.

The top of Figure 12.2 depicts the usual view of a *project* portfolio with timelines we would normally associate with gates like 'end of build' and 'test and roll out', together with actual versus planned spend and resource

FIGURE 12.2 Managing a product portfolio

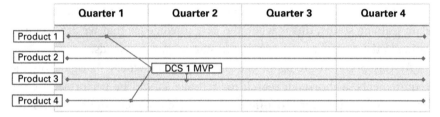

utilization. The overall portfolio would ultimately guarantee that a company's investment delivers on promises and supports management in deciding what investment is at risk or how to prioritize a new project in case of saturated capacity. The goal for the *product* portfolio is the same, but here there are continuous flows of delivery that, assembled together, deliver a certain requirement. DeXOM is still the fundamental how-to, but now the full data consumer story might be fulfilled at different stages, so data consumer story 1 (DCS1) achieves its MVP only in quarter 2 when a specific sprint of product 3 is completed, even if the product 1 and 4 dependencies had already been fulfilled.

As in many other parts of data excellence, here too there is room to leverage advanced tools, (i.e. AI). The latest advancements in generative and, more fittingly, causal intelligence, with a good level of data intelligence to start from, could deliver a good first pass of the opportunities for reuse and interdependencies between stories. This is what the architects could use as a convincing basis to gain acceptance to reuse data products from their data consumers.

Having gone through the establishment of data productization as the enabler of value, we are now ready to move to the item of cost. The value realization, like the performance of the data athlete, is something that the DPT does not contribute to directly: the DPT is an enabler and, although the DPT and DAs are part of the same organization, it is unlikely that the

DPT or their teams will be the ones using the data to directly produce the value, just as it is equally unlikely that a personal trainer would run the marathon on behalf of their trainees. However, final realized value must be weighted in relation to the cost that went into its creation. The DPT has a key role in understanding and optimizing that cost to maximize the net benefit to the company, and that is what we are going to focus next: in essence, was that worth it?

COOLING DOWN

- A product is made to be used, and its usage brings value to someone.

- Data can be likened to a product.

- A data product is for the data athlete and is a crucial enhancer of their performance.

- The data consumer stories, or the data epics, define the data products and their features.

- The orchestration of the data portfolio is key to switching to proper data productization.

- Product reuse means lower cost and time to insight, but it is difficult.

- The data domain owners are product owners of the data products in their domain.

13

Value from data

When the data athlete is at their best

WARMING UP

- How do we fund data products?
- How do we evaluate data products?
- How does the DPT support the perfect business case?
- What is the best approach to reduce the data debt and keep it low?

The importance of the funding model

To properly delve into the final part of our voyage in the setting up of data excellence, it is important that we discuss the other cornerstone of all business endeavours: funding. As a digital neo-humanist, I naturally see the first cornerstone as the people, the new roles, hence the new expectations in terms of actions towards data were discussed extensively above. Now that we have gone through data productization and before we solve the riddle of the data business cases, we want to understand how we fund the transition to data products. The complexity of the funding is of course proportional to the complexity of the organization. A single-entity, single-country, single-currency, domestic-market-only company would have a simpler solution and an easier transition than a multinational corporation. Nevertheless, I will provide you with some financial essentials directly related to the management of investments in companies, to illustrate what type of set up can be put in place to enable data excellence from a resourcing point of view.

Allocating investments

Essential to the portfolio management process is the allocation of an investment. You can liken the portfolio management office to your fund manager, providing the intelligence to invest in the highest return shares and monitoring the market in order to notify you when it is time to sell, hold or buy. In our case, our portfolio management is looking at strategic intentions and gauging which one is worthy of investment, given that demand for investment always outstrips capacity. So organizations have in place prioritization processes that require teams wanting funds to submit the already mentioned business cases. One of the differentiating elements is the cost–benefit analysis (CBA), articulating the return on the investment. Once a business case is approved it receives *discretional spend approval*, meaning that the requestor is given access to resources, based on the ask, either allocated to their existing operational cost centres, or allocated to a specific investment cost centre – here the choice really depends on how the finance team is managing its processes and chart of accounts. In normal circumstances, once the approval is given, a process of financial governance is applied to the cash flow of the initiative, whereby spending is properly accounted for and the amount of spend incurred over time is measured by the key 'plan vs budget' indicator, as a sign of financial health. The expectation is that the initiative follows its path and delivers what has been promised in the business case, whether that be a new product, a new process or, of course, a new data product, on time and to budget.

The concept of capitalization

An important concept to keep in mind when building something new that will benefit the company or its third parties is capitalization. It is an accounting practice that allows for financial statements to reflect the fact that a substantial investment to create an *asset* – in the widest possible sense – has been sustained, as the asset created will be utilized for an extended length of time to generate value. Imagine new machinery bought to automate a production line, or new software to expedite the approval process of customer requests. So, to reflect more accurately the fact that the benefit of usage is returned during the life of the asset, capitalization is accumulating the cost incurred during the *construction* of the asset (capitalization period) so that it does not hit the profit and loss of the company and then released in instalments over the useful life of the asset (depreciation period).

Strengthened by this knowledge and even before discussing how the DPT enables more accurate CBA, we want to help our finance teams to overcome the obstacles to properly funding data excellence.

Funding data excellence

If we go back to our favourite metaphor, a data athlete undertakes the virtuous journey of data excellence, works with the data domain owners and data domain architects to practise the Data Excellence Operating Model and really endorses the data disciplines and sub-disciplines, etc. However, following normal finance processes, the first brave athletes might find themselves paying for the whole investment to create the data excellence apparatus, as the new resources (e.g. DDO) and new capabilities (e.g. data intelligence repository) would be charged to the project or initiative that is establishing them. This would be the equivalent of making a personal trainer charge the first trainee through the door for the entire building and running of the new gym – something that would dissuade even the most determined athlete from subscribing to their services. On the other hand, we need to sympathize with the finance team, who are obliged by accounting practice to recognize costs and depreciate assets properly.

Admittedly, only a small number of our DPTs will find themselves in the enviable position of having a solid team and an adequate, centralized budget to establish all the foundational elements, capabilities and roles needed. In my experience that is really the exception, and more often, as discussed in Chapter 2, the DPT will need to fund their journey through initiatives, hence the potential issue of overcharging the first customer. In this case, I recommend two linked actions when you start with data in general, and data productization in particular, to encourage the new behaviour and to comply with acceptable finance practices.

First, for as long as is necessary in the data-training phase we need to capitalize the inception of the identified data products and their associated development costs. Finance should treat data product development as research and development (R&D) costs, though not all expenditure might be capitalizable, such as certain infrastructure costs. So the DPT should put in place measures to maximize the eligibility of the costs, for instance setting up a timesheet system for the resources involved in order to keep an accurate account of labour costs. The company's asset capitalization policy, if there is one, might need to be revised, otherwise the DPT should be advising the finance team in creating one with data products in mind. Such a first step would decrease the initial impact on company profit and losses, but the DPT should also seek advice from technical controllers to minimize the risk of *asset impairment*, which happens when the capitalized amount of an asset does not match its present or future value, in our case a data product that nobody uses or that generates no demonstrable value. In that case finance would be compelled to record the difference with a detrimental impact on the profit and loss (P&L) statement.

THE DATA EXCELLENCE GYM MEMBERSHIP ALLOCATION MODEL

Second, to distribute the costs more evenly and also to promote buy-in to data excellence practices, I recommend establishing a 'data citizenship tax' to levy across the organization based on a relatively simple allocation model proposed in Figure 13.1. Perhaps better sold as 'data excellence gym membership', in any case the allocation model reinforces the perspective that data is not for free and that everyone contributes to the organization's overall data fitness. At the same time an allocation model would be ideally suited for the franchise model discussed in Chapter 3, which entails a distributed creation of data products. Beside the economic appeal of sharing the

FIGURE 13.1   Allocation model of the data excellence costs: data excellence gym membership

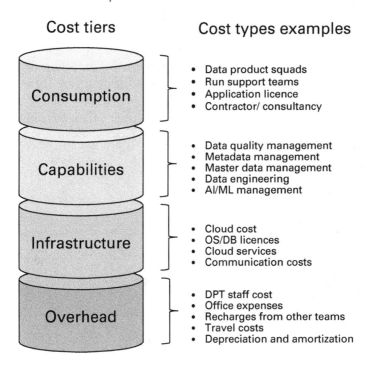

Cost tiers

Consumption

Capabilities

Infrastructure

Overhead

Cost types examples

- Data product squads
- Run support teams
- Application licence
- Contractor/ consultancy

- Data quality management
- Metadata management
- Master data management
- Data engineering
- AI/ML management

- Cloud cost
- OS/DB licences
- Cloud services
- Communication costs

- DPT staff cost
- Office expenses
- Recharges from other teams
- Travel costs
- Depreciation and amortization

overhead cost of development and maintenance across the multiple parties using them, the model officially recognizes as enterprise data products the ones produced by the franchisees, further fostering the sense of belonging to a cross-functional data tribe.

The grouping of costs could be tailored, but the logic of the model is to allocate costs based on how many consumers are using a product or an analytic application (top tier) and apportioning costs that are not directly for consumption (the bottom three tiers) based on the relative weight of the consumption activity. Figure 13.2 shows a working example.

The top tier of the figure represents the company's fictitious business units (BU_i) that are consuming a mix of data products (DPR_j) and analytic systems (SYS_k). The idea is to allocate to the unit a portion of the total cost to develop and maintain the asset, but the cost is split in two parts. The direct cost represented on the top tier is apportioned on a user percentage key, which means that the larger the relative user count of a BU, the higher the direct cost charge. On the other hand, the indirect or enabling costs, such as infrastructure, office and personnel costs, are allocated to the specific DPR/SYS based on relative direct costs of the different products, which means that the data product that receives the higher direct investment should logically attract a higher portion of the enabling costs. So formulaically, the items of cost charged back to the unit BU_i are:

$$D_{ij} = DPR_j \text{ direct costs} * (x_{ij}/x_{tj})$$

FIGURE 13.2   Assessment principles: working example of how to calculate data excellence gym membership

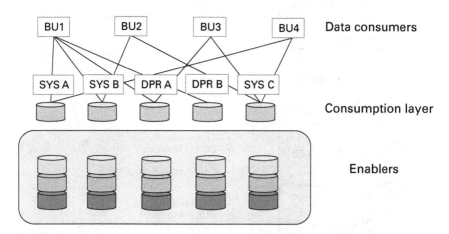

KEY: BU = business units; DPR = data products; SYS =analytic systems

where D_{ij} is the element of direct costs charged to the BU_i using the DPR_j, and the allocation key is based on x_{ij}, the number of BU_i users registered on DPR_j, in proportion of x_{tj}, the total number of users registered on DPR_j. In addition, the enabling cost share of DPR_j is calculated as (with Σ meaning 'the sum of'):

$$C_j = \Sigma \text{ enabling costs} * (DPR_j \text{ direct costs}/ \Sigma \text{ DPR direct costs})$$

This means that a data product that represents 10 per cent of the total costs of all data products development will attract 10 per cent of the enabling costs, and that cost will be charged to the unit based on the user allocation.

I want to emphasize that the model still stands whether business units are also providers of services and/or developers of products, in which case with a simple recharge to the overhead tier and a straightforward ledger of investments vs recharges they will have recognized their contribution to the overall data excellence investment, thus financially supporting the franchise approach mentioned in Chapter 2.

As a final point, the data excellence gym membership allocation model might not be extremely sophisticated, but it will serve the purpose of simplifying an essential accounting need to appropriately distribute these investments across the organization. I have witnessed finance teams working for months, trying to attach a single engineer's hour of labour or server software licence cost to the dashboard used by one team member. Although that would be an excellent data consumer story to deliver for the majority of the consumers about 'How much am I paying for my data?' information, it is a very tall order for a company in a data-reactive or training phase. The model above is a more than satisfactory MVP, that, maybe one day in a data-driven company, could be replaced by an ultra-comprehensive activity base-cost model.

Data product evaluation

The other notion that we must clarify before finally tackling the data business cases is the evaluation of the data products. We now know what they are, and we know that our data athletes need this gear to perform. We are even able to distribute their costs across teams, but it is important to be able to put a value on this. Why? Because in many of the processes that will involve our data athletes, they should be equipped with the notion of what their gear is worth.

Inventory value

The worth of a data product comes from two facets, exactly like any other product. One aspect is linked to an evaluation of the expense that went into creating it. I call this the *inventory value*, which is in effect a cost label that is associated with our data product since its first release. This takes into account the different components of cost that went into its manufacturing, such as the labour of the squad, the extraction costs, the quality cleansing cost, etc. Once more, this value evolves in tandem with the data fitness and intelligence of the organization, and it grows in precision and comprehensiveness with data domain completeness and the mastery of the data disciplines. It is obvious that the allocation model described above would benefit from this additional piece of data intelligence, as it would make the reusage of data, i.e. the use of the same product, on multiple occasions, a quantifiable benefit, based on the cost avoidance associated with the inventory value of the existing product.

Market value

The other aspect, like to the frenzy around AI, is often chased before the organization is truly ready. This is the *market value*, which serves as a prelude to the much-popularized data monetization. Understandably linked to the current inventory value, the market value is the price that a third party would be willing to pay for the data product, and it is a much less straightforward matter. Bringing an external party into the process commands a much higher proficiency, like going from donating makeshift equipment to your primary school soccer team to being signed as the official footwear provider for a Premier League football club. Minor flaws that are totally acceptable in the first case become infringements of contractual clauses in the second. The good news is that the data excellence methodology, as set out in DeXOM, is naturally extendable to data monetization, as everything described so far could be used to prepare data products for external users, including what I present in the next section on the refinement of business cases. However, attention will need to be paid to articulate at what point in the journey of data fitness and intelligence a data product might be fit for external usage, and the legal team will be a necessary party to bring to the table in drafting contracts containing data quality or data control clauses.

In practical terms a data product would be ready to be monetized when:

- its build is completed beyond MVP
- an effective set of data controls are in place
- its inventory cost is recorded on the balance sheet
- a marketing strategy is formed and enacted

- a pricing policy for the data product is agreed
- the data product is officially part of the company product master
- a contract template is agreed
- data product service SLAs are confirmed with the product development squad

If the company already has a software sales business model, there will be elements that could be leveraged, but I would recommend that the DPT joins forces with marketing and sales leaders to ensure that an overall operating model binding together the above-mentioned points is established.

Data debt and data value

Finally, we are ready to tackle the last challenge illustrated at the very beginning of this book: the business cases for data are disappointing expectations, as our data athlete is not able to predict what is going to be the quid pro quo for their performance. In business terms, they do not have the ability to pinpoint a causal relationship between better data and better value. As better data means cost and labour, their cost–benefit analysis is often unreliable, and either very often negative or immaterially positive. I mentioned above and I ought to repeat that the final mile of value creation is not directly owned by the DPT, as it is the data athlete who owns the intent, i.e. the next intended action that should produce value, and who finally competes to win. With the data consumer story and our Socratic *maieutica*, we should have paved the way for our pupil to convert thought into action and action into value, and yet they might discover in the moment of truth that perhaps their hypothesis was not correct. In Data Workout 2, we would have believed the consumer that controlling the delivery schedule within SLA would have increased customer satisfaction, but what if that was not the true root cause and, after all the work done, the NPS score did not improve at all? Everything the DPT can do before and after that moment to support their data athlete following the three pillars of data excellence will be critical – especially when the time has come to revisit and adjust the business case. This is because the best athletes are the ones who are resilient in the face of defeat.

To inch even further in the direction of unlocking value, I would like to conclude this chapter by presenting a novel approach to refining the business case. This formed part of a study conducted with Professor Michele Staiano, long-time friend and Senior Researcher in Applied Statistics at the University of Naples 'Federico II', about balancing data value and data debt.[1]

How to create a high-quality business case

Let's start from the simple assumption that an agent who is intended to achieve value (V) would need data at a certain acceptable level (L), whilst the data is currently of a certain status or quality (Q) (see Figure 13.3).

Let's call M the amount of capital, or, interchangeably, effort (as effort can be transposed in capital) that needs to be employed to bring Q up to level L, which we can write as a very simple data debt equation:

$$M = \mu\left(L - Q\right)$$

In this equation μ is a gradient that represents the unit of cash spent per quality discrepancy to fix. As we learnt from the data consumer stories, our data consumer might express their expectations regarding multiple features of the data product, and moreover a story could require multiple data products, so a more mathematically correct formalization of the data debt components would be:

$$M_{ij} = \mu_{ij}\left(L_{ij} - Q_{ij}\right)$$

where i and j indexes are specific amounts of data debt required to bring the feature i of product j to an accepted level L_{ij}. It is easy to extrapolate that having tens if not hundreds of data debt components would not help our data athlete/consumer understand what is good enough for them and what is the most effective way to achieve this. So, in the search for a more scientific approach to rationalize the reduction of data debt, Professor Staiano suggested that we looked at the Kano Model.

FIGURE 13.3 Value is in the eye of the consumer: the relationship between value, acceptance level and quality

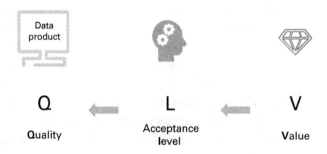

DATA DEBT REMEDIATION APPROACH: THE KANO MODEL

Noriaki Kano is a professor and writer in the field of quality applied to customer satisfaction. In 1984, together with his colleagues Seraku, Takahashi and Tsuji, Kano came up with the idea that not all product or service quality features are created equal.[2] Through the lens of customer experience, the model divides the given properties of a product into several categories. The first is defined as *must be*, without which the product is not viable as the basic customer needs are not met. In the next category, *one dimensional*, are those properties where the more there are the better. The last category in the Kano Model touches on something that I was keen to capture in our Consumer Story, that is the previous categories are usually explicitly requested by the customer, but there is also a more important 'unspoken' nature to the intent of our data athletes. The model defines these features as *attractive*, as customers are unlikely to ask for them outright, but a world-class product or service demands an accurate analysis of customer needs that identifies that all-important 'wow factor'.

To illustrate the Kano Model using an example drawn from the world of hospitality, if we take the experience of staying in an hotel, the *must be* feature might be the cleanliness of the room, as it is plainly a prerequisite, whilst the numbers of pillows on the bed could be a *one-dimensional* quality expectation, and, only then, the little chocolate laid on the pillow could be an *attractive* offer that the customer was not expecting and which they will be delighted by. Clearly, pillows on the bed or a surprise chocolate would not compensate for a filthy room.

Thus, to draft more accurate business cases and to achieve value more predictably, the recommendation is not only to have a reliable evaluation of the underlining data debts, but also to adopt the Kano Model as a classifier of data consumer expectations. This approach creates a faster path to value via a more coherent management of the data product backlogs that are now vectored on 'customer satisfaction'.

In Data Workout 3, which follows this chapter, I will take you through a numerical exercise to visualize the approach, but first I would like us to look at how the model provides more insight into the cost part of the cost–benefit analysis. The cost of creating a new data product can be written now as:

$$C_t = C_0 + \sum_{i=1}^{N} M_i$$

The total cost of a given data product C_t is the sum of the set-up costs C_0 plus the sum of all the N data debts identified. We will leave to one side for the moment the set-up costs and focus on the data debts by applying the Kano Model categories to the product features based on what emerged in the data consumer story.

$$C_t = C_0 + \sum_{i=1}^{N}\left(M_i^m + M_i^o + M_i^a\right)$$

To adopt this formula, it would be necessary that the requirement Q_{ij}, in the data debt formula, so far expressed with common data quality measures like completeness, validity or timeliness, should be further referenced to the Kano Model's categories. Now, for the *coup de theatre*, let's adapt a cost/value chart (commonly used in stock analysis) to plot the relationship between the cost of implementing the data product and the value deriving from the data product through the eyes of the data consumer (Figure.13.4).

Let's assume for simplicity that C_0 is constant, i.e. there are no running costs, and that during the set-up phase no value is available at this point in time ($V_0 = 0$). At the end of the set-up cost, the data product is accessible in

FIGURE 13.4 Building data products: value vs cost with Kano model

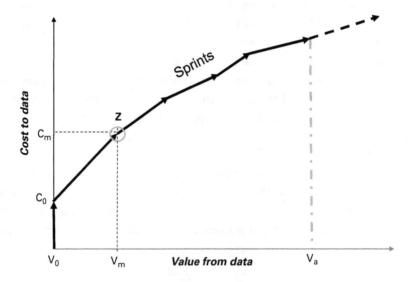

its structure, i.e. it could be consumed, but it is riddled with data debts. The data debt remediation gets underway and, hypothetically, value could already be generated, but in reality, and as per the model, until the point where all the *must be* L_{ij} are satisfied, the data product is *not good enough* to be *operational*, i.e. it is not ready to be used in a live business environment to generate value.

The point Z in which all the data debts M_i^m have been cleared at a cost C_m is in effect the point at which the data product has reached minimum viability. So our agent has got an MVP, because the minimum expectations for consumption are met. This almost geometrical truth should help resolve or at least ease the initial paradoxical conversation we were having with our trainees ('If it's not perfect I can't use it'), and it is corroborated by the zeal that went into précising the data consumer story.

So it is worth highlighting that the additional efforts required to move from the MVP quality to satisfy *one-dimensional* needs are usually comparatively less costly than the former *must be* debts (as the less steep segment between V_m and V_a depicts). These types of debts are usually linked to a characteristic that is less expensive to remediate, at least until they cross the line of the unspoken needs. Once the V_a point is reached by *saturating* the quality standards of the data set, additional unexpected value can only be created by increasing quality in a fashion not previously envisioned by the data athlete themselves. Practically speaking, by capturing in the data consumer story a deeper understanding of the DA's value chain, the DPT is able to recommend that a data product feature previously not delivered is identified as beneficial to increase value, and although that would require extra cost, it can be presented to the data athlete as a self-funded value adding initiative. This in turn would reinforce data consumer trust and satisfaction.

Finally, it is useful at this point to draw the data athlete's attention to how data excellence can mathematically improve their cost–benefit analysis and unlock more value. Indeed, from the formula above I can plot a direct correlation – if not causation – between a lower C_t and an organization's capability, maturity and data fitness.

Starting from the set-up cost C_0, a lower implementation cost will be dependent on:

1 Agile architecture: A substantial amount of the building cost of data products is associated with the creation of the pipelines to replicate and process data coming from the different sources. Leveraging modern cloud

computing and with consistent and robust design standards of architecture, this can greatly reduce storage and maintenance costs.

2 Portfolio management: The capability that oversees the execution of different priorities detects opportunities for further productization and fostering reusage of components by appropriately sequencing the demands. Hence new initiatives would leverage set-up costs of previous projects/products.

3 Delivery methodology: Whether Agile or Waterfall, having in place robust, mature and coherently adopted methodologies for change (like DeXOM), increases first time right outcome and minimizes resource and time wasting.

4 Communication: The binding agent that has been the focus of this book since the beginning, the adoption of processes and standards is only possible if strong communication amongst all the parties is in place and hence goal alignment delivers efficacy.

Whilst we already know that data debt has an inversely proportional relationship to data intelligence, in order to lower and keep the data debt low, the following behaviours and structures are essential:

- Data fluency: A culture that appreciates data and acts in accordance with the data charter fosters an environment that preserves gains of intelligence and discourages the multiverse of data that tends to add complexity and data debt.

- Data resilience: DeXOM and the connected capabilities of domain ownership, data design authority and risk management constitute a holistic, virtuous circle that continuously builds on data intelligence and strengthens the resistance to adverse changes.

- Effective data controls: An environment that maintains the gains achieved and provides assurance to build trust in reusage of products that are kept at a nominal level of quality and performance will avoid the long-term erosion effects of good data, and will keep the curve of data debt on a downward trend.

After a quick cool down, let's now practise with data debts and business cases in the third and final data workout.

COOLING DOWN

- The DPT must make the finance team controllership work for data.
- Data products can be funded through the data excellence gym membership allocation model.
- Data products can be evaluated at an inventory value and at a market value.
- DeXOM supports data monetization, but data monetization requires a specific business model.
- The Kano Model is used as a classifier of data debts to achieve value faster.
- A data product MVP is the point at which all the *must be* debts have been repaid.
- Data excellence makes data cost–benefit analysis more beneficial.

Notes

1   R Maranca and M Staiano. A generalized approach to data supply chain management: Balancing data value and data debt, AIRCC Publishing Corporation, 2021, 11 (11), 4.

2   N Kano, N Seraku, F Takahashi and S Tsuji. Attractive quality and must-be quality, *Hinshitsu*, 1984, 14 (2), 147–56.

Data Workout 3

Effort vs rewards: Calculating data debt and planning for remediation

In the third and final exercise I would like to stretch your data muscles by exploring the concept of data debt, applying what we just learnt about data debt calculation and improvement of business cases in Chapter 13. For simplicity, I am going to build on the example used in Chapter 7, regarding the team who were trying to improve sales using customers attributes. See this exercise's compacted data consumer story below.

DATA CONSUMER STORY

Sales increase project

As the pricing leader, I would like to support the sales team's ambition to generate an enticing offer for each one of our existing customers, providing them with a tailored discount rate based on specific customer characteristics. They are going to apply this discount to a complete set of quotations covering all current customers and then the quotations will be emailed to the customer business email. It is our combined expectation that a percentage of these quotations will be converted into sales, hence generating additional top line revenue. In order to calculate the correct discount, I have analysed the customer data and decided that the best data elements on which to base the calculation of the discount are the customer classification (CC) and the market segment (MS). To produce a quote I need *both* CC and MS to be valid, and, according to the data domain standards, I learnt that means CC must be a number between 1 and 10, whilst MS must be a number between 1 and 20. In

FIGURE DW 3.1 Sales increase project – new data flow

Source	Extraction	Quality Checks	Consumption Point	Outcome

CRM

MAS

Is Customer Class ∈ [1..10]?

Is Market Segment is ∈ [1, …, 20]

QE

Quotes produced with Discount:
$D\% = f\ (Customer\ Class,\ Market\ Segment)$

Customer Proposal

On average **8%** of proposals **convert into a sale**

the current system architecture these two data elements are present in two databases, customer relationship management (CRM) and marketing system (MAS), but we are missing a capability to perform bulk quotations so we have commissioned the implementation of a new software, the quotation engine (QE). Therefore, in collaboration with our data domain architect, we define the new data flow design (Figure DW3.1), in which we will extract the data attributes from the source systems, perform on them two quality checks to screen the records and then send the valid ones to the quotation engine. The engine will produce the quotations that will be delivered to the customer. Dear data personal trainer, we welcome your support.

Increased turnover

There are 100,000 records in the company's CRM, and they are confident that they should be able to turn 8 per cent of all the valid quotes into a sale, with an average of €500 per sale. So, the theoretical increased turnover is:

$$V = 100,000 * 8\% * 500 = €4,000,000$$

The project to build and commission the new quotation engine and the data quality checks has been appraised at a nice round sum of €2,000,000, which sounds expensive. However, the company is really keen to beat the competition, and they are intending to pull out all the stops to have the solution up and running in matter of weeks, built by the best software engineers, who are expensive resources.

The data debt

So, the return on the investment could be as high as two million, right? Not so fast! As the DPT, you have been requested to review the project and although you are pleased that, having partially applied DeXOM, the project manager has diligently tried to control the data domain standard for MS and CC, you then ask them whether a data profiling of the two fields has been executed. Regrettably that had not been done yet. The request for profiling is made and after three days the profiling results are in (Figure DW3.2).

FIGURE DW3.2 Data profiling results

Data Profiling Results

	Column 1	Column 2	Definition
Name	Customer Classification	Market Segment	
Physical Name	*Cus_Class*	*Mkt_Segment*	
Type	Numeric	Numeric	Data type
Number of rows	100000	100000	Total number of records in data set
Empty rows (nil values)	26643	50010	Number of records with no value
Highest value	10	20	Max value in data set
Lowest value	1	1	Min value in data set

Although the value spread seems to match the valid sets (1–10 and 1–20), almost 50 per cent of the MS is missing and more than 26 per cent of the CC is missing too. Unfortunately, due to the limitations of our profiling tool, we are not able to count the records that might have both the fields missing and so reduce the number of invalid records. So, we need to assume the worst-case scenario that the defects do not overlap, hence the assumption of increased turnover must be lowered to:

$$V = (100000 - 26643 - 50010) * 8\% * 500 = €933,880$$

Which, compared to the proposed investment (I = €2,000,000), would be a disastrous loss of more than one million euros.

Fixing the data debt

The project team panics. But the confident DPT then suggests evaluating the data debt and a data sheet (Figure DW3.3) is provided by the Six Sigma team, based on a previous analysis of the company's activity base costing:

FIGURE DW3.3 Data sheet

Customer Classification and Market Segment

Time to fix (mins/defect)	30	45	Average time required to fix one data defect
Hourly labour cost (€/hr)	32.0	35.0	Average labour cost
Correction effectiveness	95%	97%	% of successfully fixed issues

For each attribute, the project team is given the average time employed by a data steward to fix one attribute and the average labour cost of the stewards. The Six Sigma team have also measured that the data stewards have a success rate of less than 100 per cent, i.e. during the cleansing work some fields might be missed.

We now have all the elements to calculate the data debt, according to the formula:

$$M = \sum_i \mu_i \left(L_i - Q_i \right)$$

where L_i is the acceptance level of the quotation system to the two attributes, which we will fix to a maximum of 100,000 records (100 per cent of the set) and Q_i is the current quality level measured in the profile. In this simplified case, μ_i is simply the multiplication of the time to fix T_i and the labour cost C_i. The data debts M_1 and M_2 will be added to the project cost to reflect the true investment inclusive of the data debt remediation.

M_1 is calculated using the data whereby, as seen in Figure DW3.4:

FIGURE DW3.4 Customer classification data debt calculation

Number of records with valid CC	Q_1	73357
Number of records with CC = *null*	D_1	26643
Time to fix Customer Classification	T_1	0.5 hr
Hourly cost for Customer Steward	C_1	32 €/hr

$$M_1 = (D_1 * C_1)(L_1 - Q_1) = 16 * 26{,}643 = € 426{,}288$$

and with the same procedure M_2 calculation yields, as seen in Figure DW3.5:

FIGURE DW3.5 Market segment data debt calculation

Number of records with valid MS	Q_2	49990
Number of records with MS = *null*	D_2	50010
Time to fix Market Segment	T_2	0.5 hr
Hourly cost for Market Steward	C_2	35 €/hr

$$M_2 = (D_2 * C_2)(L_2 - Q_2) = 17.5 * 50{,}010 = € 875{,}175$$

After the data debt remediation, the number of quotations produced will be:

$$P = 100{,}000 - (100{,}000 - D_1 * (1 - 0.95) - D_2 * (1 - 0.97)) = 97{,}168$$

where the two factors in parentheses multiplied by the initial number of defects D_1 and D_2 take into account the performance of the stewards, hence the final number of valid records is less than 100 per cent. Applying to the quotes the 8 per cent conversion into sales:

$$S = P * 8\% = 7{,}773$$

which, multiplied by the average sale amount, yields the total increase in turnover:

$$T = S * 500 = € 3{,}886{,}500$$

And finally, we are able to calculate the true return from the project:

$$R = T - (I + M_1 + M_2) = € 585{,}037$$

Our data debt remediation managed to turn the business case into a positive benefit.

Conclusion

Although the exercise is based on a very simple case, once used in a true pilot case it became a powerful eye-opener for our data athletes, as it strengthened the credibility of business cases while creating that virtuous circle of reduction of data debt, increase of data intelligence with reduced cost and time to actionable insight.

14

Total data for total performance

WARMING UP

- What is the value of data beyond monetization?
- What does it mean to be an impact company?
- What is the DPT contribution to avoid depletion of resources?
- Why are companies hiring philosophers?
- What is next for data-driven companies?

A different type of value

During my career, and especially since I have dedicated it to data, a wider sense of belonging to a higher mission has been nurtured in me. Perhaps because I have been fortunate enough to live in a golden era when the few pioneers were keen to pass the baton of the data challenge to a small cohort of newbies. Perhaps because of my classical education and the insightful philosophical conversations held with my mother (herself a keen student of philosophy) on upholding humanistic values in a world dominated by technology. Perhaps because I really believe that data can solve the paradox of growth for everyone at a sustainable cost, I have been steadily drawn to the concept of the 'impact company', a different way of pursuing value, whereby for-profit companies are implementing strategies that, while producing said profit, are also delivering societal advancement and environmental improvement. This is a trend that appeals to people like me who believe that data can be a force for good – although we are at a perilous fork in history, leading to either a data utopia or a data dystopia. As a consequence, I have personally sought to be associated with companies that have at their heart a meaningful mission. So, I have striven to enable their missions with my data personal trainer approach.

Aside from personal ambitions, being a company that makes a positive impact is becoming less of a choice and more of an expectation, as in a globalized world companies with an international reach cannot completely control how they are perceived. Once you are exposed to worldwide markets and you want to attract worldwide investors, you need to be sensitive to a wider range of issues, and that sensitivity, if neglected, will negatively affect the share value. Equally, on a smaller scale, with unfortunate exceptions, it is generally more difficult to put pure monetary profit ahead of anything else. In fact, you might argue that the more local the envelope of a company's activities are, the more the relations with the local community have to be nurtured. Last but not least, in the permanent competition for talent, being an impact company is a necessary condition to be seen as an employer of choice, and young talent are very effective at performing due diligence on the value proposition of their prospective employer, thanks to the abundance of information that can be easily accessed. But what has this got to do with data? A lot!

If we go back to the main mission of our personal trainer to accompany our data athletes in the accomplishment of their ambitions through the practice of data excellence, the ambition of becoming an impact company presents a new challenge. Most of the management of said companies have been brought up in a world of relatively simple metrics that are basically proportional to what was sold. Notwithstanding a certain type of politics or the conjunctural fluctuations of attention around environmental themes, with a wider base of small investors that are making sustainable funding choices and with social media pressure applied constantly to brand reputation, executives are grappling every day with decisions that are now multidimensional in nature and ethically based. What I mean here is that it is not immediately measurable what the return on sales will be for a diversity and inclusion strategy. Equally, companies might be asked to prove tangibly claims of 'transparency' and 'simplicity' that cannot be put simply into percentages and indexes. Adding to these challenges, there is additional regulatory pressure coming from regulations like the European Corporate Sustainability Reporting Directive (CSRD) that would make an equivalence between the auditability of financial market disclosure and the newly required environmental, governance and social (ESG) metrics disclosure. It is as if our 100-meter sprinter had been asked to race up a steep mountain slope running backwards, and expected to clock the same time!

If there was one objective I wanted to pursue in this book, it was to give the data personal trainers support to prepare their data athletes for this coming challenge. I maintain that the three pillars of data excellence, if properly practised, provide a solid basis to prove to the outside world what value is created in the direction of missions like the United Nations' Sustainable Development Goals.[1] These goals, such as 'no poverty', 'climate action' and 'industry, innovation and infrastructure', are seen by many as the true north of an impact company. Given the agency issuing these goals, they are unsurprisingly formulated as incredibly high ambitions on a planetary scale. However, the DPT should not be afraid to discuss with the daring data athlete how they might demonstrate impact value aligned to these goals. Even if 'solving world hunger' from a business perspective is usually viewed as the kind of challenge that is too big to even attempt, each of the goals can be treated like *Epics* for equal numbers of data products to capture in evolving data consumer stories. If you take gender equality (Goal 5), an initial story could be the measurement of head count broken down by gender, evolving then to a measurement of the gender salary gap and the evidence of fair career progression. Again, higher data fitness and data intelligence will drive the sophistication of a data product that could one day link gender equality to better sales performance in a causal model.

The DPT using data for impact

Even if the company the DPT is training has not been looking at wider forms of value yet, the DPT themselves can still think about their 'impact', and more specifically about lessening the impact of their activities on humanity. If you think that considering 'humanity' is too emphatic, I will draw your attention back to the section in the opening chapter of this book about 'responsible data', in the preamble on the emerging needs for data. Here I mentioned that in the course of our work we often forget that we effectively produce data on data. Beyond the already mentioned data quality information that is added to the information itself in the form of quality metrics, DeXOM itself could be seen as a process that is inflating the data strictly needed to accomplish a story by creating more precise and detailed *artefacts*. Data profiling, or the data quality assessment as an important DeXOM step, could produce data sets that are as sizable as the initial set, if not larger. Data intelligence being a structured digital representation of the organizational information is ultimately more digitized information. While we have also been exploring methodologies used to close data debts, and our data athletes have definitely felt the cost incurred in capturing and structuring the data, they are much more oblivious to the cost of simply storing such data, thanks to ubiquitous and cheap cloud storage and computing. However, in line with the spirit of making an impact, we are now starkly reminded that in 2021 (owing to digitization and AI), data centres surpassed general aviation in terms of CO_2 emissions.[2] The study shows how emissions from data centres have reached and surpassed the substantially flat 2.5 per cent created by general aviation and shipping, with uncertainty about the current levels, which could already have increased to 3.7 per cent.

Although that does not seem like a catastrophic portion, in emission levels everything counts, which confirms the existence of a hidden non-monetary cost to storing data, furthermore given the frenzy about and expectations of AI, the upward trajectory of the trend is a seemingly unstoppable one. New data centres are now designed with clear requirements to lower their carbon emissions and to reduce the usage of water, and amongst many data colleagues the concept of *green data* or *data frugality* has started to emerge to counter the 'big data' mindset of 'the more data the better'. We should not collect and hoard data just because we can, and I do hope that the 'big data' days will give way to the 'right data' days, in which we would constantly be adjusting the supply of data to what is measurably needed, another superpower that data intelligence could bestow on us.

One simple step that the DPT should recommend in changing course towards the right data is the adoption of a simple frugality measure for every data product or delivery our data athlete is committed to achieving, such as the Consumption Efficiency Index (CEI) (Figure 14.1). I define the CEI as an index between 0–1, obtained by dividing the number of gigabytes served at a specific consumption point by the total number of gigabytes of data hosted in the data architecture supporting said consumption (inclusive of course of the ones served). The aim is to minimize the redundancy and the complexity of the data supply chain feeding data to a consumption point and to drive the CEI as close as possible to the theoretical limit of one. Although focusing only on storage and not also on central processing unit (CPU) power (which has a greater impact on emissions), I would still maintain that the index is an indicator sufficiently precise to steer data design practices in a direction that minimizes unnecessary usage of data centre facilities and therefore drives emission reduction.

The key promoter of the CEI should be the data design authority, which should be certifying efficiency ratings of each data design based on how much the projected efficiency of the design minimizes the carbon footprint. For ease of reference, the CEI could be mapped to an A–G scale similar to that used for environmental credentials of commercial or residential buildings, or those commonly found stuck to the front of appliances. See Figure 14.2 for an example of a CEI.

FIGURE 14.1 Pictorial view of the Consumption Efficiency Index

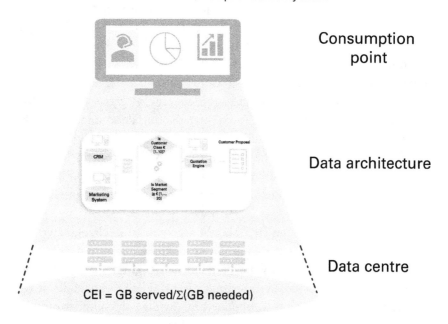

Consumption point

Data architecture

Data centre

CEI = GB served/Σ(GB needed)

FIGURE 14.2 Example of a Consumption Efficiency Index

Green data rating	CEI values
A	1–0.8
B	0.79–0.2
C	0.19–0.1
D	0.09–0.05
E	0.04–0.01
F	0.009–0.002
G	0.0019–0

In the scale above, a data supply chain serving 10GB of potential consumable data to its data consumer and tallying 100GB in total between the different tiers of the application and database infrastructure, would have been assigned a C rating (10/100=0.1).

The data design authority will recognize in some cases that the actual entitlement of a solution might be lower than optimal, for instance where data sovereignty requirements compel the jurisdictional duplication of infrastructure and hence data. However, the DDeA should in any case set a minimum bar, or at the very least might request an analysis of improving actions to be considered in a cost–benefit comparison. The key recipients of the ask will of course be the data domain architects, who would be sharpening their digital pencils and be incentivized to leverage reusage of existing infrastructure, be rigorous in managing the non-production environments, as well as enforcing retention schedules of test sets or lab environments, which are all demanding in terms of space.

Finally, the finance team could be further encouraging the improvement of designs, allocating proportionally more budget to teams that are demonstrating a higher data frugality performance. In terms of acceptance of such guidelines, I found people generally to be very sensitive to the issue. One of the best-performing data retention exercises happened when we explained to an HR team that on average a retained email would have generated 10g of CO_2. That notion created an absolute deletion frenzy, so much so we had to remind everyone that certain records should not be deleted too early. People want to make an impact.

The DPT's greatest contribution

I met Marie Wallace in 2018 when she was still in the IBM research team. Though I cannot recall which conference it was, I do distinctly remember that we wholeheartedly agreed that, given the immense impact data was likely to have on humanity (and this was years before ChatGPT), the industry had no code of conduct. The conversation continued rhapsodically in a few more conferences or meet ups, up until the point we took matters into own our hands and decided to co-author something that one day would hopefully become the pledge of every data personal trainer. We called this the Data Practitioner Pentalogue, and I faithfully reproduce it here:

I solemnly pledge:

- to *practise* my profession with conscience and dignity
- to *respect* the privacy of the people whose data is confided in me
- to *maintain* the utmost respect for the individuals whose data I am analysing

- to be *transparent, open and honest* about the type of analysis I am applying to their data

- to never use my knowledge to violate *human rights and civil liberties,* even under threat[3]

I am sure that, since then, other oaths or pledges have been written and shared over social media. I am not going to claim copyright, but the important point is that data practitioners across the world are increasingly aware of the power they could exert, and they are explicitly acknowledging their commitment to abide by a virtuous code of conduct. I have to underscore the term explicitly, because it would be unwise to assume that ethics is just common sense. As I outline in Chapter 3 in the section 'Toning the top', the code of conduct must be vocalized, even at the cost of embarrassing audiences, as I did at the CogX conference in 2018 when I asked all the attendees to stand up and take the pledge together with me!

Exactly like going through the DeXOM circuits, the role of the DPT in pushing through the pain of rewiring neuropathways is essential to the ethics of data. The DPT should not underestimate their role in what is seen as a completely reasonable expectation on whoever is devoted to the data sciences. Taking centre stage now in the conversation is the fact that the new technological advancements are now giving corporations the ability to do everything with people's data.

A couple of years ago when my daughters were about to finish high school and we started to have conversations about jobs and employability, I bet them that in ten years' time companies would be hiring philosophers. I feel I have already won that bet, if you consider how people like Luciano Floridi, Professor of Philosophy and Ethics of Information at the University of Oxford, have been advising many companies on the subject of information and computer ethics.

Data excellence nirvana

Projecting forward into the future, with all our efforts to become data-driven, to deliver value and to be an impact organization, what would that company look like? I hesitate to predict what infrastructure and architecture or what organizational model will be in place. However, it is not too difficult to picture that at its digital centre a very powerful, adaptive and dynamic corporate brain will have formed. Over time, the data intelligence collected through the many data product sprints would have accreted into one single mega-product as complex as the corporate reality that it intends to represent – and one connected to all the possible sensor data continuously feeding it with change information. A true enterprise digital twin, of course, connected to the other twins in the ecosystem that can deliver instantaneous situational awareness, strategic simulation and business impact analysis. If this seems too far-fetched, just ponder the fact that IBM has chartered their strategy for a 100,000 qbit quantum computer to be achieved by 2033, which sounds just what a pandedomenistic world needs![4]

Final cooling down

Congratulations – you crossed the finish line. You can slow down and take a few deep breaths. You have concluded our marathon through data excellence! What a journey that was. The course was testing and the conditions not completely favourable, but you made it, so you deserve to feel good about it and in a little while you should feel able to go farther and faster. It was tricky, I concede, heading suddenly uphill through the cultural dimension of the modern company, and being confronted with the slightly painful realization of how much is lurking beneath the surface that could hamper our performance. However, understanding that there are identifiable phases – data-reactive, data-training and data-driven – helped as the data fitness assessment positioned you so you know exactly where you are and how progress can be measured. When you were a bit tired, reciting the data charter and the discipline helped to focus you. And finding yourself in the company of data domain owners and data domain architects, with everyone encouraging each other to go further, meant spirits were lifted. Then you got to the change, and with muscles fully activated you went through the Data Excellence Operating Model like it was downhill, maybe a bit lightheaded at the end, but fully focused on your data consumer stories, data requirement and data design. And here it comes, the part you were waiting for, the value. Your muscles are aching a bit by now, but it is a case of mind over matter, and data productization gives you a second wind to go through a few tricky formulae. Finally, the last data workout – like the final lap in the stadium – crowns the end of the race.

I had promised to take you on a journey in data excellence, because, if you are reading this, I believe you have the ambition and the passion to use data to make your organization a successful digital company of impact in the 21st century. And so, I hope this book was not just a passing experience, but rather, through the structure of the Pillars and the data workouts, as a newly certified data personal trainer you will find it useful to return and gain new inspiration on how to solve a particular problem in your daily quest of training data athletes.

There are two points I made in Chapter 1 which are important to remember here. Firstly, data is not AI: AI has enormous potential as a tool to handle data better, but it is fundamentally a product that can be useful if designed and operated properly. But products obsolesce; focusing on the means (AI) rather than the end (data excellence) will put you at risk of obsolescence too. Secondly, regarding digital neo-humanism, I firmly believe that by concentrating on the true agents of change and the creator of values, aka the human being, this book is future-proofing your know-how. For as long as there is a human in the loop needing to make a decision, even if augmented by artificial intelligence, then the tenets of data excellence still apply, and your data athletes will benefit from your assistance. In fact, in our new role as 'chief decision officers', we will need to train them to perform in a world where interaction with the machine is not going to be mediated by code anymore, and the outcome delivered will be commensurate to their ability to grasp and articulate the causal nexus between decision and value, a no-code decision excellence environment. This is the next chapter of data, in which human decision making, turbo-powered by almighty technology that interacts and operates based on natural language, will be able to model and interpret reality in stunningly unimaginable new ways: the human factor will once again be the key to excellence as a habit, and not a one-off act.

Notes

1 United Nations. United Nations Sustainable Development Goals, nd. sdgs.un.org/goals (archived at https://perma.cc/3L3X-M25E)
2 H Lavi. Measuring greenhouse gas emissions in data centres: The environmental impact of cloud computing, Climatiq, 2023. www.climatiq.io/blog/measure-greenhouse-gas-emissions-carbon-data-centres-cloud-computing (archived at https://perma.cc/KGQ9-MRB3)
3 R Maranca and M Wallace (2019) The Data Practitioner Pentalogue, s.n., London
4 J Gambetta and M Steffen. Charting the course to 100000 qbit, IBM, 2023. www.ibm.com/quantum/blog/100k-qubit-supercomputer (archived at https://perma.cc/DP2F-NME7)

ACKNOWLEDGEMENTS

It is now time to confess that I have approached the writing of this book, ironically, in the same way the stereotypical data athletes I described approach data. I thought that just because I had data excellence in my head for years and I spoke about it and I taught it, it would be a relatively fast and painless race to the end. Instead, it became a long marathon during which, more than once, the temptation to throw in the towel was real. If I have managed to complete this endeavour this is thanks to the guidance and encouragement of my WPTs (Writing Personal Trainers) Monika Lee, Charlie Lynn and Ellen Capon.

A heartfelt thank you goes to my family who supported and cheered me along, putting up with my mood swings when chapters were not converging, and finally to my mother, whose passion for philosophy and humanities has been a source of inspiration to centre data excellence on the most interesting element of planet Earth, humans!

INDEX

Looking for another book?

Explore our award-winning
books from global business
experts in Business Strategy

Scan the code to browse

www.koganpage.com/business-
strategy

More from Kogan Page

ISBN: 9781398619593

ISBN: 9781398617773

ISBN: 9781398622012

ISBN: 9781398606128

From 4 December 2025 the EU Responsible Person (GPSR) is:
eucomply oÜ, Pärnu mnt. 139b – 14, 11317 Tallinn, Estonia
www.eucompliancepartner.com

www.ingramcontent.com/pod-product-compliance
Lightning Source LLC
Chambersburg PA
CBHW070938050326
40689CB00014B/3259